Dymphna Stella Rees is the daughter of writers Leslie Rees and Coralie Clarke Rees and now manages her parents' literary archive. For many years she was Principal Officer: English and Humanities in the New South Wales vocational education and training sector. During her time in TAFE, she created the first Diploma of Aboriginal Studies and drove other innovations in post-secondary curricula. Dymphna holds a Master's Degree in Aboriginal Studies and postgraduate diplomas in education and counselling. She is an elected member of AIATSIS (the Australian Institute of Aboriginal and Torres Strait Islander Studies). Dymphna has also been an advocate for families affected by mental illness and has worked as a counsellor with women and children escaping family violence. She lives in the Hunter region of New South Wales and delights in her large family.

Published Works by Leslie Rees and Coralie Clarke Rees

WORKS BY LESLIE REES

Children's Literature

Digit Dick on the Great Barrier Reef (1943)
Gecko the Lizard Who Lost His Tail (1944)
The Story of Shy the Platypus (1944)
Digit Dick and the Tasmanian Devil (1946)
Karrawingi the Emu (1946)
Sarli the Barrier Reef Turtle (1947)
Mates of the Kurlalong (1948)
Bluecap and Bimbi, Australian Blue Wrens (1948)
Shadow the Rock Wallaby (1949)
Kurri Kurri the Kookaburra (1951)
Digit Dick in Black Swanland (1953)
Two-Thumbs the Koala (1953)
Aroora the Red Kangaroo (1953)
Australian Nature Tales (1956)
Koonawarra the Black Swan (1956)
Wy-lah the Black Cockatoo (1957)
Digit Dick and the Lost Opals (1957)
Russ the Australian Tree-Kangaroo (1964)
Mokee, the White Possum (1973)
The Big Book of Digit Dick (1973)
A Treasury of Australian Nature Stories (1974)
Bluecap and Bimbi, Gecko and Mokee (1975)
Digit Dick and the Magic Jabiru (1981)
Digit Dick and the Zoo Plot (1982)
Billa, the Wombat Who Had a Bad Dream (1988)
The Seagull Who Liked Cricket (1997)

Drama and Theatre

Australian Radio Plays (editor) (1947)
Modern Short Plays (editor) (1951)
Towards an Australian Drama (1953)
Mask and Microphone (editor) (1963)
The Making of Australian Drama (1973)
A History of Australian Drama (1978)
~Vol. 1 *The Making of Australian Drama*
~Vol. 2 *Australian Drama in the 1970s*

Young Adult Fiction

Quokka Island (1951)
Danger Patrol (1954)
Boy Lost on Tropic Coast (1968)
Panic in the Cattle Country (1974)
Here's to Shane (1977)

Autobiography

Hold Fast to Dreams: Fifty years in theatre, radio, television and books (1982)

Plays

Sub-Editor's Room (1937)
Lalor of Eureka (1938)
Mother's Day (1944)
The Harp in the South ~ with Ruth Park (1949)

WORKS BY CORALIE CLARKE REES

Plays

Shielded Eyes (1928)
Wait till We Grow Up (1947)

Poetry

Silent His Wings (1945)

Children's Literature

What Happened After? Nursery Rhyme Sequels (1972)

COLLABORATIONS BETWEEN LESLIE REES AND CORALIE CLARKE REES

Adventure Travel

Spinifex Walkabout (1953)
Westward from Cocos (1956)
Coasts of Cape York (1960)
People of the Big Sky Country (1970)
Australia the Big Sky Country (1971)

DYMPHNA STELLA REES

A Paper Inheritance

The passionate literary lives of
Leslie Rees and Coralie Clarke Rees

UQP

First published 2021 by University of Queensland Press
PO Box 6042, St Lucia, Queensland 4067 Australia

uqp.com.au
reception@uqp.com.au

The excerpt on page 30 from *Women on the Warpath* by Dianne Davidson (University of Western Australia Press, 1997) reprinted by kind permission of the publisher.

The excerpt on page 109 from *Eileen Joyce: A portrait* by Richard Davis (Fremantle Arts Centre Press, 2001) reprinted by kind permission of the author.

The excerpt on page 155 from Miles Franklin's personal diary (January 1950, ML MSS 364/2/43) reprinted by kind permission of the Mitchell Library.

Cover design by Christabella Designs
Front cover photograph of Coralie and Leslie by Noel Rubie Pty Ltd, 1948
Back cover photographs: *Father and Daughter on the Shellcove Waterfront* by Charles D Maclurcan, 1948 (top) and *Coralie and Leslie in the Bush* by Dymphna Stella Rees, 1956 (bottom)
Author photograph by Joe Craig Black Label, 2019
Photograph on page 289: *Three of Us* by Dymphna Stella Rees, 2020
Typeset in 12/16 pt Bembo Std by Post Pre-press Group, Brisbane
Printed in Australia by McPherson's Printing Group

The University of Queensland Press is assisted by the Australian Government through the Australia Council, its arts funding and advisory body.

A catalogue record for this book is available from the National Library of Australia.

ISBN 978 0 7022 6320 0 (pbk)
ISBN 978 0 7022 6494 8 (epdf)
ISBN 978 0 7022 6495 5 (epub)
ISBN 978 0 7022 6496 2 (kindle)

University of Queensland Press uses papers that are natural, renewable and recyclable products made from wood grown in well-managed forests and other controlled sources. The logging and manufacturing processes conform to the environmental regulations of the country of origin.

MIX
Paper from responsible sources
FSC® C001695

For my Dear Ones who have gone before – they have shown me the way
and
for my children and grandchildren – this is part of their story, too.

When I am dead, my dearest,
Sing no sad songs for me;
Plant thou no roses at my head,
Nor shady cypress tree:
Be the green grass above me
With showers and dewdrops wet;
And if thou wilt, remember,
And if thou wilt, forget.

– Christina Rossetti

What a reminder to future generations of the significant heartbeats of the past!

– Leslie Rees in a letter to Coralie Clarke Rees

Contents

Prologue

Shellcove: that place of tender memory and delight. One sunny winter's day, through circumstances I would not have chosen, I walked right into the setting of my early life. I could not remember the last time – how many decades – since I had been on foot in this part of the world, the geography of my childhood, etched like a Google map upon the landscape of my heart. Neutral Bay slopes down to the harbour from its junction with Military Road. I was born right there, on the corner of Yeo Street and Wycombe Road 'under a jacaranda tree', as my mother would wistfully recall. She was always prone to hyperbole.

Shellcove Road forks off to the left several blocks down the hill. There's an Anglican church called St Augustine's on the corner. My sister, Megan, and I both went to Mirradong, the nursery school in the basement, and less than thirty years after that we sat in the church above with our father, sharing our frozen disbelief at our mother's funeral service.

But the road has a more public history. It once had a work of literature named after it: a stage play by Alex Buzo, a satirist, who

1

sent it up as one of the most expensive streets in Sydney. My father thought that a great joke, an absolute irony. He and my mother had lived there for almost thirty years, paying what they described as 'a peppercorn rent' for the privilege. They would have hated the idea they might be considered among the plutocrats. To them, any sort of social pretension, any class stratification, was anathema. And their lifestyle was determinedly, brazenly non-materialistic. They'd never had much money anyway. My father had grown up in threadbare poverty and both had lived through two world wars and the Great Depression. They had learnt to live on just enough and, despite that, to create a richly interesting lifestyle.

However, there's no getting away from it. Shellcove Road is a favoured street. That is because, as you move down to the lower end, the left side of the road fronts that narrow finger of water called Shellcove that fits between the two promontories of Kurraba Point and Cremorne Point on the northern shores of Port Jackson. It is one of the most desirable small bays of Sydney Harbour. The western side of the road boasts gracious homes with formal lawns and plantings while those on the water side have gardens rambling down to a boatshed, jetty or harbour pool. These properties look across the bay to the Cremorne side, which has, from midway down the incline, a bush reserve that stretches down to the rocky shoreline and provides a winding pathway right along to the point, a place that was so much a part of my early world.

Hardly a weekend would pass without taking that bush walk at least once with our father. Along its length is where he taught my sister and me the musical names of trees – angophora, lilly pilly, casuarina – where we learnt about the different banksias and ti-trees, where we watched for small scrub birds and identified their songs. It was here we grew to savour the colour and texture of Hawkesbury sandstone, the feel of the glowing rocks scattered along the shoreline, their small crevices alive with crabs, periwinkles and filmy sea lettuce. Once, but only once, I even took that walk by myself. I was probably only eight when I trundled my doll along its leafy length and as far as the ferry wharf on Cremorne Point. At the small kiosk, I handed up my sixpence for a roll of LifeSavers. On the way back I cautiously eyed several passing strangers who must have hidden their smiles at this small child walking alone, head down, through the filtered afternoon light, pushing an old doll's pram with a rubbery-limbed faux baby inside.

More than half a century later, here I was, wandering along Shellcove Road, pointing out to my companion the various places that held memories for me: where a school friend would invite me to play; the portico of a Spanish-style mansion where our father, on one of those weekend walks, had ushered us in to shelter from a sudden downpour, much to the surprise of the owner who cautiously opened the front door and gazed suspiciously at a man and two girls dripping onto the quarry tiles. I would like to report that we were invited in for tea and cakes but that did not happen. She surveyed us wordlessly then shut the door firmly in our faces.

Getting to the lower end of the road, our walk brought us to No. 9, the property where I spent my first twenty years. On the face of the sandstone block wall fronting the footpath I was surprised to see a brass plaque. It read, in raised letters:

Coralie Clarke Rees and Leslie Rees, writers, lived at Flat 1, 9 Shellcove Road, from 1937 to 1966 with their daughters Megan and Dymphna. Relaxing in the flats' harbour swimming pool on Shellcove between typing drafts, Leslie wrote thirty children's books including the *Digit Dick* and *Shy the Platypus* series, and histories of Australian drama. Coralie collaborated on travel books and radio scripts, and wrote *Silent His Wings* and *What Happened After*.

North Sydney Council
North Shore Historical Society

The plaque was dated 2003 but until that moment I had no idea of its existence.

Like most kids, I always thought my childhood was ordinary. While I now know that everyone's beginning is unique, not all families score a historical society plaque on the front fence. AA Milne, the creator of Christopher Robin and Pooh Bear, was emphatic when my mother interviewed him in his study: 'One writer is enough for any family!' But we had two in ours. My parents wrote separately for years and then together. Establishing themselves as individual names was hard enough, but then they collaborated on a series of works and found that a dicey business. Nonetheless, they became a power couple – 'one of Australia's best known literary partnerships'.

When I was a child they were part of the thriving literary community, which included that lady of letters later to grace our ten-dollar banknote, Mary Gilmore; the novelists Dymphna Cusack, Miles Franklin and Frank Dalby Davison; collaborators Marjorie Barnard and Flora Eldershaw; and the playwrights Betty Roland and Max Afford. There was the poet and literary editor Douglas Stewart; Gwen Meredith, writer of Australia's longest-running and most popular ABC radio serial, *Blue Hills*; the critic Tom Inglis Moore; and Pixie O'Harris, a writer as well as an artist. Ruth Park and D'Arcy Niland, another literary duo, were close friends – their older children came to our birthday parties and we went to theirs. Vance and Nettie Palmer in Melbourne appointed themselves our honorary grandparents, and in my parents' home state of Western Australia Katharine Susannah Prichard, Henrietta Drake-Brockman and Mary Durack remained friends of long standing.

Two of those writers, Miles Franklin and Dymphna Cusack, were to become my literary godmothers, for they bestowed the gift – or burden – of their names upon me. In 1938, Sydney celebrated its sesquicentenary with great pomp and fanfare: a hundred and fifty years since HMS *Sirius* sailed into Sydney Harbour and planted the English flag on Gadigal land. In response, Dymphna and Miles produced a book they called *Pioneers on Parade* – a satire that ruthlessly sent up Australia's colonial past and its reverence for the British aristocracy, which was still clinging to positions of power and authority. At the end of 1940, my parents produced a second daughter and decided to name me after their friend, Dymphna Cusack. Her erstwhile collaborator, Stella Miles Franklin, strenuously objected.

'Give the child a decent name! Call her Stella.'

So began my life – as Stella Dymphna Clarke Rees.

1

My Paper Inheritance

My mother, Coralie Clarke Rees, was a beautiful and alluring woman. More than that, she was blessed with intellect, vivacity and grace. She used her talents to become an actor, playwright, editor, overseas correspondent, broadcaster, poet, travel writer and intrepid adventurer. She might have reached greater heights in any of these fields had not chance intervened in her young life, demanding of her not gifts but deep wells of courage, dignity and endurance.

My father, despite a rough beginning, had true good fortune. He had buoyant health, prodigious energy and an inquiring mind. But his greatest blessing was finding a partner who could share his passion for literature, theatre, travel and family life – who would be his devoted lover, critic, champion and 'word friend'. Of course he was talented and determined – even driven. But my mother's support, belief and generosity of spirit played no small part in the life he devoted to the written word. He started writing as a boy of twelve – an adventure story of finding gold nuggets in the Yukon – and published his last new title, *The Seagull Who Liked Cricket*, when he was ninety-two and a great-grandfather.

Leslie Rees was a prodigious and versatile writer across genres. He produced journalism, plays, radio documentaries, adventure novels, travel books, autobiography and a tower of literary criticism including four weighty volumes recording the history of Australian drama from its convict days. Most celebrated was his contribution to children's literature: twenty-six titles, the first appearing in the early 1940s. Many were published again and again in various forms and editions over decades. The most recent versions appeared in 2016 – translated into Russian.

During my childhood, my father enjoyed enormous popularity as a writer of children's books. He was very well known – and my identity was forged as 'Leslie Rees's daughter'. *Digit Dick on the Great Barrier Reef*, his first book, was a fantasy about a tiny adventurous boy, set on Sunshine Island and in the waters of the Reef with all its colour and life. The book immediately became a bestseller and was quickly followed by another, becoming a series.

My father's publisher, John Sands, then invited him to try writing stories about Australian indigenous creatures, accurately depicting their life cycle and habitat. Walter Cunningham, a talented artist, would supply the illustrations. There were few Australian children's books available during World War II and in the period of austerity that followed. Certainly there were no others that celebrated our wild animals and birds – or not without turning them into caricatures of human behaviour. Blinky Bill featured koalas in frilly aprons and referred to them as 'bears', while May Gibbs delicately transformed eucalyptus caps into kewpie dolls and banksia cones into bogey men. Most Australian kids were more familiar with animals of the English woods: rabbits, badgers and squirrels. *The Wind in the Willows* introduced us to otters and moles, while Peter Rabbit might have seemed cute to English children, but in Australia he was an introduced pest to be shot on sight.

Suppressed resentment about this cultural cringe foisted upon the young no doubt led to the reading public's delight when Shy the Platypus came out of her burrow in 1944. *Shy* was the first of a series of animal and bird biographies that changed the nature and context of Australian children's literature and had influence for years to come. *Karrawingi the Emu, Sarli the Barrier Reef Turtle, Two-Thumbs the Koala* and the other titles that followed went on being read and published throughout last century and into this. Children treasured them; teachers and librarians lapped them up. They were books remembered and loved.

What makes a book endure for decades, even centuries, when the majority of titles have a shelf life of months? What in a book influences people and changes their lives? When *Shy*, now considered a classic, was republished in 2012 by the National Library of Australia, a man at the launch rose from the audience and spoke – his eyes glistening with tears – of how my father's books had led to his life as a conservationist and environmental scientist. Writer Jackie French spoke of how, as a child, she borrowed *Sarli the Turtle* so frequently from the local library it practically fell apart. When growing up in Africa, Mem Fox was sent a copy of *Shy the Platypus*. In 1990 my father had received a letter from the self-described '44-year-old writer of a book called *Possum Magic*'. Mem Fox went on to write:

> Well, I thought you were dead, the hero of my youth, the man who turned me on to books, to reading, to Australia, to writing [...] I owe you my love of literature, my present fame, my wish to become a writer – and JOY of JOYS, today I discover that it's not too late to say thank you – a million times over! Dear Leslie Rees, my eternal gratitude!

Delighted with this letter, my father responded by inviting Mem to a meal at his home – by all accounts a joyous meeting.

What made my father's books so popular and timely? Was it the scrupulously researched detail depicting native creatures in their own environment? Or was it because all the stories follow a pattern? They are constructed within the arc of the universal life cycle, with its dangers, triumphs, challenges and adventures, so they mirror the trajectories of our own lives. Importantly, they also shadow the dark side: the desecration of habitat through human interference, the ruthless two-legged threat that has led to species' vulnerabilities and extinctions.

But they do more than that. They shine with engaging narratives and beautiful writing – often lyrical and poetic. Although written for a certain age group, they assume intelligent reading. My father never watered down his vocabulary for children. Nor did he romanticise the bush. But his enchantment with the Australian natural world and its creatures, his awe and reverence for our landscape in its many forms – what he called his 'intoxicating faith' – is everywhere apparent.

My mother was also a successful writer, though my father's reputation tended to overshadow that fact. Her gender was against her, too, as were her time and place. And, unaware, she carried a genetic marker that would have a grievous impact on her work and her quality of life.

Coralie Clarke Rees also showed a versatile talent. As a young woman who had already written and performed in her own play, she established herself as a journalist and editor and went on to create one-act plays, short stories, works for children and a book-length elegiac poem. A scriptwriter over decades, she also collaborated on a series of travel books.

My mother's style was quite different from my father's. He was a narrative writer, like a Robert Louis Stevenson *tusitala*, a teller of tales. My mother's writing had more psychological depth, with subtlety and sensitivity, though she was also capable of flashes of showy brilliance. I sometimes thought she was the better writer – though of course I never said so.

Towards the end of his life, my father anointed me as manager of their joint literary archive. 'You'll have to deal with all this when I'm gone,' he announced. This meant taking care of their publishing contracts and manuscripts, and protecting the copyright of their works, which continues for seventy years after the creator's death.

When the time came, I found myself burdened by the impost of this bequest – weighed down by the sort of resentment a person inheriting the family farm might feel. This uncharitable response was heightened by a sudden and painful awareness that my own hourglass was rapidly filling. What about all those elusive possibilities: floating down the rivers of Europe, exploring more Australian deserts, playing my piano instead of just dusting it, devouring all the books I never had time to read, even polishing my own manuscript that loitered under the bed? Instead I found myself the recipient of a diverse literary archive reaching back nearly a hundred years. But I had no idea what riches I would expose.

My most precious discovery was the love letters between my parents in the years 1929, 1930 and 1936. Suddenly I was privy to their early life. I could witness how passionately they loved each other as they explored their dreams of a literary partnership. But finding these letters carried its own dilemma. This was private correspondence. My parents never thought their letters would see the light of day – let alone be read by their future offspring. How could I justify my overriding urge to transcribe them, to bring them out of the darkness of their dusty envelopes and into the light of the twenty-first century, to share them and make them integral to my parents' story? How could I smother the guilt of a filial voyeur?

The letters were buried in the unmanageably large and disorganised assemblage of paper my parents had amassed over their lifetimes. Books, press cuttings, photographs, manuscripts, radio scripts and notebooks all spilled haphazardly out of bookshelves, drawers and a tower of cardboard cartons. Though my parents had strenuously resisted gratuitous consumerism, it was clear this did not apply to anything containing the written word.

I was tempted to hand the material over to the Mitchell Library in Sydney where my father had already begun the Coralie and Leslie Rees Collection, depositing his correspondence with George Bernard Shaw, Somerset Maugham and other famous writers, along with some of his own memorabilia.

But I was patently not ready to share this collection, let alone give it up. It was my precious link with a lost world.

~

Holding on to my paper inheritance proved to be the right decision. Raking through my parents' literary archive, I've come across jewels of discovery, some that light up my smile for days, others that leave me questioning or digging for answers.

It is true that all writing has its pitfalls, but writing about one's parents can be truly hazardous. One should be careful not to elevate the dearly departed into sainthood, nor – if from a challenging upbringing – to paint them as unreservedly evil. One has to grapple with finding the right emotional distance to describe what is an intimate relationship. In this work, I have tried to avoid the risks – where possible – by letting my parents tell their own stories.

This book is about Coral and Les, their writing partnership and literary lives. In my authorial role, I'm looking over their shoulders, observing, narrating. For other parts, I've transcribed firsthand accounts faithfully from the faded ink on paper so dry and crackly it almost falls apart at a touch. Every biographer and researcher knows that primary sources are gold. And, given that both my mother and my father were highly accomplished wordsmiths, it would be presumptuous of me to assume I could relate their experiences better than they could themselves, particularly the earlier parts of their lives that I did not share.

So their story is told – not by one writer or even two – but by three of us.

2

Genes Worth Having

Coralie Clarke and Leslie Rees had very different childhoods. Leslie's was such that he couldn't bring himself to speak or write about it till nearly the end of his life. Coralie, on the other hand, needed no encouragement to reminisce about hers.

The Clarkes were a large, riotous, expressive family who lived in a sprawling Federation home in the suburb of Mt Hawthorn, its wide verandahs overlooking the dusty paddocks towards the small city of Perth. Sylvia and Guildford Clarke (known to their irreverent brood as Syl and Gil) produced six children. Coralie was the first born, arriving an embarrassingly short time after their marriage in 1908. She used to say that position in the family makes a significant difference to one's experience of growing up, no doubt because in her childhood 'there was always a baby crying somewhere'. But she was not complaining. The family had great fun together.

It was before television was in every home, even before radio. Words were their currency, music filled the air, laughter shook the walls. Gil sang in a rich baritone, Syl played, and on Sunday nights they would gather about the piano for a singsong, or play pencil and paper games round the kitchen table. There were weekend picnics up in the hills, first in a sulky pulled by 'that reluctant nag' Sparkles, then, as the family grew, in a motorbike with an enormous sidecar, four of them crammed inside. When that became overcrowded, they moved to a Model T Ford with a canvas waterbag hanging off the front bumper bar.

The Clarkes adored nicknames, the more cryptic the better. The youngest sister, Roma, was known as Chas (originating from Charlie Pushcart). When they were older the children called their father Bass (short for Bassendean, the Perth train station before Guildford, his real name). I never heard the derivation of my mother's nickname. Fancy reducing Coralie to Codge! Nor did I hear why two of Sylvia's sisters, Helen and Rose, were called Toss and Rid. Cousin Beryl bore the unfortunate moniker of Bedge, while another cousin, Margaret, was forever known as Pidgee.

As they grew up, all the Clarke children developed into engaging and eloquent speakers, writers and raconteurs, oozing wit, wordplay and the family hallmark: sardonic humour, preferably self-deprecating.

This was not surprising as Sylvia, their mother, relished language and was a hive of colourful expressions, rhyming slang, acronyms and hyperbole. An uncommon event was 'rare as Halley's Comet', an angry person had 'thin lips', a person of inner strength was 'SUV' (steel under velvet), and an old person had 'one foot in the grave and the other on a banana skin'. People of dubious intent 'worked underground like the white ants'. Forthright characters were 'OPs' (outstanding personalities). A persistent admirer of one of Sylvia's daughters was dubbed 'Ubiquitous'. In her senior years, Sylvia's financial mantra was 'POPs NTC' ('poor old pensioners never touch capital') – advice she obviously self-administered as she left each of her seven grandchildren a tidy sum, in my case enough for half the price of a grand piano.

Sylvia Clarke was the only one of my grandparents with whom I enjoyed a relationship (the other three were dead by the time I was nine) and she was a significant influence in my life. In 1959 I travelled overland to Perth in the first Pioneer coach to cross the Nullarbor Plain, the road a seemingly endless narrow track in the red dust. My grandmother, by then widowed, had invited me to stay for a couple of months in the family home, where my mother and her siblings had all grown up. The long holidays after my second year of university provided this opportunity and my parents obviously thought it was time for me to travel across the continent on my own, meeting various far-flung relatives along the way.

During my time in Perth, not only did Nan have me laughing at her rich language and dynamic phrases but she passed on her accrued wisdom. She taught me her favourite song with its important message: *The world belongs to everyone; the best things in life are free.* She explained to me the art that had helped her through a long and at times gruelling life: *live one day at a time and practise gratitude* (advice that pop psychology seems to have just discovered).

An attack of rheumatoid arthritis in her twenties crippled her hands, feet and spine, but Sylvia lived to ninety-eight. By the end of her life she had buried all six of her children. My father said he had only ever heard of two women who had suffered grief to that degree. One was Elizabeth Cook, long-suffering wife of Captain James Cook, the explorer. The other was Sylvia Clarke.

Sylvia's sense of humour was all the more miraculous because her life was a journey of epic loss. Her youngest, Max, was killed in a flying accident in World War II; her partner, Gil, fell dead into the arms of his son when playing a bowls tournament at the age of sixty. Her four daughters, Coralie and her sisters, Marjorie, Jess and Roma, all died of illnesses in middle age and within one decade. Her remaining son, Ron, died not long after she moved into his home as a ninety-year-old. She was no doubt grateful for the sterling daughter-in-law who continued to care for her in her last years.

Coralie used to say that Nan would have made a great journalist. She had the facility with words and she had the genes; her father was editor of Perth's *Sunday Times*. Before moving to Western Australia, he had been a senior editor on Melbourne's daily *The Argus*.

There were two striking differences between my parents' formative years. One was position in the family. Coralie, as the eldest of six, blazed the trail for her siblings: she was the first to gain entry to Perth's only selective high school, the first to attend university, the first to travel out of the country, and the first to marry and have children. Leslie (his full name was George Leslie Clarence Rees) was the youngest of six and came as a surprise package after a brief reconciliation between his estranged parents, when his mother had probably thought four sons and one daughter was quite enough, especially as she had to raise them singlehandedly.

Leslie once referred to himself as 'an islanded boy', but he also told me he never missed having a father as he had four older brothers. He said little to us about his childhood but one story revealed important clues. He was about sixteen when told by an elder brother that his father was dead. He said he felt nothing but 'the greatest, the profoundest relief'. Then he added, 'He wasn't much of a father, but his genes are worth having.'

Leslie's father, John Henry, known as Harry, was a trained teacher and a gifted musician. Apparently he also had a Celtic facility with words. Harry's parents, Mary Loveluck and John Davis Rees, had also been teachers, one headmistress of a girls' school, the other headmaster of a boys' school. They migrated to Tasmania from Wales, bringing with them only a heavy family Bible (which I have inherited – it is inscribed in immaculate copperplate, *Mary Loveluck, October 1860*) and a little pouch of gold sovereigns donated by the grateful people of Merthyr Tydfil. Obviously competent and self-motivated, on arrival in Lebrina they set up a school and an Anglican church, as well as an apple orchard on the property they named Resica – home of the Reeses.

Like his forebears, my father was a born teacher, so much so that I credit him with a significant part of my education, despite having had the benefit of two excellent public schools and four universities. He passed on his own intellectual curiosities and passions in a way that was both enlightening and memorable. Perhaps that is why the occasional critic has suggested a strain of didacticism runs through his works for children.

The other striking difference between the Clarke and Rees families was material comfort and stability. Coralie readily acknowledged her true good fortune to grow up with committed parents who delighted in their children and supplied an abundance of nutritious food, educational opportunities, music and laughter. Though not prosperous, Guildford (his mother was German, his father Australian-born of English derivation), diligently provided for his family. Trained as an accountant, he once stood for Federal Parliament. The Clarkes enjoyed the pleasures of a comfortable home and a large garden, with pets and the usual chooks up in the back corner. By the time Coralie was at university, her father had a car and had taught his eldest daughter to drive it, both rarities in the 1920s.

This secure background, along with Coralie's looks and academic brilliance, no doubt contributed to her resounding self-confidence as a young woman. She thought – she knew – the world was her oyster.

Leslie, on the other hand, grew up in a rented workaday brick cottage only a few kilometres away in the suburb of Subiaco. He gave this grim picture of the area (now a ritzy inner suburb) in his autobiography:

Outer Perth was then raw and rough-roaded, with new collections of dwellings facing up to a blistering sun (and only 'Coolgardie safes' to keep the butter from melting) or driving winter rains, and spreading its tentacles over low-level woodlands of small jarrah, banksia, grasstrees and ground-hugging zamia palms. And everywhere sand – paddocks of grey sand, bright chrome yellow sand to cover buffalo lawns, sugar white sand dunes by the sea.

Mary Elizabeth Rees, my paternal grandmother (she met me when I was a baby but I never really knew her) was clearly a strong and dignified woman who was determined to give her family the best, even though there was little available to give. She nursed tender feelings for her husband, but his drinking and violence destroyed whatever chance of happiness they might have had together. Her children, including young Leslie, had not the slightest affection or respect for their father, who had been sacked by education departments in three states. He terrified them all when drunk and brought shame upon the family.

It was not till his late seventies that Leslie published this graphic account of one of the more terrifying moments of his childhood. He was about eleven and home alone one night:

Suddenly I woke to the sound of a hoarse voice – his voice, dreaded above all things – outside the window and assuring the neighbour in a thick tone that 'it was all right', he knew what he was doing. The next moment, in the silence of the dark night, there was a horrendous crash, unbelievably close, glass splintering and shrieking and whirling to the floor beside me. Wrenched from sleep I could nevertheless guess in a flash what had happened. 'The Old', having tried all the doors and windows and raging mad, had decided on directest action. He had seized a brick and crashed it through the window, so as to be able to handle the lock inside.

I lay like a corpse on my bed. I could not move a muscle. I felt myself a tiny child, helpless. I was certain I was going to be murdered. Had I been able to drag myself from the bed, I could have opened the locked front door of the house and disappeared into the night. But I could not move an inch and just waited for the end.

The window pushed up, my visitor had no trouble in jumping into the room and crunching over the broken glass towards the light switch. The electric globe flared and he pulled me from my bed.

'Where are the others?' The words were threatening.

When I could find voice, I choked out, 'I don't know.'

To his credit he didn't try to murder me. Instead he rushed me to the kitchen. Apparently he was ill. From the pantry he demanded a bottle of medicine which he said had been prepared for him. I found it. He stared at the instructions without spectacles but couldn't read them. Neither in my terror could I. He ordered me to take the bottle into the house of the neighbours on the other side and find out what the instructions were. Coming into the street, in my pyjamas, I took a quick gape up and down the two lines of front fences and will never forget the spectacle of people in their pyjamas standing there, peering my way and wondering what in hell that almighty crash of glass had been about.

The neighbours, a middle-aged man and his wife, were waiting tremulously on their verandah. I showed them the bottle and they told me what it said. Here was my second chance to escape but some mesmeric force pulled me back. I told my father what was on the label: Take one teaspoonful. He grunted with contempt, raised the eight-ounce bottle to his lips and impulsively drank half of it. He put the corked bottle into his coat pocket and left the house by the open front door. He had not uttered another word.

Leslie's mother struggled to put food on the table. At one stage she managed by renting a 'run shop'. The family lived in the back while she flew into the shop when the bell rang to serve those who needed to 'run to the shop' for daily necessities. She never had a home of her own. All Leslie's brothers had to work as soon as they were able. They were just teenagers. Then World War I broke out and they enlisted. One was only sixteen. Averil, the only girl, had to leave school at thirteen so she could look after the unexpected baby Leslie.

It was a sacrifice my father spent the rest of his life trying to repay.

3

Mod and Tin Pot Alley

Leslie and Coralie went to the same secondary school, 'Mod', as Perth Modern School was affectionately known. Coralie explained:

> It was then a very up-to-date secondary school to which you had to win an entrance by scholarship [...] which I did and Leslie did too. But he was two years ahead of me all through our secondary education at this co-ed school and he was not one of the senior boys with whom I fell in love. I was absolutely unaware of his existence and he was with mine.

Perth Modern School is still Western Australia's only fully academically selective co-educational high school. As it was in my parents' day, the entrance process is by exam, now managed by the GAT (gifted and talented) state education program. In its history of over a hundred years the school has produced a galaxy of alumni who have made their names in the world, including Labor prime minister Bob Hawke and two senior Liberals: leader of the opposition Billy Snedden and Paul Hasluck, who later became governor-general.

Leslie described it as 'a good school that could have been better'. Whatever the school's failings, a number of his contemporaries made significant contributions in fields as varied as ornithology, biochemistry and agricultural science. He counted among his high school friends three who became professors, and one vice-chancellor. Nugget Coombs, his lifelong buddy, was also a student at Mod and went on to become governor of the Commonwealth and Reserve banks and economic advisor to successive prime ministers. More importantly, as far as my father was concerned, Nugget involved himself in cultural projects and was committed to the advancement of Indigenous Australians when few in positions of influence took any interest.

When asked to contribute to the school magazine, *The Sphinx*, teenager Leslie prophetically came up with a piece titled 'How to Write a Book'. He was beginning to excel at manipulating the language just as Coralie was, though she put her efforts into poetry. In her final year she co-edited *The Sphinx* and in her Leaving exam was awarded the English and history exhibition at the University of Western Australia. The scholarship paid for books and expenses and her parents were able to keep her at home, which meant she could do her degree as a full-time student.

On the other hand, Leslie, after finishing school – the first among his siblings to have had that opportunity – would have loved to spend all day at the university indulging his new passions for literature, philosophy, economics and the history of fine arts. But he had to earn a living while he studied. He began his career as a cadet journalist on *The West Australian*, Perth's only daily paper, and worked his way up to being its art and drama critic. It took him five years as a part-time student and full-time journalist to complete his degree.

From the challenges of his own experience Leslie formed the view that being a full-time student is an absolute luxury. When my sister and I began our university studies, our father made it clear to us that if we enjoyed that privilege and flunked our exams, we would be reduced to part-time study. The rule was invoked. For Megan it was after her second year at Sydney University when she had been diverted from her studies, partly by her love life but mainly by her devotion to the student newspaper *Honi Soit* (the following year she became a cadet journalist on *The Sydney Morning Herald*). For me it was after my first year at New England University at which I had – according to my father – 'majored in extra-curricular activities'. I was brought home to continue my studies under the parental eye and roof.

It was likely, if not inevitable, that Coralie Clarke and Leslie Rees would meet at UWA because in the 1920s very few people, particularly women, had the benefit of a university education. The university had not long been established and was still in temporary premises, which Coralie described as 'a collection of tin sheds quite close to the city, in Irwin Street, Perth'. There were only about three hundred students in all. To them it was known as Tin Pot Alley. Both Coralie and Leslie were on the Guild of Undergraduates, which was comprised mostly of men. Interestingly – perhaps typically – my mother and father each recorded quite different accounts of how they met.

No doubt because Leslie was a working journalist, after three years he was appointed honorary editor of the university journal, a prospect he embraced with enthusiasm. *The Black Swan* was a substantial hard-backed publication that came out three times a year containing poetry, stories, sketches and articles of general interest.

He wrote about meeting Coralie in the chapter of his autobiography entitled 'Black Swan, Blonde Editress and a New Prospect':

Coralie Clarke was appointed as assistant editor without my knowledge. I hadn't so far met her but did when I called a meeting of the new *Black Swan* staff. And in walked a blonde young woman of eighteen or so, with lively figure and an anticipatory smile, a broad brow and wide-set large greeny-grey eyes. I was a bit scared of her at first: she was a scholarship winner, so I'd heard, top of the State in English and History at Matriculation level. With her masses of curly hair and bright looks she was obviously a student personality.

My mother, in her oral history recorded for the National Library of Australia in 1968, described their meeting in a far less reverential tone:

Of course being interested in literature, it was only a short step to being interested in drama. I joined the Dramatic Society and in my second year was offered a part in a comedy, *The Whole Town's Talking*, which we were putting on at the Assembly Hall, the only venue in Perth to stage an amateur play. I played the lead, Mary Westlake, my leading man Paul Hasluck, then a fellow student. Plays given by the University Dramatic Society were seriously reviewed in those days.

The critic from *The West Australian*, the major newspaper in Perth, was always sent along and usually wrote about three-quarters of a column analysing the play and performance in great detail. After the first night, the notice came out the next day and, what surprised and delighted me, I got a rave notice about my performance. I was just walking on air and could see myself with my name in lights on Shaftesbury Avenue in the West End. The following day I was at university in the gravel quadrangle and a young man stopped me and said hello. I didn't know him, didn't know his name, but he said, 'I saw you in the play last night.'

I said 'Oh well' … After all a lot of people saw the play last night and I'd been having a great morning after being presented with flowers the night before. This young man looked at me rather critically and said, 'Yes, I liked your performance. Did you like what I wrote about you in *The West Australian*?'

I'm afraid I dropped the brick of all time. 'Did you write that notice?' I questioned. 'I thought a *real* critic wrote it.'

So that was how Leslie Rees and I met.

4

The Dawn of Women's Rights

Coralie was born in 1908 – the very time when women were questioning their place in society, and their options. Suffrage had been achieved – in Australia at least – but would it in fact change anything? Would women be brave enough to step out of their gendered roles and expand their expectations? Would they still have to choose between marriage and children or being 'an old maid' with a career?

Women writers were exploring these issues in their stories. In the first year of the new century, Stella Miles Franklin's first novel, ironically titled *My Brilliant Career*, presented the feisty Sybylla Melvyn grappling with 'the rubbishing conventionalities which are the curse of her sex'. Sybylla wanted to be a writer and on those grounds felt it imperative to turn down the hand of a man liberally endowed 'with virile fascination', even though he offered her, as part of the matrimonial package, a study and 'a truckload of writing gear'.

The Lone Hand, a monthly illustrated journal set up in Sydney as a sister publication to *The Bulletin*, solicited stories, poetry, articles and illustrations from the public. My Morocco-bound volume of this remarkable journal is a compendium of all the issues for that year (published by Angus & Robertson in 1907 and inscribed inside the flyleaf in pencil: *Exceedingly Scarce*) and contains absolute treasures. Interleaved between full-page advertisements of items no longer imagined, stories by Henry Lawson and poems by Bernard O'Dowd and Hugh McCrae, 'decorations' by Hans Heysen, and Norman Lindsay's ink drawings of maidens with bosoms carelessly exposed, is a thin sprinkling of contributions by women. Not only the stories and articles but the illustrations themselves hold the mirror up to the times and expose the way male contributors thought about women and how women envisaged themselves. Some items show women comfortable in their age-old domestic roles, but at least one writer, Grace Palotta (also an actress) explores 'the new breed of Australian women'.

In her short story, 'A Woman's Way', the heroine is described as 'rich, lovely, with all the charm of woman and the brain of man' though in the illustration she looks like Boadicea in evening dress. Rose is endowed with a generous inheritance (pounds rather than paper) and vows to turn away a line-up of suitors in favour of the Cause of Women. Despite this intention, she briefly lays aside her political activism to marry Otto, a de-titled Austrian prince who has fallen on hard times. She wins a seat in Parliament, but her success spells problems for their marriage as Otto finds her work personally 'degrading'. ('I want a wife, a mother, not a Member of Parliament.') Rose presses on with her career but is miserable and lonely. When Otto is injured in a mine accident somewhere outback, Rose uses her newfound skills and authority to arrange medical assistance and rushes to his side. As his life hangs in the balance, in a plaintive voice he asks when she'll be going back to her work in Parliament. She decides, at that moment, to give it all away and nurse her man back to health.

When I first read that story forty years ago, I found the ending pathetic, disappointing – Rose had caved in. Reading it now, I see Rose's dilemma as prescient. By solving one problem, women have created another, which often involves agonising choices: choices that my mother had to make, that I've had to make and that my daughters are still confronting, too.

In the early twentieth century, females in Australia were a minority. In Western Australia there was an even greater imbalance, due to the gold rushes of the 1890s in Kalgoorlie and Coolgardie. This was how both my parents' families came to be in the west. My grandmother Sylvia's father had quit his newspaper job in Melbourne to try his luck on the goldfields, leaving his wife and six children without financial support. She used to tell me how, when a letter came from their father, her mother would shake it first to see if there was a sovereign or two inside to keep food on the table. My Rees grandfather also left his wife and five children with his parents, in Lebrina, Tasmania, and made his way to Western Australia perhaps with the same intention, though he managed to land a teaching job instead. Breadwinners from all over the country were deserting their dependants in the hope of making it rich. Most eventually brought their families over to settle, despite not ever getting within sniffing distance of a gold nugget.

However, minority status did not stop the groundswell of the women's movement. The Women's Service Guilds of Western Australia (WSG) grew into a powerful voice of advocacy with branches all over Perth, and one south in Albany. They called their journal *The Dawn*, inspired by Louisa Lawson's feminist paper of the same name, which she had produced from 1888 to 1905 using her own printing press in Sydney. It had been the first Australian magazine to target women's advancement, so the West Australian first-wavers probably thought it right and proper to inherit the title. In 1929 *The Dawn* (by implication: of women's rights) became a monthly magazine, at first circulated only among members, but later expanded to a national and international readership.

Coralie had recently graduated and was looking for a full-time job as a journalist at the same time as the WSG was looking for someone with writing experience to be their full-time 'editor' – which meant being their writer, manager, distributor and publicist as well. Though she was conscious of the women's movement and sympathised with its aims, Coralie was not an activist. She was more driven by the challenge of stretching her creative and literary muscles and, in the limited job market of Perth, this was the opportunity that presented itself. Her referee was Professor Walter Murdoch, under whom she had studied at UWA. In a letter to Coralie, he revealed that he was sending his reference with a note to the woman who would have the deciding voice. He added:

> I hope you get the position since you seem to desire it. I have seen copies of the DAWN and must confess I have not been impressed.
>
> But perhaps you could reform it.

And reform the paper she did. In her book about feminists of the first wave, Dianne Davidson described the contribution of Coralie Clarke's time at the helm:

> During her editorship, she injected some much needed polish into the layout and journalistic style of the *Dawn*, giving it a snappier and more professional look. She also concentrated more on informative articles and from the time she commenced working on the paper such articles gradually replaced much of the inspirational material so prominent in the 1920s.

As editor, Coralie made sure *The Dawn* was neither parochial in outlook nor dreary in content. She gave it a new subtitle: *A monthly journal containing news of progressive movements effecting social welfare in the Australian Commonwealth and other countries.*

Regular features were introduced: 'Women from Other Lands', 'Social Welfare and Political Topics', 'Our Gallery of Women', and 'Reports from Abroad'. There was plenty of stimulating material for the readership – mostly middle-class educated women who were engaged in political or social reforms or were sympathetic to their aims. Coralie's initiatives widened the scope and circulation of the journal.

Her time on *The Dawn* sowed the seeds of a lifelong belief in equality for women. The term 'feminism' was not widely used but its implications were born, its foundations laid. Coralie was not a tub-thumper, but she incorporated the ideals of the women's movement into the way she lived her life.

As a young adult cut off from the rest of the world in the isolated small city of Perth, my mother had no way of knowing that across the hemispheres in London, Virginia Woolf had just published *A Room of One's Own*. Woolf argued that every woman writer should have economic independence and a room of her own – preferably with a lockable door – and then she would have the freedom and time to give voice and shape to her ideas. Given these conditions, female writers would at least equal, if not eclipse, the output of their male rivals in both quality and quantity.

At twenty-one years of age, Coralie was desperate to achieve financial independence. She longed to extend her creative output and to forge ahead with the career of her choice. At that stage of her life she was not interested in marriage. However, her resolve would be seriously challenged when she was drawn not to a lapsed royal but to a drama critic – one who shared her dreams of becoming a successful writer.

~

I first wrote about Coralie Clarke editing *The Dawn* in the 1970s for a seminar at Macquarie University called 'Women in History'. The second wave of feminism was raging in Australia and with a mother like mine it was inevitable I would be an ardent 'women's libber'. Little did I guess what I would discover decades later, buried in my paper inheritance: the carbon copy of a typed letter my mother had sent when working in London, a mere two or three years after her time on *The Dawn*. The letter was addressed to Virginia Woolf at the Hogarth Press in Tavistock Square, London, from my parents' digs in Randolph Gardens, and it was dated (inadequately) 'Nov. 11'.

> Dear Mrs Woolf
>
> I am an Australian journalist, at present engaged on a series of interviews with outstanding women writers, and I should very much appreciate the privilege of a short talk with you sometime soon.
>
> I admire your work very much, and the ideas expressed in 'A Room of One's Own' interest me particularly.
>
> Hoping for the pleasure and honour of meeting you,
> Yours very truly,
> Coralie Clarke Rees B.A.

Coralie had folded the copy of the letter in half and on the back and for six accompanying pages, she wrote notes in ink on what she had gleaned from reading *A Room of One's Own*. She was obviously lit up with what she had found in Woolf's text, the arguments and the choice quotations from literature that showed how women had been publicly demeaned over the centuries and kept in society's lowliest ranks. These notes were her preparation for the interview she hoped would eventuate and the article she would write. She also picked up some salient details about Woolf herself, helpful background for a conversation. Coralie noted that Virginia 'apparently likes good food and wine and cigarettes'. On the challenges of Modernist poetry Woolf had said 'one cannot remember more than two consecutive lines'. (She obviously preferred a good rhyming couplet.) Coralie also made a point of writing down that Virginia received an unexpected legacy from an aunt at the same time as she got the vote 'but she regarded the vote as more important'.

My mother always displayed an unyielding belief in women's innate strength and limitless potential. And there is no doubt she was adamant about the basic doctrine: equality. Equality of personal worth, of opportunity, equality in relationship, in responsibility. When she took my father's name on marriage, she insisted that he took hers. They both became 'Clarke Rees', though this did not last. As my father once explained, when they collaborated, there were too many names to fit on the spine of a book. My mother was a realist. She appreciated the males in her circle despite her observation: 'Men come and go in your life – your women friends are always there for you.' Neither was she cynical about marriage: she valued hers but not in a sentimental way. She once described her relationship with my father as 'Two OPs warring for supremacy' and warned that, since my chosen mate was also an OP (outstanding personality), I might expect the same. She also cautioned us: 'You don't get it all in one package – neither does your partner.'

In my late teens, Hollywood films and the new medium of black-and-white television in Australia spread the symbols of twentieth-century Western romanticism. It had some dangerous tenets. Female stereotypes on screen 'fell in love' after a chaste kiss or two and, with fluttering hearts, pined to hear those elusive words: *Will you marry me?* Once elevated into the desired status, they swiftly metamorphosed into perfectly coiffed housewives dancing around their kitchens in frilly aprons, striving to achieve perfection in their homes in the cleanest and shiniest way possible. (If you didn't achieve 'the whitest wash', you were doomed, your self-esteem in tatters.) Unwittingly, these prototypes slipped into domestic bondage and would need to be careful with the housekeeping money while they struggled to find some small outlet for their creativity and talents.

As daughters, Megan and I were blessed in our role model. She gave us a different example to follow – one that reflected individual skills and talents without tying them to gender. Our mother would frequently remind us: 'I've never seen it written on anyone's tombstone: *She was a perfect housewife!*'

5

Love Must Wait

I've searched all my father's public and private writings for some small indication of his early feelings for my mother. He did not seem overly enchanted in his account of their first meeting when she was appointed his assistant editor. But then, patently, neither was she. However, that early teamwork in many ways laid the cornerstone of the literary partnership they would create. They were forced to work closely to bring out three editions of the university literary magazine each year and soon discovered they were both infatuated with words, if not with each other. My mother records that it was not only editorial work demanded of them. She was required to produce articles, short stories and book reviews.

Then Leslie wanted a play for *The Black Swan* so I wrote a play called *Shielded Eyes*. It was the first West Australian play to be published and was also produced in a programme of one-act plays, again at the Assembly Hall, not by the University Dramatic Society but by the Perth Repertory Club. I played the leading lady, my leading man Paul Hasluck.

As Coralie and Leslie were working side by side over a common interest, it was not surprising their relationship ripened into a collegiate friendship. Happenstance intervened when they discovered they were both spending their Christmas holiday at Rottnest, that idyllic island eighteen kilometres off the coast where Perthsiders flock to escape their blazing summers, savouring leisurely swims in natural rock pools, bike rides round the salt lakes and ambles through the bush with quokkas scuttling out of their path. The island worked its magic. In my mother's words: 'All that weekend we spent a lot of time talking in the sandhills and our future was sealed at that point.' (Neither would have used as banal a phrase as *falling in love*, so often indicative of a sudden and perhaps indiscriminate obsession.)

No, their passion was for literature. It underpinned their relationship and enriched every corner of their lives, as did their shared determination to make their own contribution. Now both journalists, they were bent on becoming writers. They understood that there was a distinction: a creative progression required, one that would extend their skills and demand the best they could give. On this, their first interlude of commitment, they read the poetry of WB Yeats to each other. After sharing John Galsworthy's story 'The Apple Tree', they decided that if they had a daughter, they would call her after one of the characters, Megan – pronounced in the Welsh way with a short 'e', as in Meg.

In 1929 Coralie had graduated with a row of distinctions and was working full-time on *The Dawn*. Though it took Leslie five years to finish his degree, he was hungry for more. Straight away he put his energies into postgraduate research. Drama was always his main preoccupation but in Perth he was limited. He could only *read* plays. He needed to see theatre, to experience it. He was greatly in awe of George Bernard Shaw, both his philosophy and his dramatic output, but he was also entranced by the plays of the Irish literary theatre, and planned his master's thesis on Synge, Yeats and O'Casey. He decided he must widen his knowledge and experience by going abroad. But how? The only way to get to England from Australia was by sea, the steamer passage taking five weeks from Fremantle. Commercial air travel was still years away. The Orient Line offered a scholarship program for graduate students to extend research in their chosen field, with a free first-class passage. A return passage was included, though not for over fifteen months, at least twelve of which should be devoted to a course of study. No living expenses were provided. Two scholarships were awarded each year, one for a June departure, the other for December.

Leslie applied for the one at the end of the year and was successful.

He was thrilled and excited, at the same time wracked with concern. Looking back on this moment, he wrote:

> I considered. I dreamed. Not without further negative tremors, though. To walk out on my family would be in the natural order of things, however much they'd helped me; not so to part with someone who had become intimately identified with my life, in a daily association with a score of affinities.

That does not sound like passion, but my father was extremely reticent about discussing intimate feelings. It was not until I read his letters from that voyage, seventy years after they were written, that I discovered this sensitive young man I had never known, how socially insecure he was and how besotted with my mother. Yet he was driven to the very real risk of leaving her behind while he explored the wider world.

Leslie had never travelled alone. He had only once been away from Perth – a quick train trip across the country with a crowd of other youngsters in the Young Australia League, an organisation to which his mother donated her services. He still lived at home the way most people did in their twenties while they were single. It was also common for young people to be virgin until marriage, due not only to the unavailability and haphazard nature of birth control but to prevailing moral imperatives. Leslie admired women and had engaged in a few tenuous flirtations but never an ongoing relationship. Always cautious with money after tasting years of poverty as a boy, he had lived modestly on his salary from *The West Australian* and had saved every penny towards his trip to the other side of the world.

Nearly twenty-four years old – he would have his birthday during the passage – Les (as he preferred to be called) would set sail on 2 December 1929 and expected to be away for at least eighteen months, maybe more. He had promised Coralie they would marry when he returned. However, they had not revealed this intention to their families or made any announcement about their plans for a future together.

The RMS *Orford*, a two-masted steamer, had been built in England for the Orient Line only the year before and was reputed to be the last word in luxury. On the day of Les's departure, a blazing summer day, Coralie borrowed her father's car to drive him, with his mother and sister, Averil, down to the port of Fremantle to board the ship. As was the custom, each clung to their ends of coloured paper streamers across the widening gap of water as the ship pulled away from the wharf. When Les's streamer finally broke, he went to his cabin and took up the pen provided and a sheet of ship's stationery. Now he was on his own.

6

Letters from the Ship: 1929

On this first night, as on every night of the voyage, after dinner Les secluded himself in his cabin and wrote to his beloved, his Coral, telling her what he was thinking and feeling, what the day had brought. This became part of his story of that voyage. The ship would make its first port in Ceylon (now Sri Lanka). He hoped there would be mail from home awaiting him there or at the northern end of the Suez Canal at Port Said. But he had already decided he would not post his swag of letters until he reached the safety of London. Then the package would take another four weeks on another ship, this one heading south, to reach Coralie in Perth by mid-February 1930.

There is no way I would have recognised the writer of these letters, the ingenuous love-struck Les on his voyage to the Promised Land, as my father and the literary figure I grew to understand. However, I can now see that the restless traveller endlessly seeking new adventures – whatever the cost – was a central part of his nature. In fact it became an entrenched part of his self-constructed identity.

Dec. 2nd, 1929

Darling, I was glad the ship went when it did. I couldn't keep my eyes off the little fluttering red figure in front of everybody else at the wharf and as I watched it I knew definitely that my poor mother, whom I had thought was equal in my heart with you, took but a very secondary place. Oh, the anguish of great love!

I watched you getting smaller and smaller but still looking at the ship. More than once I looked overboard to see how far it would be to swim to land. At last the ship hove to outside the breakwater, the pilot boat came alongside, the pilot changed decks and the little ship was off – the last link with the darling of my heart broken.

After a while I saw Rottnest – even that was passing and then I went to the cabin and fairly wept.

Dec 3rd

At breakfast this morning I was in a fix. Table is set like this: I've drawn a little sketch for you. Now what would the little knife and fork marked 'A' be for? There was nobody at my table; the assistant purser had finished and Miss Brady doesn't come down to breakfast so I couldn't find out and left them there.

There's just been a terrific noise – bells and gongs clanging; what does it all mean? I ask a fellow passenger and he replies 'Boat Drill'. I go to my cabin, ring for the steward and he helps me into a rigmarole that would drown a man in the water. I get on deck then there's a terrific buzzing of a siren and the whole crew rushes about the decks – the only time one sees them all – cooks, stewards and workaday-looking chaps that must live down in the holds. They line up, the boats are lowered and they get in. Suddenly it struck me that the boat was going down and I was getting left. Life on this ship's very terrifying, mystifying. Everyone on board – except the passengers – has a face like an underdone scone. Why is that?

Have tried to make a start on the play but I'm afraid I'll do nothing but write to you on this voyage. Cheerio, darling. Will write again this afternoon.

~

I must tell you how I got through my first night of ballroom society. I went down to dinner and found that the funny little knife and fork had been added to by a spoon. We later ate ices with the spoon but no-one touched the funny little knife and fork – perhaps no-one knows what they're for. After eating consommé, fish, chicken, pudding, ices and nuts, I went up to the Lounge where everyone goes.

The officers were in their white dinner coats looking very like stewards. It is a sumptuous place, quite the last word in luxury as indeed the whole boat is. But for me, very boring, not knowing anyone. I sat and pretended to be interested in the punch. Then a waiter brought some black coffee which I refused. I went up to the deck and then I went to bed where I am now.

Well, goodnight, girl of my dreams, 'dream-dimmed' girl, wonder of the western world, pride of Australia, envy of the English-speaking, beautiful, lovely, warm-hearted, generous, wonderful Coral – who is keeping herself only for me.

Dec. 4th

I suppose you are just thinking of leaving your office, tired and hungry after a day's work. May my thoughts reach you and brighten you up. I have just been talking to a girl who is going to England to be married. I told her how lucky she was and how I had left you behind at home. She doesn't seem very thrilled. I wish you were in England instead of Australia, then this trip would be worthwhile.

I have your photo before me – the full length one – and yesterday I covered it with some powder so that when I kiss it, it smells like you. For I do kiss it and even put my arm around the back of it so that I seem to be embracing you. But what a shadow compared to the sacred reality of three nights ago. Oh darling, what a treasure I have left behind! If only you were with me. May the days speed by and the nights. I love you, dearest, Love you, LOVE you. Be sure to wait for me till I return. I feel positive that I shall wait for you.

That last night together. What a memory it is! I wouldn't have missed it for fortunes. And to think that you have chosen me of all men, singled me out to shower with your wealth of gifts. Conventional thought? But true, darling, if it was ever true.

If you were here, I should be revelling in the luxury of this ship. As it is, the ship is for the most part simply boring. By the way, I found out what the little knife and fork is for. It's for fruit but we never get any, being in the middle of the ocean.

To change the subject to something nearer to our hearts, I got on writing a fair bit of the play today. But I don't think it will be any good. Perhaps you are to be the playwright and I the critic. At any rate, criticism just flows out of me whereas creation doesn't.

We are now over Capricorn in the tropics but it is not hot. On the contrary, almost chilly, very cool today. I have two swims, the most pleasant diversion of the day, apart from writing to my darling.

Dec. 6th

Darling,

I deferred writing this letter to read the last of Vance Palmer's plays. Jolly good plays they were, too. Very similar to Louis Esson's;

in fact, as far as I can see, the same man might have written the two volumes. Better than the plays, I like a short story of Palmer's in my *Australian Short Story* book called 'The Birthday'. Very subtle. I have been wondering whether a subtle theme requires carefuller handling than a common or obvious theme: in the one you have to be careful not to miss bringing out the point and in the other to be careful to disguise the point.

Tonight I got down early for dinner – the officer eats so quickly that I'm often cut short – and had that khaki-coloured soup (basque something), fish, roast mutton and Pêche Melba. Then came the hideous walk upstairs – I dread it every night – to café (which I still don't have) and those awful vamps joined us. I always shut up like a trap when they're there. Tonight, after one of the bored silences of the company, one (divorced) woman, Mrs Johnson – I bet it was her fault – said to me 'D'you ever talk?' in an insolent tone. 'When there's something to talk about and someone to talk to,' I replied with equal insolence.

But no! That's a lie. Your poor Les had neither the wit nor the impudence to say such a thing (I thought it out afterwards) and all I said was 'Very little.' If she knew me!!

Extremely hot today, like a midsummer day in Perth. I had two glorious swims. I don't know what I'd do without the pool. Also I wrote 'CURTAIN' at the end of my play. I feel much more pleased about it than a day or so ago but I still have hours of work. And it's jolly hard work too. Still it cheers me to think that with effort I can get to the end of writing a play. Strangely enough, it is like your play [*Shielded Eyes*] in that most of my characters are women whereas most of yours are men.

The news that I am an Orient Scholar is gradually spreading over this ship.

Thought for the day is 'the first picnic at Armadale'. Ah, Darling, I can remember a better one – when you decided to have a swim and we looked up at the stars at night. Dearest! Memory is wonderful.

The sea outside is a marvellous mystery and at times haunts me. Don't be alarmed when I tell you that I often have funny impulses to jump overboard. I say don't be alarmed because the opposite impulses of self-preservation are much stronger.

I think of you working on your paper. So how is the old *Dawn* going? I suppose the next issue must be pretty well due. Don't slave your insides out, but being both the editor and the main writer is good experience. I certainly think another 18 months – or at least 12 – on *The Dawn* won't do you slightest harm. It will consolidate what you have learned, apart from teaching you much more and then some editor may lift you into a women's section sub-editorial chain. I think you're making a marvellous start. Between us, we should really make the world.

Darling, I'm simply longing for the hour when we shall meet again, to part no more; meet again to perform our great work for Australia, ourselves and for literature. Life is going to be more marvellous than ever it's been – and it can be marvellous. Never forget, it can only be marvellous with me.

Dec. 9th

I have been upstairs watching the dancing tonight (had one dance to be honest) and looked through an English magazine which gave me an idea for *The Dawn*. I think you had already agreed that the book review, although a good innovation, provided a rather sparse literary feast for a month. Well, ask your readers to recommend books and print the list of recommendations or make a digest from the hundreds of letters you receive.

We crossed The Line sometime this evening. There were no celebrations. In these tropics, one wakes up in the morning feeling like a limp collar, almost suffocated, enervated. Then after breakfast the weather seems to cool off and at lunch time it is quite tolerable. Then in the evening hot again though this might be due to the evening dress one is forced to wear.

I had intended to go to Kandy but now find that there must be a party of four. Will have to find another first thing in the morning or the trip is off. I don't mind. I'd save 30/-.

Dec. 10th

It is still fearfully hot, so much so that the temperature of the water in the deck pool which is straight out of the sea is about the same as the atmosphere. It's very queer to look up on a starry night while on deck and see the Milky Way swinging to and fro like a lamp and the moon like a bouncing balloon.

I am thinking of turning my adventures with the Menu into capital, so you may see an article in *The West Australian* on the subject; I will ask the editor to let you have it for *The Dawn* if he doesn't want it.

Well, darling, this must seem all very dry and disinterested stuff to pour down your neck. But one almost grows tired of repeating the same old longing. Don't imagine that I have stopped feeling it, although when my surroundings are more lonely and less luxurious, I am sure I'll feel it more still.

A dozen times a day I think of you in different positions beside me – at dinner, on the deck, dancing, in my bunk – laughing, effervescent, ever sympathetic and wonderful at listening. It is perhaps the very certainty of our liaison that stops me from talking about it so much in these letters. I never for one moment doubt our eventual reunion and am thinking of 'eventual' in not too indefinite terms.

That professor! He's a scream but I must reserve his description until there is more time. On second thoughts I may write a sketch about him instead of telling you. The essay-article itch is getting me again. I have in mind writing a short story and am also trying to think of a subject for a romantic prose play. Romanticism hasn't had a voice in Australia yet. It's a field to be explored.

You must expect my letters to get shorter when I reach England though it won't be for lack of inclination.

December 14th

Darling, I'm afraid you are monopolising all my writing time. I have got as far as making out a list of people to whom I should write but I never get the time to write to them – even to Mum.

Am typing out the play and getting more faith in it as I go on. Marvellous how all the little difficulties gradually smooth out, isn't it, you being the experienced playwright? Mine will be considerably longer than yours. But still your play had a deal of substance, mine is very light social comedy. If possible, I want to send you a copy from Colombo, but it may not be finished.

Everyone on this ship seems to be looking for ways of passing the time; if I tell anyone I've been working, their eyes nearly fall overboard into the sea. But for me, I am glad to say, the days are still too short. Apart from your absence, this is really the ideal life, the life that I have been longing for, for years. I read for 20 minutes before breakfast, work on the play during the morning until noon, swim until 1 pm, lunch, read till 5 pm, swim and sunbathe till 6.30, dress for dinner, dinner.

Then comes the great need of the missing woman. I miss you and feel lonely and want to talk to you and sympathise and have you sympathise. So great is my need to talk that I tried to tell the Brady woman about my play and explain some of the difficulties of writing it. But one might as well address a tree. She's a cultured (in the narrow sense) well-brought up girl but absolutely idea-less.

Lord knows how her man will get on with her when he wants to explain (he's a doctor) how he's found a new unidentified sac in the human intestine.

I am so certain that I am coming back to you, darling, that I constantly forget the need for any reminder of my constancy, loyalty, love. But I know that it's nice to have the iteration and as often as possible. This Brady woman never speaks of her fiancé but is constantly telling me that the jazz music brings back memories of her dear boy pal in Melbourne. Don't you go getting any boy pals like that!

Four long weeks till I hear from you but I seem to hear your voice and see your face and feel your presence all the time. And so, dearest, I end the first chapter of the book of messages that I shall write to you on this trip. May this find you glorious in health, lovely as a star (as you always were) and the same dear girl.

Think of me always, dear

Les

7

The Girl He Left Behind

Coral would eventually have the opportunity to tell her side of this story.

Les went off to London. He said 'I'll come back in a year's time and we'll get married.' But I thought no – what an intolerable situation for a marriage that would be. He would have all the overseas experience and I would be the girl he left behind in little Perth. No, that didn't suit me at all. So as soon as he was gone I had to get busy to get myself over there.

Years later Coral was to turn the whole episode into part of her constructed story. She would even recount it on national radio to an audience of listeners from all over the country as part of a series of broadcasts, based on their unpublished manuscript *Seven and Sevenpence, Please.*

High up on deck Les had waved the tattered bunch of paper ribbons in his hand and clutching mine I waved back till my arm ached. Then his face grew smaller and smaller and all I could see as the great stern of the ship began to turn was a clockwork arm waving broken streamers. Then he had gone. And I was left behind.

Something in my mind pinged at that moment. A surge of protest rose and nearly choked me. Was I cast for the role of the girl he left behind him, the little woman who would keep for him in Perth, a place full of quiet breathing, until he came home after a year and we could be married?

In a disembodied way I began to drive my father's old but useful car homeward, with Les's mother and sister Averil as passengers. I looked across to the sandhills of Cottesloe where Les and I had lain, reading Yeats. The words murmured within me:

> Oh what to me my mother's care
> The house where I was safe and warm
> The shadowy blossom of my hair
> Will hide us from the bitter storm.

The *Orford* was just passing Rottnest Island, the hot dry magical island off the mainland where two years previously Les and I had discovered each other in a blinding flash, after a long and desultory friendship. In the days and weeks that followed that revelation we had talked and planned far into the night. Driving along the Perth-Fremantle road I pulled myself sharply out of a daydream. How could I get myself to London – and quickly? I was 21 years old with a Bachelor's Degree and a leg-in to journalism as both editor and staff of *The Dawn*. My salary was £3 per week. After a year on *The Dawn*, I had saved nothing.

Nor were there likely to be better opportunities. A city of about 200,000 people, Perth had one morning newspaper, one evening newspaper, a Sunday paper and a couple of sporting rags.

Women were not admitted to general news journalism and that left only the women's social columns with their small fixed staffs.

My only hope was to be awarded one of the free-passage scholarships given by the overseas steamship lines to the university for poor but worthy graduates wanting to study abroad, similar scholarships to the one that had just taken Les away. But these were annual awards. Some months must elapse before the next batch – not a whole year – as Les had left Perth at the end of his permissible off-season period of travel while I ... I might be able to leave at the beginning of the next period, if only I could win favour. This would depend on how many graduates were in the field and how outstanding they were.

I applied at once. Fortunately my record as a student was good. So I approached our professor of English literature in whose department I had majored. I asked him to support my application. Professor Walter Murdoch's writings as a quizzical essayist and common sense philosopher were relished from one side of Australia to the other. He was a rare, warmly human personality. He also had discernment. He smiled at me across his table, roguish eyes over thin-rimmed spectacles, bushy grey moustache and thatch of hair. In that cockle-warming Scots burr he enquired: 'Do you two intend to make a match of it?' I hadn't expected such a non-academic question but on recovering my breath, whispered, 'Yes.' Murdie, as we called him, being a romantic gave me his blessing. My application had, of course, to go before the Senate.

By mid-February 1930 a trickle of letters – sometimes a wave – began to arrive in Mt Hawthorn from Les in London. They did not always arrive in the order they were posted. When the package of Les's letters from the ship was delivered, Coral carefully arranged them into sequence and pasted them into a book. Les had written to her every day, sometimes twice a day, for thirty-five days in a row. Now it was her turn for the nightly ritual. Every evening after dinner Coral would repair to her desk and pen her letter to Les. Sometimes, she would present him with a poem, written in rhyming quatrains in the vein of the Victorian romantics they had studied and admired.

To Les

You are the breath of fragrant nights
When summer hangs on flower and lawn
And the pale moon's half-swooning lights
Haunt shadows, like lost dreams forlorn.

You are the heavy scent of dew
Which rises from dank violet beds
The wet earth's vapours, there are you
And the ripping showers which winter sheds.

Your voice is in the breeze of spring
Which rustles the lips of tall gum trees
Of your glad mating magpies sing
Their sunshine-bursting melodies.

The russet browns of autumn's leaves
Are warmth upon your cheek and heart
As fitful sunshine oft deceives
The sadness that we are apart.

In all earth's beauties do you shine
And live with me through every day,
And while there's still a breath of mine,
There'll be a prayer for you to say.

At other times she gave her own account of what was happening in her much smaller distant world, including her daily challenges on *The Dawn*, which seemed so demanding and so humdrum compared to the 'thrilling deeds' Les was relating in his letters.

But besides reports and the endless iterations of his love and devotion, Les's side of the correspondence gave him the opportunity to air his ideas and discuss his literary works in progress. To these, Coral would respond with enthusiasm and warm encouragement, setting a pattern that would last. She would also, tactfully, offer suggestions. They separately articulated their plans – how they saw their future careers. The letters also gave them both time to work out some of the ground rules of their relationship and to find a path through their differences by negotiation, skills they would need to refine for any literary partnership to take shape and survive.

8

Full of Love and Literature

In the mêlée of the Clarke household Coral often found it impossible to get an uninterrupted moment or enough quiet to concentrate. One night she was trying to write with a party for her sister Jess's sixteenth birthday going on in the adjoining room. As she complained:

> – not at all a fitting atmosphere in which to discourse sweet nothings or rather passionate and important somethings to my darling. They're making barbarous noise in there now. It's very distracting having a flapper party in one ear. So you will make allowances, dear?
>
> It really means that I require a harmonious atmosphere in which to commune with you – it would be sacrilege to try to tell you all the beautiful thoughts and emotions aroused in me by your wonderful letters while this dreadful party is going on.

Now that she had applied for the scholarship to go to London, Coralie was desperately raking over ideas to earn extra cash, over and above her salary at *The Dawn*. She was already coaching younger students at night plus running an exercise class, but now she had the idea of freelance writing. She reworked pieces of prose and poetry for submission, some of which she would try out on Les by enclosing in a letter. She was realistic and imagined she was ready for any success in the venture, or none at all.

> Darling dearest Les – my lover, husband, hero and author – you're
> the biggest interest in my life – without you all the literary success
> in the world would be as 'a sounding brass and a tinkling cymbal.'
> Goodnight, beloved, Coral.

As soon as Les hit London, he had wasted no time in getting to the West End. His budget was meagre – two pounds a week to cover everything – but he would rather cut out a meal than not see a play, even if there wasn't an actual seat. He once stood for three hours to see Shaw's *The Apple Cart*. The seats were so far up in the gallery he said 'the players looked like well-dressed ants on their hind legs down on the stage and the words were hard to hear'. Shaw's are plays of ideas and the exact words are important. He went again and stood for another three hours just to catch the dialogue.

Les wasn't writing up the plays he saw for a newspaper – not yet. But they were filling his letters to Coral. She was envious.

> Darling, it must be marvellous to be seeing all those good plays
> wonderfully acted – the feast of a lifetime! And to think that
> there's been nothing but wretched pictures in Perth since you left!
> And all for 7/9 – the plays – one week's tickets – that's amazing.
> I'm longing to hear your impressions of George Bernard Shaw as
> a person and as a speaker. Was he disappointing? I don't think he
> would be.

By the way, I've just read a priceless anecdote about Shaw and Barrie. Apparently they used to live opposite each other in Adelphi Terrace which must have been a rather narrow lane, because one day Shaw looked out of his study window and saw Barrie pacing up and down wrapt in pensive thought, so he threw an apple across. It did not hit Barrie but fell upon his manuscript. He affected to take no notice and bided his time; when Shaw in his turn was immersed in the fever of creation, Barrie then threw a fat pink uncooked chop at him through the window. Rather subtle repartee – because Shaw is a vegetarian. But I believe they are great friends.

Apparently, between seeing plays, Les was busy writing one. Not the one-acter he put together on the ship but a full-length play set in the newspaper world with which he was so familiar. (This work would eventually end up as *Sub-Editor's Room* and become – in 1956 – the first Australian play ever produced on Australian television.)

When he explained about this work-in-progress in his letters, Coral cautioned him to be realistic about its prospects. She cited examples of other plays that took a long while to find a market.

And, as far as your big three-act world-revolutionising drama 'The Press' is concerned, about which critics are going to rave and make blazing Broadway lights – permit me to be comforting, darling, just in case they don't at first. You must never tire of trying to get 'The Press' produced. But you'd be missing part of the business if the first manager accepted it!

Actually, I'm dying to hear more of this epic of newspaperdom – have you really completed it, or did you die on the idea? Am I allowed a suggestion, dear? Don't call your drama 'The Press' if it is about newspapers and newspaper people. 'The Press' would be attractive if it was used metaphorically to refer to say the crushing weight of family tyranny, or some big machine that tries to stifle individuality in man's life. Obviously, I too am influenced by Shaw (you seem to be very).

I'm almost as thrilled about your play as you are, darling. A glorious brother-playwright feeling, the pride and comradeship, and not a whit of jealousy – only stimulation to get busy myself again. I'm longing for the next lots of letters to know how the great work is going – and do hope you haven't cooled completely off the idea.

Les suggested she try to sell her one-act play, *Shielded Eyes*. But there was no time for that now that she was pinning her hopes on winning that scholarship.

Thanks for the tip about selling one-act plays, Love. However, if I'm off to Europe in June, there isn't much time to work for anything (except cash). When we return to Australia, darling, nothing will stop us establishing and endowing an Australian, all Australian and nothing but Australian theatre. Old Yeats and Lady Gregory will be put in the shade. I feel the power of certainty within me, don't you Love?

For the first time, Les revealed in a letter his deep antipathy for organised religion, stemming from the time as a child he was pushed into attending a badly run Sunday school. He said he didn't believe in God; he worshipped only her.

Coral found this confronting, even shocking. It was the first deeply held point of difference they would have to negotiate. She had a strong faith, a Christian view of God based on the Church of England liturgy.

All the reasoning and philosophy in the world cannot make me lose my childhood faith. It is all I have to cling to when I am in trouble or doubt which goes beyond human understanding or sympathy.

She also made it clear to Les that worshipping her was not a healthy alternative.

You must not let *me* be your religion, dearest. Very often one sees an overwhelming passion bring about a person's downfall. However, you are far too balanced to let even me overrule you, aren't you dearest? And for that I must frankly confess my gratitude and admiration. I know now how much better and more valuable it is for your love to be more critical and less abject and I recognise that in that lies its infallible attraction for me. Only foolish girls revel in unqualified worship. How on earth can they take a man's word that they are goddesses when they must know themselves that they are not.

That does not mean that you're to drop an ounce of the reverence from your love for me, dearest, and lapse into a platonic sort of camaraderie. Even if you contemplated such a thing (and I'm sure you have no wish to) that is not what I mean for an instant. It's the happy mean between mutual admiration and love in spite of faults and blind worship that we must strike — a state of enlightened devotion or of sure love incurred with the divine essence of self-abnegation and sacrifice [...]

Darling, I too have found myself imagining that you were dead or crippled, and I independently came to the same conclusion as you did — that it would make no real difference. Poverty, failure, nothing could part me from you — only death. And when the time comes, may we go down together like the couple in that film we saw — *Atlantic*. Even physical death could not part our spirits, beloved – for I know that if you died first my spirit would go with you even if my body had to keep walking on this physical plane. And if I died first I would be beside you in spirit always – until you too left your body – and then forever after that.

Through their studies of literature, both had spent years deconstructing other writers' notions of love and observed the way memorable characters experienced it, dating right back to *The Canterbury Tales* and that eternal motto *Amor vincit omnia* – love conquers all.

From the time she first came upon it, Coral embraced Shakespeare's sonnet 'Let me not to the marriage of true minds admit impediments', and she went on quoting it all through her life. This became her ideal: a marriage of true minds, an intellectual as well as an emotional partnership that rides out the storms and endures – 'even to the edge of doom'.

Oh, a thousand times a day I offer prayers of thanks for this love of ours. Do you realise how blessed we are to be experiencing it? You say that countless people through the ages have felt as we are feeling, dearest, but I can see and think of many who have not. We're phenomenally lucky to have one another – don't let's forget it. We must never tire for one minute of making ourselves worthy of each other, of the priceless jewel which binds us together.

My heart's heart, you ask me to live on until you return. Beloved, I shall live only on my hopes and plans for an ultimate life with you. You are the very breath I draw.

I think I'll stop writing now for tonight, beloved, and go to bed. How very often since you went away have I done nothing but spend whole evenings with you. It is as great a measure of compensation as is possible. Never mind – if I get the scholarship, it won't be long before I shall be with you in the flesh, dearest.

Until then may my never flagging love and devotion wrap you around always.

Coral could now spell out the details of her surprise. Yes, she had won the scholarship! She would be leaving for London at the beginning of June. But Les would not know about it till the letter arrived in five weeks' time.

Oh at times like this, imagination and memory are a torture – it shall be wonderful, wonderful to be with you again, dearest – don't let's be matter-of-fact for a second. Let's try never to get over the breathless excitement of having one another. For the first six hours after I arrive in England don't let another person come near us. Just ourselves for a long timeless stretch until we can bear to separate ourselves in the presence of outsiders. Say you feel the same burning yearning as I do. How can I wait?

Les, meanwhile, was working on another play. Coral was fulfilling her role as chief encourager. She apparently still had her eyes on the stage and envisaged playing the lead in Les's plays when they hit Shaftesbury Avenue on London's West End.

My wonder playwright! I shall not be surprised if by now you have enough one-act plays to fill No. 1 of your collected works of drama. For the lead's sake send me copies of this work of genius 'Mother's Birthday' as soon as possible. Your fecundity is amazing, dear. I feel like an arid desert when I think of what you are doing.

(The play Coral refers to here became the basis of *Mother's Day*, which was first published in a book of collected plays in the 1950s. It has also seen stage performances – though not with Coral as the lead.)

It is delightful to discover married literati. But I can't imagine how people can keep up a violent interest in each other with no common ambition. Have you ever now the effrontery to wish that my interest and ambitions were not identical with yours? If I were a musician or an artist, how could I sympathise with you with a genuineness born only of personal experience, when you wrote your plays, poems and articles? We might admire one another's work with broad discrimination but we could never understand it or each other as we do now, could we?

To Coral, the sharing of their work as writers was central to their relationship. The only problem: she herself was not getting any writing done – due both to lack of time and to what she regarded as the more menial tasks demanding attention. This would become her familiar lament; indeed, the story of her life.

Are you disappointed and surprised at the little, in fact almost entire lack of, freelance writing that I find time and energy to do, dear? – that is apart from *The Dawn* and these letters to you? If the number of words in each of these sources of literary activity were counted they would be found to run into several volumes, I'll warrant. It's disgusting that I never have time to think of anything but *The Dawn* from as soon as I wake in the morning until about 8 pm at night and then I write to you and sometimes go out and after that I'm too tired for anything. It's a wretched state of affairs. I often have the most brilliant ideas for articles and plays and am forced to put them aside for the time being, and that means for forever – for I scarcely find time to go back to them. I know that 'procrastination is the thief of time' but what can one do with an octopus like *The Dawn* around one's throat and you so far away that I have to take hours over painful transcription of a few of the things I long to talk to you about.

I feel a tremendous power to write within me, dear. If only one weren't forced by competition to a time limit. However, I shall make big efforts during the next few months.

No more for tonight, my dearest love,

I am Coral, your betrothed, and full of love and kisses.

9

Betrothed

It seems that right up to the time she was getting ready to go overseas, Coral was still considering a stage career – though she only ever envisaged herself as the lead, a fact that reveals her boundless optimism and alarming degree of self-confidence. In immediately putting in for a scholarship so she could join Les in London, she had not faced up to certain realities. How was she going to support herself? It was clear Les would not be able to help. He was living frugally off his savings and already going without the odd meal. Of course they could not live together – that would be unthinkable – so she would require her own accommodation. Under the contract offered by the shipping company, they could not marry for at least a year. Of course she would apply for jobs – but the Depression was biting already, even in Perth, and Les had told her that in London many journalists were already now out on the street.

There was another thorny problem. Although both their families knew that Les and Coral had become close, marriage had not been mentioned. Perhaps Coral was being super cautious as she had already had a brief engagement with someone else.

As youngsters, we used to laugh about this. It was part of the legend my parents wove about themselves. My father used to say:

> The best thing I ever did for your mother was to save her from that dreadful fate. She would have been bored to tears and never written a word if she'd become the wife of a school master in some remote little town in Western Australia. Can you imagine it! Coralie – your mother – living a life like that?

Apparently he convinced her, too, because an end was quickly put to the previous arrangement. But it was not entirely forgotten. My sister, Megan, who used to write funny rhyming verse for special occasions, immortalised Mr Rejected as 'Poor old Hal Adam / who just missed being Pa'.

Although women and their assets no longer passed to their husbands on marriage, the social conventions in Australia in the 1930s were surprisingly similar to those of Jane Austen's time. The business of marriage was hedged with protocols and processes that one did not easily ignore. There were important steps to be undertaken. First, the suitor needed to approach his future bride's father and ask him to give 'the hand of his daughter'. The father would interrogate the anxious swain about his financial prospects before any permission was given. 'Can you keep her in the manner to which she is accustomed?' he would sternly ask. If he gave his consent, the couple could announce their engagement and seal it with a ring. They might put a notice in the paper. This would allow their friends and family to get accustomed to their approaching status while signalling to any other contenders they were both now off limits – bespoke. It would also allow the bride time to build up her glory box, filling it with necessities like teaspoons and doilies, vases and silver trays. She also had to collect a trousseau with a 'going away' outfit for her first appearance as a Mrs and, more importantly, fine underwear and nightgowns ready to entrance her new husband as they took that first step into unknown territory as sexual partners. 'The marriage bed' had its own mystique. Some women approached it with delight, even relief. Others (Les's sister, Averil, among them) regarded it as an alien landscape where the distasteful obligations of matrimony had to be endured.

But the situation in which Coral and Les now found themselves, afforded no time for ceremony, let alone convention. Coralie must have written hurriedly to Les – maybe even sent him a cable. *I'm on my way but we must be engaged.*

When Les heard the news he was bowled over:

> It had taken me quite a time to adjust to the news (brewing for some time) to realise what a tremendous difference the change would make to my life, as well as hers. Gradually there grew the expectation of a season of daily companionship as we faced our problems of make-do together.

So in Perth, Les's mother, Mary, duly received a letter from her son announcing their engagement. Mary invited Coralie to tea. She had written a reply to Les on his important news, a letter for Coralie to take with her.

Les was particularly close to his mother. He wrote to her every week from London and she wrote back, recounting what was going on in Perth and with the family. But now he was taking on responsibilities for another person, Mary decided it was time for her son to understand some home truths about her life, facts she had never before spelt out in order to protect him.

> But darling it's this way. I know you have not understood half of the worry I had to go through when you were born and after for many years, in fact until the boys were able to help a little towards

home expenses I had a fearful battle as when you were just a baby (9 months) I had to turn out to work for you all which meant that your sister Averil had to take charge of you (she was just 13) so you really have to thank her a lot as she practically brought you up when you were a young baby. Things should have been different, Les. Your father was a well educated man and gave promise when we were married of becoming a great man both in teaching and in music and he held his first-class certificates. So you see you have really him to thank for your brains. I was very proud of him I can assure you and loved him and still hold his memory dear. But his fault or weakness was the demon drink. It got the better of him and his ambitions. Today we could have been in a good position and I might have been able to do such a lot for my dear children. But no! I have had to endure shame and to fight for your bread to eat at times. I don't like to think of the terrible times I had for a few years after my arrival in this state with all my children growing up. As soon as they could work they have done their very best for me. So now dear as the years are going by, I have had no regrets for you have all turned out so good and it has been my great comfort. So now dear you will understand perhaps what made me seem hard at times. It was I could not give you what I would have liked to help you in your young life because it has been a constant struggle to live and keep out of debt which, thank God, I have done.

I congratulate you Les on your choice and I can assure you I shall be very happy to have Coralie for my daughter-in-law. You are a very lucky man to get such a fine girl in every way and you certainly have everything in common which is a great thing in married life because each is such a help to the other as long as you both love each other. I am expecting Coral to tea tomorrow (Sunday). I have not seen her since I received your letter about getting engaged. What about her Father and Mother? Perhaps they may not give their consent.

She enclosed in the letter a gift of twenty pounds as her 'little present – it is hateful to be short'.

Coralie's father, apparently, had not been so impressed when his eldest daughter brought Les home to meet her family. 'That young man has a lot to learn,' he told Coral. Maybe Les, who was not used to having a male parent, had shown a little less respect than the restrained paterfamilias demanded. And now his daughter said she was engaged to this man and was about to disappear to the other side of the globe to join him. Guildford Clarke penned a letter, making it clear to Les that he expected him 'to make good in one or more of the avenues which you have selected as a means of advancement'.

However, he softened a little to end his missive with a drop of cordiality:

I just briefly wish to acquiesce in your engagement to Coralie and feel sure that both of you are destined to have many happy years of companionship adorned with all the material advantages which your respective talents are reasonably certain to ensure.

Sylvia, Coralie's mother, also wrote to Les:

I would just like to add a few lines and say there is no one I would like better than you to take care of 'Coral' – I took a fancy to you the first time I saw you and feel that I know you very well by now and I also know that since you have been away Coral has not been the same girl and I'm sure it is her longing to be near you that has urged her on to work for this scholarship. I am sure you are both going to be very happy as your tastes are so much the same.

Coral has been a wonderful daughter and naturally we feel the parting very much but as you may some day know that parents feel all the joys, hopes and sorrows of their children so that her happiness is our happiness. She has always been ambitious and worked hard and this just seems a fitting climax to her scholastic career.

I feel so relieved that you will be there to greet her and be with her until she gets used to things and now Les I am only going to wish you both success, health and happiness in the future.

I remain,

Yours affectionately

S. Clarke xx

Just to make sure all looked above board, when my mother safely arrived in London, the Clarke parents put a notice in *The West Australian*, announcing Coralie and Leslie's engagement.

10

Luxury and Freedom

Coral was later to say of the Orient Line scholarships that took them separately to London:

> They give you a free passage, a first-class passage ironically enough; and considering that we only had such a little bit of money and so few clothes, it would have been better, really, if they were tourist-class passages.

This might have been true for Les who, judging from his letters, squirmed amid the sumptuous first-class décor and its unfamiliar protocols. But when Coral set off on the SS *Orsova* at the beginning of June 1930, she found herself not only at ease in the opulent surroundings but lapping up every aspect of shipboard life. There were endless elegant meals, dances after dinner, picture shows, a fancy dress ball and other evening entertainments, games on deck and a sea pool.

> It is positively staggering the way excitement upon excitement piles up when one is doing a trip like this [...] it's also amazing

how the time just filters away from one during these days aboard ship. I don't know how anyone could find them dull. For me they are never long enough.

Then there were the other passengers, among them a seemingly inexhaustible supply of admirers willing to share in the enjoyments of the trip and offering to escort Coral while exploring various ports. She revealed them all openly in her letters to the family and with a degree of insouciance, as if having a string of willing suitors was every girl's natural right.

At Colombo, their first port, Coral's eyes opened wide with her first experience of a foreign country and its different peoples. She was shocked to see the underprivileged Tamils who were loading coal into the ship by hand from an adjacent barge in mid-harbour. A party from the ship planned to go ashore for the day and she with them. But, perhaps by design, her escort for the day, Dr Riccardo Robotti (later referred to as 'Richard' and then 'Ric') was delayed in getting his passport stamped and so they were separated from the boat party. They missed the car and train taking them to Kandy.

Instead, Richard suggested they explore on their own. Their day together began with a visit to an impressive store of treasures, 'a riot of rich colour and silky attraction' where Coral bought some silk underwear for a friend in Australia. After negotiating the challenges of the postal service, they hired a rickshaw. Richard was already familiar with Colombo and wanted to show his ingenue the Cinnamon Gardens with their luscious blooms, and then the museum. After that, he took her on an hour's journey through the countryside to Mt Lavinia, a seaside resort with a gracious hotel right on the beach. They had lunch on the cool terrace.

The vista was very novel to me: full-sailed Arab dhows now and then on the ocean before us and on either side stretches of carved, yellow-sanded beach, down to the very shore on which bent thick groves of coconut palms.

It was then back to the bazaar for Richard to buy some luxurious women's pyjamas for his mother and sister – or so he told Coralie – and then to the ice-cream parlour and back to dinner on the ship.

Richard wanted to take me rowing on the Harbour but there was not time for that so we lounged upon the cool deck, surveying our last of the twinkling lights of Colombo until the anchor was withdrawn, the ship had turned and was again gathering speed outside the harbour.

When they passed through the Suez Canal, Coralie was utterly entranced. The way she described the scenery in her letter home foreshadowed the travel writer that would emerge in the years to come.

The colour experiences were among the most beautiful and unusual impressions left upon me by the Canal. The way the whole colour of the water varied from bright turquoise blue to equally bright and clear Nile green – the variation was graded of course and not sudden and depended on the angle from which one looked. In contrast to this were always the desert banks of the Canal – now cream in tone, now mud brown, now faint pink, now with soft purple and blue shadows on their distant ridges.

The ship docked in Port Said late in the day and after dinner Coralie went ashore with Ric to explore. He first took her to an enormous store – a cave of local artefacts: carved ivory, leather work, wood and silk. And perfume. Of course, he bought some for her. Then it was off to the Casino Palace Hotel for 'a marvellous evening'.

Coralie had never seen anything like it. She was stunned by the excesses of the décor. Ric told her there were many hotels like that in Europe but, as she wrote to her family, 'with my bankrupt Les' she doubted she would ever have the chance to see them.

The dancing floor was hung from the ceiling with cascades of gold lotus flowers. We took a table and drank champagne and danced and at intervals watched the beautiful marvellously dressed aristocratic women of Port Said.

Her Italian doctor friend left the ship at Naples, although she managed to see Pompeii – with or without him is not recorded. When the ship berthed at the Mediterranean port of Toulon, Coralie walked the town in the company of 'a young Russian doctor from the ship – an extremely model gentleman, brought up all his life in London'. They took a taxi together to explore the town.

It is one nestling mass of cream, pink and grey stone buildings, all rather weatherbeaten, built in high stories and so close together [...] They all have flat faces and shutters, sometimes coloured green or blue and little balconies from which the mats are beaten and the washing hung.

Back at the waterfront they met up with 'another man friend from the ship' and the three of them sat at a little café, 'watching Toulonese life go by and sipping French wines, Dubonnet and Roussi'. She described the port city as 'a place of sunshine on cream stone, and grey shadows which are the narrow streets'.

Their last port of call was Gibraltar. Coralie wrote: 'I went ashore with a man who has wanted to spend rather a lot of time with me since Ric left the ship. He's a typical fresh-complexioned fair-haired Oxford-accented young Englishman with light horn-rimmed spectacles.' They took horse-drawn hackneys to drive around the town, which was blatantly a military stronghold – soldiers everywhere.

But the attentions of this man were not entirely welcomed. Coral sometimes needed to avoid him so she could find time in her cabin to write more of the play she had started. The end of the journey was near. Soon she'd be reunited with Les. She started to think about the reality of her future life, their lack of money, the challenges ahead. 'I'm afraid, by what Les says, this will be my last bit of luxury and comfort for a long time. Well, no-one can say I haven't appreciated every moment. I've fairly revelled and even if it's only been for a month, I'm very grateful for it.'

Although this would be the first of a lifetime of journeys for Coral, she would never again experience such luxury – or such freedom. From now on, travel would be second class or even less – a tent, even a swag under the stars.

When I read her letters of this first adventure on her own, all excitedly typed single-space on small frail pages and rich with descriptions, I am struck by the fact that, even though she is writing to her family and sending a carbon to her closest friend, Dorothy, she seems at pains to mask her naivety, to quickly smother any suggestions of vulnerability. In narrating her experiences, she is already creating a literary persona, one she would extend and reinforce as her writing career took shape.

Only as the journey was coming to an end – a fantasy of being squired around by charming sophisticated European men in exotic places she never even knew existed – could she be herself, a twenty-one-year-old girl who grew up in one of the most isolated cities in the world, cosseted by the security of a devoted family.

I think of you often, my dear ones, and at some moments feel very alone in the world and very far away from anybody who really cares about me. But that's no use so I furbish up the old pecker and try to look hardened again.

I also need to meditate on my rapid approach to dear old Les. I'll be with him in two days' time. Incredible! He seems to be something to which I'll always look forward but never quite reach, and he says he feels the same about me.

Coral arrived in London on 3 July 1930.

When I stepped from the boat train at St Pancras amid a welter of luggage and porters and passengers greeting their friends, an enthusiastic figure came running towards me, teeth gleaming and his old Australian felt hat held high in one hand. London was obliterated. Then he said: 'Why did you bring so much gear? I told you not to bother about things like tennis rackets!' thus foreshadowing in that moment of ecstatic reunion the beginning of our 30-years' war over luggage.

My father remembered this occasion quite differently. It must have made a lifelong impression because, when he recounted it to me forty years later, tinges of his dismay were still palpable.

'When your mother stepped off the train after we hadn't seen each other for eight months, I greeted her with a jubilant, "Here's my girl!" To which she replied, "I'm not *your* girl. I'm *Coralie's* girl."'

11

Seven and Sevenpence, Please

Within fifteen months of Coralie's arrival in London, she and Leslie had fulfilled the study conditions of their Orient scholarships and Coralie had kept her promise to Professor Murdoch. They were free to marry and with some relief could now live publicly in coupledom. The following four and a half years spent in England were to prove critical to their careers and to their story. They milked these experiences again and again, recounting them in articles, talks, broadcasts, books and interviews. As writers, they had quite separate and distinctive styles so in the book they wrote together about this period of their lives they developed a technique that would allow each to express their individuality and authentic voice, even when collaborating: they decided on alternating chapters, each identified by their initials. It was a technique they would also use, to great success, in their series of travel books.

The following four segments are taken from a full-length memoir – a 'co-autobiography' – they called *Seven and Sevenpence, Please*. It took its title from the cost of their marriage certificate that was handed over right on closing time by a crusty bureaucrat at St Pancras Registry Office in London on 19 September 1931.

For reasons unknown to me, the publication of this work was halted before it saw the light of day as a book. Undaunted, my parents turned their text into a series of radio programs that were broadcast on the ABC in 1968 with each of them reading their own narratives.

It would be downright impudent of me, as a fellow writer, to paraphrase my parents' account of London life when they wrote it first – and they wrote it better. So I've transcribed these chapters from the fragile yellowing typescript loitering in my paper inheritance. Now, with their own voices, once again Coral and Les can present their authentic selves, their unvarnished truth.

1. An Impecunious Student – CCR

When I arrived in London, I needed accommodation. The second-floor bed-sit that Les had booked for me was in Torrington Square at the back of the British Museum. It was clean but cheerless with Victorian-era sepia framed prints which we rapidly removed to the top of the wardrobe and put up Gauguin postcards instead. The landlady was Flemish and full of outward *politesse* and inner money-grubbing. She had trim feet and ankles, wore jet earrings and what was called 'a transformation' – a wig. She used to intone after me in her high-pitched sing-song: 'Yees, mademoiselle, no mademoiselle. Certainlee Mees Clarke, bath are fourpence the each.'

My next-door neighbour, a gentleman called Mr George, had a bath every Sunday morning. I couldn't help knowing all about it because the maid would knock at his door and call: 'I'm now going to put on your bath, Mr George.' Presently she would return and say: 'Your bath is on, Mr George,' and five minutes later 'Your bath is now ready, Mr George.' All that ceremony for fourpence!

I objected to paying 2/4 per week for the daily privilege of soaking off London's soot as I also objected to my ablutions being turned into a public festival. I began to achieve astonishing feats with a cloth and jug of hot water which the maid left at my door every morning.

The twenty-five shillings a week rent did not include breakfast so I concocted and heated meals on the gas ring in my room. Breakfast was usually bread and 'lower fruit standard strawberry' jam which was actually cabbage pulp, sugar and red food colouring, fourpence ha'penny a jar. Les's room was close by, a much smaller dog box for eighteen shillings a week so no 'facilities' – i.e. gas ring. We shared the cost of food bought at a local market and cooked up cheap meals in my bed-sit. It was the first time I had batched or lived away from the family hearth. The freedom and independence of it was intoxicating.

But I was there to study. Now I had to call on Allardyce Nicoll, Professor of Dramatic Literature at East London College of London University. He was the only professor of his subject in England and said to be a world authority. So that was the first of many fivepenny bus rides from Holborn out to Mile End Road, Stepney Green where the college was housed in the former People's Palace building. Past Chancery Lane and the black and white Tudor houses at the foot of Gray's Inn Road, past the Old Bailey and the huge GPO. Down Cheapside, past Milk Street and Bread Street and so to Bank. There was something so fundamental, self-assured and impregnable about the Bank of England, symbol of security throughout the yet unshaken British Empire. Bank, not Westminster, became for me the hub of the universe as I looked down from the bus on the Underground exits, belching up swarms of ants in their city clothes – cheap morning trousers and bowler hats – from the miles of intestinal railway below. On past Gresham's Royal Exchange, down Cornhill, Leadenhall Street and so into High Street Whitechapel where soot-streaked office blocks gave way to terraces of grubby-faced small shops: shops selling unnaturally red meat and shoddy clothes strung up on lines above the pavement. East End was East and West End was West and I could ride from one to the other over the high-pressure heart of the Empire's commerce for fivepence.

I found Professor Nicoll a spindly boyish-cheeked man of about forty with dancing brown eyes and a shy embarrassed smile: a don who wore his shabby gown as if it sprouted from his shoulders like wings. He was warm and courteous to me, partly because it was his nature and partly because I fancy he liked having a student sent to him from one of the remoter parts of the Antipodes. We planned the lectures I was to take; he mapped out a wide course of reading for me to do in the British Museum, advised me to take my notes on cards for easier indexing, requested my attendance at his evening seminars and set me essays to prepare.

From now on, during my student days in London, the British Museum Reading Room became my chief spiritual and physical home. Nearly every day I claimed sanctuary in that great domed chamber, ringed with names of celebrated writers and thinkers. Immediately you showed your ticket to moustachioed uniformed attendants and passed through the imposing doors marked 'Readers Only', a sense of privilege settled on you. Admission tickets were free, provided you were properly recommended and could vouch that you had a *bona fide* purpose. We got the Agent General for Western Australia to back our applications and what a key to incalculable riches they provided. For even then the BM was claimed to have a copy of almost every book published in England and the best selection of books in any foreign language as well.

Les often joined me and used to take lush delight in having his desk piled with twenty reference books at a time. He'd fly from one to another like a bee visiting flowers. He was fulfilling obligations in return for his free passage by taking a course of lectures on the history of art at the Slade School. Very dull they were, so he assured me. William Dobell was a fellow student, not that we met him till later. I hadn't the same itch for quantity though I loved to be able to ask for a Beaumont and Fletcher first edition with the same ease as the minor works of the social dramatist I was studying – the Norwegian Henrik Ibsen.

I doubt if we would have appreciated the books so much if the Reading Room had not been so handsomely if dowdily upholstered with creature comforts. The chairs, if you arrived early enough to secure one in the original spokes-of-a-wheel plan, were pneumatically inviting. Each place was supplied with a blotting pad, inkwell, pen, paper-knife, green-shaded reading lamp, footstool, hat peg and adjustable book-rest. How few of the penurious scholars working there could afford such equipment in a private study! And later, when winter came, there was central heating, free warmth not only on your shins but all around you – a luxury above price.

There were disadvantages, of course, in this haven of research and the main one was that it took almost an hour for an attendant to bring you the book or books you ordered – so complex was the organisation and so vast the mileage of books housed behind those swing doors, in the dome balcony and in catacombs below. Forty-six miles of books. Four million of them.

While you were waiting, however, the Reading Room was second to none as a place to cope with your private correspondence. I wasn't the only one to recognise this, judging from the assorted scribbling into assorted writing pads that went on about me in the interstices of serious reading. I remember overlooking by accident a letter that was lying on the desk next to me and being shocked to read that 'by the time you receive this I shall be well out of this damn cold jobless world and you'll find my head, if you're still interested in it, in the gas oven.' I looked anxiously about for the occupant of the desk but he was nowhere to be seen. I remembered that his clothes had been thin and ragged and that he'd had a disturbing cough. There were several depressed-looking men wandering among the catalogues. The owner of the letter did not return to his desk all that afternoon. Perhaps I was already too late.

The readers in the British Museum presented a cosmopolitan and varied cross-section of humanity. I often used to wish it was required to wear name tags on the lapel, as one does at conferences. Fame jostled obscurity, shoulder to shoulder. There were aged men with respiratory difficulties such as haunt every public library I have ever been in. They would wade through enormous tomes with magnifying glasses and then fall asleep with little sniffling snores. But despite these somnolent characters and their eccentricities, the Reading Room had an aura of thinking, striving and knowing that lingered from the past.

The oldest book in the library at that time was perhaps the fifth century manuscript of *The Bible*, the *Codex Alexandrinus*. The two original copies of the *Magna Carta* (1215) were there. In that room knowledge was piled high in a great impersonal tower, high above individual human life and individual human endeavour. Macauley, Dickens, Carlyle, George Eliot, Ruskin, Samuel Butler, Swinburne and Gandhi had all been regular readers there. So too had Karl Marx, perhaps in the seat I was now occupying. Ironical that Marx, a permanent expatriate from Germany and living with his wife and four children in poverty, would perhaps not have been able to do the research and writing for *Das Kapital* if it hadn't been for the amenities provided by a major capitalist country. For years he had sat there from nine till six collecting economic and historical material to illustrate his doctrines, his stomach rumbling from lack of food. Lenin, too, had been a daily reader though he was forced to give a false name (Richter) to get a reader's ticket. It was one of the periods when he was in political exile after subterranean conspiracy in Russia.

Sometimes to stretch our legs in the middle of reading, Les and I would stroll out into the main body of the Museum, take a turn among the Elgin Marbles, view the Portland Vase or the galleries of Italian majolica. When the Museum closed at six we would buy two fourpenny chops, a pound of potatoes, a cabbage and perhaps a small tin of soup. Back in my room we would cook everything on the one gas jet, heating the soup, then boiling the vegetables in one saucepan then frying the chops. We reckoned our meals cost about ninepence ha'penny on average and better value by far than a 'Lyons Ordinary' teashop. After hastily clearing away the newspaper tablecloth, we'd bolt to Shaftesbury Avenue to take our place in yet another Gallery queue at one of the many theatres.

2. Storming Fleet Street – LR

The air in the crowded room was heaving with the stench of old damp unwashed clothes and unwashed bodies. In the middle were set out on vertical stands that day's issue of six or seven London newspapers. With pencil and paper in hand I queued behind scores of unemployed men for a swift glance down the Positions Vacant column of each paper. Every morning during the early springtime I had made for this reading room attached to the local municipal library. Many of the men here had slept the previous night on seats in parks or gardens. Now they were wordlessly, patiently scrutinising the newspaper columns for a suitable job – any job at all. It was for most of them a mockery, fruitless, sickening. The number of jobs was decreasing every week. By the time the reading room was open and the men could edge up to the newspapers in turn, many of the jobs would be filled.

As for me, I would scribble out the details of any opening connected with writing or office work, then scuttle back to my room, seize the typewriter and get my application in to the post by noon.

If I wanted to stay on in London with Coral, who was still in the midst of her post-graduate course, I would have to find a job. And quickly. No more glorious days of freedom. In the bank I had about £12.00. Not yet destitute but I had often observed that it is not complete lack of funds which causes panic in the human breast. No doubt most people in jobs haven't more than five bob in the world the night before payday. It's the certainty of receiving another pay envelope that allows them to sleep soundly. With no hope of new income I had the feeling that within another four weeks I'd be on the streets. And Coral had practically nothing to lend me. Hunger marches were going on in Hyde Park. I was on the brink of joining them but typed out one more application instead.

Naturally I wanted to get back to journalistic work. But Fleet Street appeared to be hermetically sealed. I had met the genial boys of the Australian Press Association (APA). No work there what with every journalist from Australia clamouring at them for help as a natural right and the Depression hard-hitting the whole of Fleet Street. I learned that 600 qualified pressmen were out of jobs in London. The cold cruelty of life in this city was to shoot its barbs deeper and deeper into my flesh.

One incident sheeted home to me the merciless conditions for journalists and others. I had been given a letter of introduction to the news editor of a London daily. The letter was from an APA journalist, a friend of the news editor and was complimentary about me. I got as far as the lift in the building. The lift man asked me what I wanted. I told him I had letter for the news editor. The lift man stood in front of me, blocking my path and saying bluntly that he'd take it up himself. In five minutes he brought it back.

'Very sorry, there is no opening ...' *et cetera*. Not even to be able to speak to the man face-to-face. That left me gaping.

Neither of us had up to this time sold a single item to a London newspaper. The walls seemed like battlements. Usually London dailies published only one magazine article a day beyond staff material. They were supplied by an unending stream of freelancing specialists. Book reviews were written by noted authors. London editors looked blankly at our particular field of knowledge. Australia was foreign to them and of no particular interest.

Someone told me that the only hope for the outsider to sell an article was to seize on a current topic about which one could mug up plenty of facts or give an angle based on experience. If you could sell one article to one paper it would be a contact for the future. A foot in the door, a job maybe. You had to be persistent. I decided to try this technique. I had nothing to lose. Article in pocket, I'd march down Fleet Street until the dome of St Paul's swung into view. Then I was in the thick of Newspaper Land. I'd enter the spick and span new *Daily Telegraph* building, enquire at the counter, send the article up to Literary Editor or News Editor and wait below on the marble bench.

After ten minutes down it would come by a boy. 'The Literary Editor is sorry ...' *et cetera*.

Dashed but by no means depressed, as there were plenty of other papers, I'd leave the fabled dignity of *The Telegraph* for the black mirror glass of *The Daily Express*. Another ten minute wait below and with the same result. So, down to Bouverie Street and the slummy *New Chronicle* building where Charles Dickens checked leaders a hundred years earlier and the place looked as if it hadn't been painted since. Here a very grubby boy took my copy upstairs, only to bring it back minus the envelope, dog-eared and with black finger daubs on the first page. A cold fatalism would set into veins where hours before optimism had flowed.

At *The Daily Mail* a tall uniformed bulldog would at once make sure I had legitimate business. Another fellow was stamping all communications that were to go upstairs. A big heavy stamp that penetrated two or three pages. When my article came back, I would have to tear off as much of the stamp as I could before offering it further. By the time I'd passed on towards the evening papers, that once immaculate article would be in a very secondhand condition. I'd never sell it now. No editor would look at it with its history of rejection written in thumb marks.

No luck this day – even though it was quite a good article. No encouragement anywhere, even from the commissionaires. In sinking desperation, a suicidal anger of heart, I'd wend my way home. But you must be able to take hard knocks. Actually once or twice over a period of two months I did sell a short piece. A *Daily Telegraph* editor surprised me by coming all the way downstairs – no doubt to prevent me from coming upstairs but nonetheless surprising – and crossly examined me on the source of my article 'School Children and the Cinema'. He then said: 'I think we'll be able to use it though I can't be sure'. To my amazement and delight it appeared the next morning, truncated but on the leader page. The cheque for two guineas arrived six weeks later.

I went to see a London agent whose business was to gather leader-page articles of 1200 words for provincial dailies. Yes, he would be glad to receive material but assured me the standard was high. I said my standard was high too and offered four subjects about Australia. He accepted three: Flying Doctors, Gold Mining and Immigration. He offered one guinea each for one publication. I felt duped when I discovered that the articles were used in half a dozen papers – I'd only been paid for one.

Pity the poor freelance journalist! I vowed that if I ever filled any sort of editorial post myself I would do all in my power to alleviate the wretched conditions of the freelancing writer. Later I had my chance, not in a newspaper office and not in London but in a long career in Australia that gave me the opportunity to do just that and to fulfil my vow.

Coral and I were reaching a point of desperation and thought our only option was to take up our free return passages to Western Australia, caving in on our dreams of establishing ourselves as writers in London. When the shipping agent offered a three month reprieve before the terms of our scholarships expired, we determined on a fresh assault on Fleet Street.

I had long harboured the desire to work as a dramatic critic but knew only too well that this sort of post was eagerly sought by scores of well-connected Honours graduates coming down from Oxford. What chance did I have, a wild colonial from faraway Western Australia? My experience had shown me that merely to apply for such a job would be hopeless, useless, even laughable. I needed to take a different approach so I hit on the idea of writing to well-known critics to say that I had admired their work and would like the opportunity of meeting them. I thought that if this ploy was successful, I would at least establish some personal contacts.

Amazingly Ivor Brown, then chief dramatic critic of the *Sunday Observer*, invited me for a conversation at his flat in Bloomsbury. I started by making it clear to Mr Brown that it was my ambition to be a critic in his own worthy tradition. He was formal but courteous and suggested I write an article for the *New York Theatre Arts Monthly*. But he could not offer any hope of progress in London. The critic from *The Daily Telegraph* invited me to the staff canteen to meet him. He gave me buttered toast and tea and then asked 'How old are you?'. When I admitted to twenty-five, he said: 'No one can be a critic till at least thirty. I wrote stuff when I was in my twenties and now realise it was complete rubbish.'

The feeling of 'What's the use?' had just settled on my soul once more when the mail brought a cutting: one of my *London Lights* articles had been published in an Australian paper. Not only that, the headline promised more: this was 'one of a series'. With a bit of luck I'd keep this going a long time. I yanked the portable typewriter onto the washstand and whipped up another *London Lights*, getting it into the post that afternoon.

Spurred on by Coral, herself churning out applications with assiduity, I resumed my attack on the dramatic critics. I wrote to George W. Bishop, editor of *The Era*, a weekly devoted to reviews of theatre, films, variety and music. Bishop replied saying he was very busy but could spare me a few minutes. When I arrived at *The Era* office on the corner of Soho Square I found that Bishop had suddenly resigned and a new man, Burnup from Fleet Street, was in charge. Burnup might well have refused to see me but from the start he appeared quite interested in what I had to say about myself. After about ten minutes, he picked up three pairs of theatre tickets. 'Would you like to review these shows?' Would I like to? I learned that *The Era*'s main theatre critic had also just resigned, deciding it was now or never to write that novel.

So here was a London editor actually in need of staff. I could not believe my good fortune. I had sailed in on the very day that gave me a chance. A day later it might have been given to someone else. I saw the plays, wrote the notices and dropped them into the office. Two days elapsed and the new issue was published. I found that Burnup had accepted two out of three of my notices. Jubilantly racing home to our moth-eaten premises I collided with a messenger who had a letter for me from Burnup. In it he congratulated me on what I had written and included more tickets for that very night. So here was my breakthrough. I was on *The Era*'s freelance staff.

The paper had a long history going back a hundred years. It had been known for decades as 'The Actor's Bible' from the fact that it traditionally reviewed every play and ran many columns on actor's 'cards' or personal advertisements. Many eminent people had written for it. Charles Dickens wrote in 1867: *The perusal of The Era is one of my greatest enjoyments ... It gives profuse and erudite criticism of plays. It attacks in fiery terms any short-sighted stiff-necked (theatrical) bigotry.*

Just before I came to write for it the paper underwent a modernising treatment. Its nineteenth century microscopic typefaces were enlarged. Block advertisements were introduced. The take-your-time wordiness of the older journalism gave way to modern brevity, liveliness and layout. More attention was given to 'talkies' – talking films then only a year or two old.

It wasn't long before I was making overtures for a regular job. The editor was in favour but he apparently had to consult an enormous man upstairs who was, it turned out, co-editor. But after many delays, I was engaged at £5 per week. My job was to review not only plays but new films pre-shown specially for the cinema renting trade. I was also required to give a hand with sub-editing and headlining the copy that flowed in from a number of freelance contributors on amateur drama and provincial performances.

These arrangements suited me well. During parts of four weekdays I worked in the office. On Tuesdays the editing staff adjourned to Fleet Street and the Argus Press, a major printery handling big newspapers such as *The Observer* as well as our weekly. In rough annexes two or three of us sub-editors licked late American cables and local copy into shape. Then with the help of approved compositors ('comps') and with the reek of printer's ink in our nostrils, we made up our pages on 'the stone'. It was a hectic day but by waiting till late we could take a fresh-smelling copy of *The Era* away with us.

I moved from being an expert on cheap admission prices, vantage points and the discomforts of gallery seats to being admitted to the stalls or dress circle on free tickets. Instead of queuing for an hour or two in biting winds, I arrived at the front entrance of the theatre five minutes before curtain up and was given my complimentary programme by the management. It was an incredible feeling: the theatre was my love and here I was being paid for enjoying her favours. Now at last I was to learn what a West End first night was really like.

At this stage I was merely a junior critic but it sometimes happened that there were first night clashes: occasionally there might be as many as four productions beginning on the same night. In the thirties, evening dress was worn in stalls and circle. There were two theatres for which the tickets actually said: 'Evening Dress Obligatory'. I have always abhorred evening dress at the theatre, believing it adds to the sense of social discrimination and so prevents the theatre from enlarging its audiences. But as a young critic in London I was in no position to upset entrenched sartorial laws. In fact, such traditions had one specific advantage for me. My dark lounge suit was falling off me: shiny on the seat, old fashioned on the shoulders, beginning to shred at the cuffs. Fortunately I did have a dinner suit which I had brought from Perth and which had been gathering dust ever since. The dinner jacket came into its own.

I quickly acquired the feeling of being part of the theatre organism. I was an anonymous newcomer, no doubt – but I was writing a review. Reviews taken as a whole, the corpus of printed opinion, could have either a drastic or a highly beneficial effect on the box office fortunes of that particular playhouse and on all involved in the performance. Therefore the critic had every right to protect an image of himself as functionally involved in guiding the public interest in theatre, pointing out faults, recording merits, helping to shape an ethos of the theatre and doing this with as much sincerity and valuable sense of purpose as did the dramatist, the actor, the producer and the entrepreneur. Taking such an attitude was possibly sheer impudence on my part but I felt sure of my ground.

Few of the critics had space or inclination to state a theory of their job. We were all evaluators, assessors, acting as guides to our own special public. A practical *ad hoc* approach to criticism was the thing: a broad tolerance for a variety of forms of theatre art and entertainment was implied and plays were judged essentially as they came to us in performance, not in the written or printed word. Sound criticism could be described as the sum of these: quality writing, subject knowledge, a range of comparative examples, acute perception and a balance between technical terminology and graceful reporting.

Despite the Depression, there was much of interest happening in the theatre world. Actors like Laurence Olivier, Ralph Richardson, Robert Donat and Jack Hawkins were making their mark alongside Vivien Leigh, Peggy Ashcroft and Flora Robson. John Gielgud was already an idol of The Old Vic. Bernard Shaw and Somerset Maugham were occasionally offering a new play. Noel Coward was at the head of the daring young wits with a succession of revues and light comedies of the town. Most playwrights of the Thirties tended to deal with the lives of middle class or professional people, the very sort who were facing the actors from the stalls or circle. However, the approach of young playwrights to cushioned middle class values and people was by no means escapist but often realistic and probing.

All in all I was now reviewing three or four plays a week. Not all of them were exhilarating but in contrast to the almost complete sense of failure, dejection and bewilderment of a few months previously, I felt that heaven was opening up before me. Winter now had lost its terror. I had saved enough to buy a new lounge suit off the hook. And I had bought a fine black hat – a critic's hat!

3. London Literary Life in the 1930s – CCR

Another winter was upon us. But in our new flat we were sufficiently cosy with a coal fire – except when the bitter east winds, the dread visitors from the North Sea, blasted our windows. 'Draught excluder' was the only answer: double strips of felt placed under the doors and in the cracks between the panes, kept there day and night until the winds moderated at which point one strip might be lifted from the windows as a concession to fresh air.

I was busy with as much journalism as I could comfortably pack into my life. I was now writing for English papers like *The Sunday Chronicle* and *The Family*. My main work was as London correspondent for papers in Perth, Melbourne and Sydney. I had my own regular column, my *London Woman's Diary*.

I was meeting celebrities thick and fast. Indeed, between the two of us, we were adding to our bag most of the outstanding authors of a generation as well as notables from other aspects of the Arts. However, it was writers that were our magnet. We never ceased the game of inquiry into how authors got their start in life, what impulses directed their pursuit of writing, what were the practical as well as aesthetic problems of living by the pen, how it feels to be successful and to what degree an author's home environment harmonises with the personality of the work created. No doubt such a line of investigation reflected our own latent ambition to be authors as well as journalists.

In the pursuit of topical subjects, l was granted an interview with Lady Hilton Young, a sculptor. She was the widow of 'Scott of the Antarctic' who had famously perished with others of his party on their return march from the South Pole in 1912. It was now twenty years later and she had remarried and to a parliamentarian, at the time of our meeting Minister for Health in the British government.

Lady Hilton had been commissioned to create the bust of Australian poet, Adam Lindsay Gordon, about to be unveiled in Westminster Cathedral's Poet's Corner. Gordon was the first overseas writer to break into the hallowed gloom of Literary Greats and so created some fluttering of attention by Australians then in England. Along with us, they attended the Abbey for the unveiling.

After my meeting with her in her studio, the sculptor confessed that she formed her conception of Gordon largely from his poems. For his appearance, she had little to guide her, only one old daguerreotype and a photo of the recent statue by Paul Montford in Melbourne.

Lady Hilton had shown me other of her works and told me she had carved a full length statue of her first husband, Scott, which is in Christchurch, New Zealand as a memorial to him. About Scott the explorer she was unwilling to speak personally, but she was enthusiastic to talk of her son, Peter Scott, then emerging as a talented artist of wildfowl in the natural environment. He had just had his second one-man show and was only in his early twenties.

A favourite novelist of my girlhood had been the Baroness Orczy, author of the Scarlet Pimpernel series. Meeting the Baroness by appointment at a Pall Mall hotel brought the disclosure that, although she wrote in English, she had been unable to speak a word of it until the age of fifteen. Baroness Orczy was born Hungarian, a daughter of the landed aristocracy. Her father was a brilliant musician and their home had been a mecca for composers like Wagner, Gounod, Massenet and Liszt. She had come to England as a girl to be 'finished'. She studied painting and even exhibited at the Royal Academy but she decided to write a short story and it was published by *Pearson's Magazine*.

I was intrigued to know how she first got the idea for the Pimpernel, that intrepid Englishman who risked death a thousand times to save French aristocrats from the dangerous consequences of The Revolution. 'It came to me in a flash,' the plump, bejewelled Baroness told me. 'Suddenly I saw the figure of Sir Percy Blakeney, complete in every detail: the curled wig, lace at throat and wrists, coat and breeches of the finest cut and quizzing glasses. Oh, I'm a great believer in inspiration. And in character – it's works of character that last – think of Dickens and Shakespeare. My method is think of the character first and then build a story round it.'

The Baroness told me how her first Pimpernel book was turned down by twelve publishers – then she turned it into a play and the play was damned by the critics. Now the books have sold more than three million copies. At the time of our interview it was being made into a film with Leslie Howard as the inscrutable Sir Percy and Merle Oberon as Lady Blakeney.

Generations have come to love Winnie-the-Pooh and his friends of the House at Pooh Corner: creations of A.A. Milne. I was invited to his home to meet him. He lived in perfectly Milne-ish surrounding, in Mallord Street, Chelsea, a street of humanised dolls' houses, though made of brick not gingerbread. From any of them you expected Christopher Robin to pop out. Number 13 was distinctive for its blue door. The little entrance hall was blue too, as was the carpet on the stairs. So were A.A. Milne's eyes as he welcomed me into his little ground-floor study. Later, when conversation became easy and more personal, he told me his nickname within the family was 'Blue', too.

Milne was at that time past his peak as a successful playwright but his reputation as an author of children's books was as bright and unsullied then as now. We began to talk of Christopher Robin, not the character in the Winnie-the-Pooh series but his twelve-year-old son who gave his name. 'Moon is doing quite well at boarding school,' said Milne. 'We always call him Moon – it was his first effort at pronouncing Milne. I don't particularly want him to be a writer. One is enough in any family.'

I asked whether Christopher Robin still liked the children's books that were written for him. 'More than ever now,' said Milne. 'He's read them all and knows huge chunks by heart.' Before I left, Mrs Milne took me upstairs to see, in Christopher Robin's nursery, a glass case on the wall. Inside resided all the famous toys: Winnie-the-Pooh, Piglet, Tigger and Eeyore.

Another celebrated writer whose home I visited was Walter de la Mare. He lived at Tallow near a serene middle reach of the Thames. De la Mare was a poet of other world fantasy, of dreams, of delicate observations of nature. But in person, he was no intense aesthete. His manner was straightforward, utterly free of affectations, gently humorous though shy when it came to talking about his personal life. In response to my request for an interview, he had written that he disliked the word 'interview' but would very much like to meet us for a talk.

He wanted to hear from us as much as talk about himself. At one point, he asked what we thought of the English climate. I told him how I deplored the long grey gloom of the winter. He, on the other hand, felt he couldn't cope with our abundant sunshine. But he did tell us something very interesting that linked him to Australia. His great grandfather, Dr Arnold Browning [Dr Colin Arrot Browning], had been a naval surgeon in charge of two shiploads of convicts taken to Tasmania in the 1840s. The doctor had showed a humanitarian interest in the convicts and during the long sea passage taught most of them to read and write. His experiences were recorded and published in a book, *The Convict Ship*.

After tea, Walter de la Mare escorted us through his garden. It was the mellow sunset hour which is particularly lingering and lovely in the English springtime. While we strolled, he compared himself to an old apple tree there which was still clinging to life, bearing blossoms and fruit. Such a wise and gentle man. He and his wife were very kind to us and hospitable, asking us to visit them again which we did.

G.K. Chesterton, essayist, poet, historian, critic, writer of murder mysteries and creator of the quixotic, bicycle-riding priest and private detective Father Brown, was a joy to meet. In his home, we chatted with Mrs Chesterton, waiting for him to appear. Then in he came, enormous in girth, small eyes behind pince-nez, droopy moustache, a muttering half-buried voice disguising the intellect behind.

He began to laugh – how he loved laughing, specially from self-deprecation. He began by telling us about some neighbours of his, past and present. One was the owner of a mansion that had burnt down the previous day. 'He was a retired factory owner. When he came here to live, he said to me: Of course you won't think much of me, I'm only a soapboiler. I replied: well, I'm only a potboiler. And we've been friends ever since.'

Chesterton was the exception to our observation that notable authors don't necessarily converse as well as they write. They are seldom as coruscating, profound or lyrical in speech as they are in the written word. But no matter what subject was mentioned, G.K. had a flow of words or ideas about it. In that low mumble of his, he would go on talking high and clever sense without a smile until suddenly, with a twinkle, down would fall the pince-nez to land on his billowing stomach and he would break into unrestrained giggling. It was a cumulative exhalation of irrepressible spirits, going on for a minute or so, Chesterton heaving with subterranean rumbles which eventually subsided as he took up the thread of his argument.

The subject turned to Hitler as it did in mostly any company those days. Chesterton was derisive about the servile obeisance paid to the Führer at public gatherings while in Britain the Prime Minister, Ramsay MacDonald, was subject to every democratic jibe. 'Apparently in Germany, when you shake hands with a friend, you have to say *Heil Hitler*. Imagine meeting someone in the Strand and greeting them with *Oh Ramsay MacDonald*.'

This was at a time when Hitler was not always treated as a joke. Some found his rulings fitted with their social and moral theories, even G.K., when we tackled the subject of women's rights. 'I believe Herr Hitler is groping towards the truth when he sends women back to the home. That's where they belong – not in offices and factories.'

I was shocked. Naturally I challenged him on such a reactionary statement.

Chesterton was a master at combining earnest argument with satirical humour. I wasn't sure how to take him. 'To my mind the so-called emancipation of women has given renewed lease of life to a number of bad institutions such as party politics. Just when men have reached the stage of seeing through its farcical procedure, women have got the vote and an avalanche of ardent schoolgirls have kept the outworn system going. I admit that the position of women needed brightening up and if that's what you mean by emancipation, I'm all for it. But I can't see that it's a step upward for women to turn factory handles and enter figures in a ledger. Their job is to marry, make homes and raise families.'

I protested as politely as I could.

'Of course, I'm not fanatical about all women sticking to the home. Joan of Arc, after all, pointed out there'd always be plenty of women to sew and spin. There will always be exceptions like her – but I won't have the normal sacrificed to the abnormal.'

So that was Chesterton on woman's status. Even if everything he'd said went against my grain, there was no doubt he was a most likeable fellow and most engaging.

My own attitudes to women's abilities were gratefully reassured when I met Lady Astor, the first woman to hold a seat in the British Parliament. Surprisingly, though she was prodigiously wealthy and the owner of three homes (all of aristocratic proportions), she arranged to meet me in her car. We were driving from the House of Commons where for two hours I had waited for this appointment. It was clear she was an extremely busy person. Her constituency was in Plymouth and after her work in the House, she was in demand for the projects she most supported such as nursery schools in London's East End. Inaugurating schools for disadvantaged children in the slums was what she regarded as her most important work. Even at the weekends she was busy entertaining in her luxurious upper-Thames home near Maidenhead. Regular visitors were members of the Conservative establishment who came to be known as 'The Cliveden Set'.

As Lady Astor's chauffeur zigzagged the Daimler through Westminster's six o'clock traffic, making for her town house in St James Square, I had to make the most of that journey to ask my questions. I began with 'Have women made good in the British Parliament?'

'Good?' she exclaimed. 'They've made more than good. And so have the women electors.' She loosed a flood of impromptu oratory upon me. 'Considering British women have only had the vote for seventeen years and there've been so few women members of parliament pitted against hundreds of men who didn't like us one bit, I think they've done remarkably well. At least they've taken their job seriously. Their diligence and constant attendance at the House have proved that.'

This petite feisty woman, then in her mid-fifties, was sitting bolt upright in her car. Her warmth of manner, direct intonation, her energy and determination all commanded respect. 'A hundred years hence there may be equal numbers of men and women MPs.

There might even be a woman Prime Minister. One thing is certain – I will never be PM. I did not go into politics for personal aggrandisement. I stood because there was urgent work for me to do. And now the three policy areas nearest my heart: housing, education and nursery schools, have really been taken up by the Government. That is my reward. If I'd been considering myself all these years, I'd have stayed home. Wouldn't you?'

I was aware that Nancy Astor had six of her own children. We talked briefly about home life. She maintained: 'The best thing a mother can do for her children is give them a clear standard of right and wrong.'

Thankfully we were held up in a traffic jam so I could ask her more about women in politics. 'Don't mistake me,' said Lady Astor with one of her quick, retaliatory, floor-of-the-House glances, 'I'm not in favour of a sex-ridden government. I can conceive of nothing worse than a man-governed world – except a woman-governed world. What I see is the combination of both, going forward and making civilisation more worthy of the name, a civilisation based on Christian values: justice and mercy – not on force and aggression. I feel men have a greater sense of justice and we of mercy. They must borrow our mercy and we must borrow their justice.'

The Daimler had reached St James. I had been given a glimpse of this woman's humanitarian dynamism. Though she was cradled in luxury, her record of public work in England was just wakening the need for social justice, for people's basic and inalienable rights. Her candour and energy had made her an institution since she won her seat in 1919. But she was not wholly popular. Her rash and impulsive jibes often got her into hot water and her anti-Jewish attitudes were well known. It was some time after my meeting with Nancy Astor that suspicions were raised about the role of 'The Cliveden Set' of which she and her husband, Viscount Astor, were leading lights. The group was rumoured to be favourable to the policy of appeasement, sympathetic to the bourgeoning Nazi Party and extremely right wing, even Fascist. To what degree its influence did actually change governmental policies to the looming threat of Hitler in the lead up to the Second World War was to become a matter of public debate and commentary in years to come.

4. The Heartache of the Expatriate – LR

Despite the low pulse of Britain's over-all economic living, the terrible state of unemployment in so many industries, these had been very full years for us. We had been lucky as well as hard-working. I had become senior dramatic critic of *The Era* and attended hundreds of theatre first nights. For three years I had a full page to myself, 'The Week at the Playhouse', to write what I liked. I had been a member of the choosy London Critics' Circle. In the latest edition of *Who's Who in the Theatre*, my name was included in a short list of London's principal dramatic critics. I had written articles for *The Times*, *The Observer*, *The New York Herald Tribune* and the *Theatre Arts Monthly* as well as some of the English weekly reviews. I was invited to lunch by theatrical managers and was frequently astonished to hear how seriously my views on theatre were being taken.

Our delight in meeting writers had not waned. In fact between the two of us, we never ceased the game of enquiry into how authors got their start in life, what impulses directed their pursuit of social and personal themes, what were the practical as well as aesthetic problems of living by the pen, to what extent writers used their own intimate experiences, how it felt to be successful, what were the problems in maintaining success, the problems of free expression and censorship.

I had been privileged to meet so many – so had Coralie. I'd met J.B. Priestley in his Georgian house once owned by the nineteenth century poet, Samuel Taylor Coleridge. He used the same study and writing room. I'd met Somerset Maugham and talked in his flat at St James and Hugh Walpole, the novelist, in his country home in the Lake District.

For me, the pinnacle of meeting famous writers in their own homes was my visit to Bernard Shaw in his flat high above the Thames. Shaw not only gave me an hour of his exuberant company but a long handwritten newspaper interview that caused quite a flurry in Fleet Street when printed in *The Era*. Coralie had met many notables herself and written them up for the newspapers in Australia for which she was a London correspondent. And together we had made a visit to Paris to talk with James Joyce.

So there'd been many good and memorable times – but tough ones, too. There'd been deaths in the family at home, the news taking so long to reach us. I'd had my troubles with the editor of *The Era*, culminating in my departure from that office. Neither of us had had a book published or a play produced although we'd tried – oh yes, we'd tried. A pile of manuscripts was testament to that. We had plenty of freelance work to keep us busy but despite this, we were unsettled. Emigrés from Australia seemed to form two main groups: those who had come to study and would want to return, or need to, after their course to find a job; those who felt their only hope of a successful career lay in the crowded centres of Britain and in competition with the British themselves.

Our homesickness was as great as ever. It had expression partly in herding with Australians, either old-established or newly arriving. Much mental and emotional confusion could be seen in our inclination to criticise many things English but also see many things Australian from a distance and a more critical perspective. The thoughts roamed, the inward hunger gnawed: when shall we be able to return home? But fear gripped, too. What risks would there be? Would we find jobs, would we regret turning our backs on what we had worked so hard to build up? It was a persistent internal tussle tearing at us, an agony of rootlessness. Should we leave before the process of assimilation swamped us and it was too late?

Then there were external influences. 1935 was a year of restless movement towards change. In Britain, Ramsay MacDonald, the spent Labour leader, had resigned as head of the National government and Stanley Baldwin had taken over. On the Continent, Fascism was a rising spectre from which most people seemed still to be hiding their eyes. Mussolini was preparing to invade defenceless Ethiopia. Would there be sanctions against Italy? Was Britain herself defenceless, being now open to new methods of air attack?

And Hitler, Hitler, Hitler – the giant question mark. Was totalitarian government the inevitable and unalterable pattern for the future? Rising tensions everywhere on the Continent but nobody in England taking them very seriously. Mosley's blackshirts selling you their paper outside Charing Cross station. European countries seemed more and more chaotic with unemployment and Nationalist fanatics. New techniques of communication lessened the space between us and them.

Other distances were shrinking, too. Scott and Black had won the MacRobertson's air-race to Australia, compressing the long months of sea travel into a micro-flash of three days. Following hard on this the England-Australia airmail had been started, first fortnightly and then every week. What a joyful sense of closer contact this new mail service gave us exiles! Coralie and I had articles on the initial airmail plane, addressed to the newspapers we wrote for. These were given prominence when published, even one of my long envelopes with scrawled lettering was photographed and reproduced full size: 'By England-Australia Airmail – Press Copy – Important'.

Various new trends of thinking were causing turbulence within me. I was becoming more and more excited by sociological phenomena and ideals. I was keen to learn what various propagandists had to say about monopoly capitalism as well as social exclusion. The loss of contact between different levels of people seemed to me at the root of the malaise in England. Wasn't the rise of Fascism just as much connected with the decay of socio-economic structures as was the rise of Communism? Surely modern writers like Lawrence, Joyce, Huxley and T.S. Eliot were throwing overboard many of the solid Georgian and pre-Georgian literary forms – widening the boundaries in unheard-of ways? I borrowed a disguised copy of *Lady Chatterley's Lover* and managed to get hold of Joyce's *Ulysses*, also in the 'Denied-by-State' (banned) list.

I had already read *Dubliners* and *Portrait of the Artist as a Young Man*. Now I spent six weeks of spare time reading *Ulysses* and then determined that before we left the northern world we should get to Paris again and try to meet James Joyce. We arranged to fly the Channel, a new adventure and dazzling experience as neither of us had been in a plane before. We found Paris embalmed. Ice-stalactites encrusted every shop front. The grey deserted streets were like skating rinks. The beloved city gave a frigid welcome.

From London I had written and received no reply. But while we were in our hotel on the Left Bank a letter came from Paul Leon. He was one of a group of writers who, under Joyce's influence, had been experimenting with language during the past fifteen years. Gertrude Stein and Ernest Hemingway were also among them. Leon had written to say Mr Joyce never saw the Press but we might like to meet him on different grounds. Leon arranged for us to call on Joyce at 3 pm that day.

We made our way to Joyce's flat, No. 7 Rue Saint Valentin Edmond in the Pont d'Alma district, under the lee of the Eiffel Tower. Ascending by a small open lift ornamented with enamelled filagree, we knocked at the door of No. 7. A servant woman ushered us into a modest-sized sitting room, furnished in genteel taste.

Joyce came in, a thin nervous figure. He walked slowly and gave me a limp hand. I introduced Coralie. Very quietly he offered us seats and himself sat with his back to a window. 'So you are from Australia? I don't usually see people but you seemed to have come such a long way, I couldn't very well refuse you. And you're not journalists?'

We immediately felt like imposters. Joyce evidently thought we had just arrived in Europe. We hadn't said we were not journalists but we had promised not to write articles. Joyce went on: 'I've suffered so much from journalists. Scandal-sheet journalists, I mean.' He followed this up by asking numerous quiet questions about Australia. 'What is the Australian accent? It always bothers me when they talk about it.' His own speech was the low-pitched Irish conversational manner with a quiet brogue. Joyce was then fifty-five years of age. He had shortish silver-grey hair brushed back from a low forehead. He had fine small hands and thinnish pointed knees, his small feet in slippers. He wore a red velvet jacket. His eyes – we could not see them. He wore one pair of glasses at a time and at intervals put another larger yellowish pair over the first pair.

I asked did he write every day?

He replied yes, if he was well enough. But of course ... his eyes. He'd had nine operations, treatment from forty doctors. He said it was all due to the rheumatic fever he'd had years ago when one eye became infected. No one could do anything until he found a specialist in Zurich, Alfred Voight, who had saved his sight. Joyce said he went every year to see him. But he couldn't see very well. 'I cannot see you, sitting opposite me.'

His tone was factual, not self-pitying. With the inadequate empathy of the young and healthy, I asked: 'How can you go on writing?' We knew that he was then engaged on an enormous work later published as *Finnegans Wake*. Joyce told us he had special attachments for his spectacles and sat at a lighted table. 'Can you dictate your work?' I pressed.

Joyce's reply was definitive: 'No-one would stand for that.' He seemed quietly conscious of his notoriety and wryly amused by it. He told us what he called his 'book of so-called poetry' *(Pomes Pennyeach)* had been published in a luxury edition with illustrated manuscript initials by his daughter. It was printed on Japanese incandescent paper. 'One newspaper said it was printed on "indecent" paper. Probably influenced by me. Quite appropriate anyway.'

From a glass-fronted cabinet, he brought out a copy of this edition and showed it to us. The cabinet, so Joyce told us, contained copies of all the editions of *Ulysses*. We looked at some of the translations and at an edition illustrated by Matisse. I asked him questions about other modern Irish authors. He had read very little of them but, of course, it was hard for him to read and he found being read to 'very unsatisfactory'.

I asked Joyce was he troubled by the censorship, banning and other ill-treatment of his books. (In America, editions of *Ulysses* had been burnt by order of the Post Office for alleged obscenity.) He said: 'No, not bitter. Just bored. Ten years before *Dubliners* could be published, that little book. Well, well.' It was clear he did not want to pursue the subject.

He seemed a man in eternal pain and, without complaining, he communicated his pain to us. We got ready to take our leave. In an unobtrusive way he helped me into my coat. A little reluctantly he agreed to autograph the copy of *Ulysses* we had brought with us – two thick paperbound volumes. When we left Paris for London by Hercules plane, I had the volumes deeply secreted in my overcoat pockets, hoping they would not be discovered by the British Customs Officers. Joyce died five years later. Only then did we permit ourselves to write about him.

Joyce was living an expatriate life and so were we. What determines a person's loyalty to a particular country? Whatever self-indulgence or social justice says, the homing instinct is strong. Here we were, myself born of a Welsh father and an English 'Geordie' mother, Coralie born of German and English forebears and looking so German at times that French people insisted she was one! Well, such ancestry gave us excitement in the traditions of England, Wales and Germany but never for a moment identification with their peoples.

We'd been born in Australia, our first score of years spent there, absorbing with our mother's milk the shapes, colours, tastes, smells, sounds and feel of those environments, the timbre of voices, the look of faces, the taste of grass and sweat and the slant of light on buildings. And Australia was the place of a thousand early growing pains, emergent curiosities and joys, of friendships, family stresses and laughter, adolescent ambitions, dejections and dreams. If we lived a century and stayed seventy of those years abroad, Australia would still be our psychological matrix, calling us back to its warmth and light and expanses as it did every exiled Australian we met in Britain.

If we went back, we'd have the reward of merging with a community where we had a right to be, where our kind of work needed to be done, where the emphasis was not on the storied past of the few, where an entrenched hierarchical form of society did not exist, at least in the same degree as in England. The ordinary man had a definitely larger say and larger place in the sun, tasks of planning and building things were going on despite the Depression and a hundred other setbacks – just as it would for the whole of our lives to come.

There were other pressing emotional needs. Coral and I had been together through thick and thin but true homemaking lay in the future. Babies had hardly been in our minds – except how not to have them. But parenthood was another buried urge that would not be endlessly denied. We had given up our plans to drive our tiny car all the way across Europe, through Asia Minor to India and on to Burma and Malaya where it could be shipped to Australia. The Automobile Association had strongly warned against border troubles as well as shocking roads.

In London there'd been goodbye parties and lunches and the last horrific sleepless all-night final packing up. For sentiment's sake we decided to devote our last evening to a play. And what more appropriate than John Gielgud's lyrical mounting of *Romeo and Juliet* with himself and Peggy Ashcroft in the leading roles. Parting is such sweet sorrow, indeed. But even before interval we could no longer keep our attention on the play. There was so much to do before a friend was calling in the early morning to take us to the station.

The bleary dawn light smeared the window. Our friend, Buck, was waiting below with the car. Half an hour later we were meeting Eileen Joyce, the Australian concert pianist, on the grimy platform and being farewelled by a group of her friends and a few of ours. We were travelling with Eileen to Fremantle on the other side of the world, three West Australians sailing home.

Returning exiles: we were a mixture of confusions – glorious anticipation of seeing familiar faces and places but also eroding doubts about whether we could stand up to the unspoken Australian challenge: *Come on, show us what you're worth.*

Well, we'd take the chance and see.

12

Coming Home with Eileen

Those years in London (from 1930 to 1936) were central to my parents' lives. They honed their craft – Coralie established her name as a journalist, Les his as a drama critic – and they made the miraculous discovery that they could support themselves by writing. They learnt, too, that they could live on very little money and still have a rich and interesting life. They also found that, no matter how stimulated they were by the culture and history of Europe, their own faraway country and their families always tugged at the heartstrings. In her years overseas, Miles Franklin used to greet other Australians with, 'Smell the gum leaves!' Coralie declared: 'I never identified with England, and never felt I belonged to it or it belonged to me.' Australia remained, as Les described it, their 'intrinsic psychological centre, of the future as well as the past,' calling them back to its physical light and colour, its different lifestyle, its challenges as well as satisfactions.

However, there is no denying that their separate and shared experiences were invaluable. Les attended hundreds of theatre performances as a full-time dramatic critic, usually reviewing three or four plays a week. And, a rare experience in the journalistic world: his copy was never edited.

West End theatre was at its zenith with actors of high calibre – Laurence Olivier, John Gielgud, Ralph Richardson, Sybil Thorndike and Peggy Ashcroft – working there. Les met them all as a representative of his paper. Paul Robeson came into his office one day seeking someone to write him a new play, as roles for Afro-Americans, even a singer as famous as him, hardly existed. He had already played a season as Othello.

With his work in theatre, Les rubbed shoulders with famous playwrights, too. He sat next to WB Yeats at the premiere of TS Eliot's *Murder in the Cathedral*. He met Eliot on another occasion when he was talking about his poetry. Les was able to ask him a few key questions. Eliot told him: 'It takes a robust character to be a poet – to survive either over-adulation or over-neglect.'

Both my parents determined to meet as many notable literary figures as possible. No doubt my father's role as a theatre critic gave him the added cachet to gain entrance to writers' homes – for this was their preferred way of conducting interviews. Maybe what tipped the balance was that they were two keen young journalists from a distant colonial outpost, a rarity in the upper echelons of the literary world, and so much more appealing than some cynical hack from a London newspaper. There were occasions when their subject was just as interested in interviewing them. When Leslie met sixty-year-old Somerset Maugham for 'a two-hour chat' and at the end of it asked him to inscribe one of his books, the famous playwright wrote in it *To Leslie Rees, in recollection of a heart-to-heart talk*. Although Virginia Woolf ignored my mother's entreaties for a meeting, Coralie scored a long interview with the renowned actress Merle Oberon. They also met Bertrand Russell, HG Wells, JB Priestley, JM Barrie and Cecil Day-Lewis.

Coralie Clarke Rees's newspaper writings had always shone a spotlight on any Australians making their names abroad. She'd written feature articles on expatriate writers Henry Handel Richardson and Mary Grant Bruce after visiting them in their homes for long conversations.

Then there was Eileen Joyce – 'the most important pianist whom Australia has given to the world for a generation. In London her name is now coupled with those of Horowitz and Solomon, Myra Hess and Rubinstein.' My mother had at least twice interviewed Eileen Joyce, a prodigy pianist who had left her home in Western Australia as a teenager and, without knowing any of the language, had studied in Germany for four years.

Success in London
From Coralie Clarke-Rees
The Western Mail of 8 February 1934

LONDON, Jan. 4. – Seven years ago a young girl between fourteen and fifteen years of age left Perth for Europe to carve herself a career as a pianist. After a lot of solid concert and broadcasting work in England during the past three years, she has at last leapt into what seems the beginnings of fame with the making of two gramophone records a few months ago.

Eileen Joyce attributes the crisp individuality of her finger work which seems her outstanding trait as a pianist to Teichmüller, the master under whom she studied in Leipzig for four years after leaving Perth. 'He gave me my fingers,' she said. For her age, she is easily one of the most brilliant pianists at the moment in England, Myra Hess and others of established reputation being nearly twice her age.

Her chief points of advice to other young musicians who are hoping to leave Australia for further study in Europe are:

'Do not go to a foreign country, like Germany, without knowing something of the language. Do not leave home un-chaperoned (particularly if the student is a girl under the age of twenty). Bring plenty of letters of introduction with you; and don't forget that your Conservatorium fees are only a small part of the expense of launching oneself abroad as a musician.'

In 1935, a full-page feature article in *The Broadcaster* (Perth) announced:

EILEEN JOYCE '*will return still unspoiled*'
by Air Mail from Coralie Clarke Rees

LONDON, Dec. 21. – In the two years that have elapsed since I last met this brilliant West Australian pianist, Eileen Joyce has scaled many more dizzy rungs on the ladder of musical reputation. Few of her achievements, however, had given her greater pleasure than her recently signed contract with the Australian Broadcasting Commission for a tour of her home continent during the middle months of 1936. She leaves London at the end of February, will arrive in Perth at the end of March and will give her West Australian broadcasts and concert performances during the first weeks of April.

She was wearing a pair of grey flannel slacks and a navy blue woollen jumper when she welcomed me into the 'workroom' of her Hampstead flat last night. 'Excuse the trousers,' she said. 'They look a bit "arty" but actually I wear them for warmth. My knees get so cold as I sit practising hour after hour.'

'Do you still practise seven hours a day?' I asked.

She nodded and went on to tell me the life of a concert pianist, particularly a successful concert pianist, is by no means 'jam'. 'People scarcely realise,' said Eileen Joyce, 'that it's a terrifically hard life — at the moment I feel that it's too hard for a young girl. I feel tired out. I'm giving the first performance in England of a Shostakovich Concerto at a Promenade Concert under Sir Henry Wood on January 4, I'm scheduled to make twelve records during January, there are my visits to leading public schools all over the country and there's my Australian tour for which I have to prepare twenty different programmes.'

She is looking forward to her Australian tour with just a modicum of delicious apprehension. 'Do they know much about me?' she asked. 'And will they like me?'

These nervous little questions at the end of the interview gave some clue to the fragile nature of Joyce's self-confidence and portended some of the problems that would emerge on the tour. Apparently Joyce suffered some sort of breakdown after the Shostakovich performance and there was a flurry of telegrams between Australia and London about the likelihood of cancelling her impending Australian tour. According to her Australian biographer, Richard Davis:

the sea voyage, the thought of being reunited with her family and friends and the prospect of a triumphant tour of her homeland (which the ABC was already tipping) dispelled memories of her recent illness and raised Eileen's spirits but what she did not realise was she was sailing into a storm.

How Coralie came to be engaged as Joyce's secretary and troubleshooter for the Australian 'storm' and how much she was privy to the dramas that preceded it has remained untold. Did these two twenty-eight-year-olds negotiate a deal at the time Coralie went to Eileen's home for that interview in December, just months before both were leaving the country? Though very different personalities they had plenty of common ground as West Australians triumphing home after carving out success abroad. Privately, each was driven by longing for family and the prospect of that joyous balm – endless sunshine.

But while other encounters with notable people in London and Europe were told and retold by Coral and Les – both within the family and for the wider public, every rich detail mined and mined again for broadcasts, lectures, articles and eventually books – some aspects of this saga remain a mystery. Besides a few published articles before and during the tour, little mileage was made of my mother's unique contract to escort and organise Eileen Joyce as she displayed her virtuosic technique and prodigious musical memory around the country.

Coralie was at Eileen's side on land and sea: for the four-week voyage from London to Fremantle, for the four Perth concerts plus a flurry of engagements, then as she toured across the nation. The red-haired Eileen and the blonde Coralie, both remarkable for their beauty, caused quite a stir wherever they travelled and were constantly written up in the papers as well as in *The Australian Women's Weekly*. But why the blanket of secrecy afterwards?

Imagine my delight when, just a few years ago, I unearthed from a dusty old manila envelope among my parents' papers a pile of letters in my mother's baroque hand. They were still in their envelopes with postmarks from three Australian cities, all in the months of April and May 1936, and all addressed to Les at 'The Commodore', his temporary Sydney digs in inner-city Darlinghurst. I hoped these missives would shine a torch on the dark corners of the Eileen Joyce tour. Carefully opening them (it seemed they had not been touched for nearly eighty years and could easily disintegrate) and piecing together their sequence with the aid of a 1936 calendar, I was not disappointed.

My mother's letters reveal how much she was challenged by working with the unpredictable Joyce. Her revelations to my father show a brave, practical and determined young woman, sometimes raw with the pain of loneliness but using all her resources to fulfil a challenging assignment. The correspondence also explains the need for her steadfast discretion about Eileen Joyce.

Eventually I located my father's bundle of letters to her during that period and found they documented his meetings with the literati of Sydney. They also record his immense frustration in working for *The Sydney Morning Herald*, a comedown after the heady literary and journalistic life of London. He relates these experiences to Coral with ebullient style and places them in counterpoint to his own loneliness. He could not bear to be alone. At the same time, he abhorred his dependence on her. It surprised me to find how insecure he was about their relationship, how jealous and possessive in their first long separation after six years.

The letters between Coral and Les are the intimate accounts of two young writers, separated but 'together, alone against the others'. They span the period 17 April to 2 June 1936.

~

It was 27 March 1936. The SS *Moreton Bay* was about to arrive at Fremantle docks. The sun was bouncing off the water. For the homing trio on the deck, Coralie, Eileen and Leslie, watching their familiar coast loom into focus was a beautiful sight. Waiting on the wharf, Mary Elizabeth Rees, a usually restrained woman, could not contain her excitement. Her boy, her youngest, was coming home. He had left as a twenty-four-year-old journalist on *The West Australian*. Now he was returning as a thirty-year-old, an accredited member of the London Critic's Circle. Even better, Les was to be under her roof again, if only for a short while.

Mary lived with her daughter, Averil, and granddaughter Ailsa at 39 Elizabeth Street, South Perth, a comfortable Californian bungalow made available to them under some suitably vague long-term arrangement, courtesy of Averil's admirer, a well-heeled gentleman with his own wife and family.

So Les was back home, basking in the glow of reunion with friends and family and soaking up the autumnal sunshine. But he was concerned that Coral might not be realistic about what she had taken on. Their sea journey did not live up to expectations. Four weeks in a shabby cabin of what they called *The Mortifying Bay* was not the rest they were hoping for. And they found themselves little prepared for Eileen Joyce's constant moods and ever-present insecurities.

Once they arrived in Perth, there were dramas for Coral to contend with, thanks to Eileen's fracas with the Western Australian press, who found she had been a little loose with the truth in overseas interviews. She had lied about her age, but they were more concerned about reports in British papers where she'd made uncharitable statements about her home town and the nuns who had taught her. Her compatriots questioned her on these and made it clear they did not appreciate her embroidery. Then there was Eileen's outrage at discovering she had signed up to perform three concerts each week – a detail that had escaped her notice when she took the contract months earlier in London. When she agreed to the conditions she had been on the point of collapse from exhaustion.

Coralie had her own personal disappointments. She found she was required to stay with Eileen in the Adelphi, Perth's glamorous city hotel, when she had been pining for at least a few days in the cocoon of her loving family. After six years away she was longing to luxuriate in endless talk, relaxed laughter and her mother's good cooking. Instead she was only allowed one day's release before the first round of social engagements she was required to attend in her role as Eileen's 'secretary'. On their second day on home soil,

Loreto Old Girls put on a dinner where president Miss Octavia Grave 'in exciting cerise and silver matt crêpe, welcomed Eileen, her mother, her two sisters and 90 past pupils'. Other functions of similar magnitude followed.

However, the Perth concerts were a sell-out, the audience transfixed. A notice in *The Bulletin* from a local correspondent recorded:

> In Western Australia, Miss Joyce seems to have swept everything before her. She has given four concerts in Perth. At her first recital the platform was hung with black curtains, and the only light in the hall was a lamp in a bell-shaped shade immediately over the keyboard. Miss Joyce came on dressed entirely in white, and, as she is only a little over five feet high and daintily built, the effect was extremely charming. At the second concert in Perth, the young pianist was recalled to the platform 20 times.

Coralie at once came face to face with the realities of *her* contract – effectively to be at the performer's side to fulfil her instant demands for every waking hour. She was required to be at all the recitals as well as the functions and interviews, dealing with the press, soothing Eileen, escorting her to and fro, arranging suitable accommodations and dealing with reviews, reviewers and any other inquiries or unexpected problems. Her most pressing and ever-present task was to make sure there was a piano – not just any piano – available for the diva to continue her schedule of six or seven hours of practice a day.

After the Perth concerts, the two young women had to contend with the commitments of the ABC's first national concert tour. On 15 April they set off for Sydney, unprepared for the strenuous months of travel ahead. There were only two options for getting from Perth to Sydney, a distance of almost four thousand kilometres.

There was the Trans Australian Railway, actually a series of distinct railway journeys, requiring changes at Kalgoorlie, Port Pirie, Melbourne and Albury over four or five days. Or there was the sea voyage from Fremantle down the west coast and across the Great Australian Bight (rumoured to be rough) to Adelaide and Melbourne, then up the east coast to Sydney. The ABC's concert schedule did not allow for this longer alternative; in any case, it would not have suited the delicately constitutioned Miss Joyce, who had a tendency towards *mal de mer.*

Les had to face the reality of being separated from Coral for up to three months. In their years abroad they had never spent a night apart. He was worried about her, worried too about her luggage, the 'Five Bob Case', a cardboard contraption of tenuous durability. The Kalgoorlie Express had barely departed when he penned his first letter to her, standing at a bus stop:

> Wrap the rug around your 5/- case and the strap around both.
>
> Cheerio, m-darling. Remember that I would be with you if I could and that I shall be with you as soon as humanly possible. Keep faithful and write often. Don't get panicky but keep cool. You're all the world to me and I want you back looking just as lovely as you ever were.

In a few weeks Les would be ready to leave the West himself and head for Sydney. He arranged a passage on the SS *Mongolia.* Meanwhile, as he had no income and hardly any savings, he was churning out articles for various newspapers and journals. And the reality of Coral's absence was biting already:

> I have been rushed off my feet since you left – scarcely a moment to sit still – except for the purposes of writing some blasted article. It's terribly hard work to do any writing in these circs …

How I am missing your conversation at the moment, dear. This morning I finished *The Daily News* article on Perth-after-six-years (not until *The News* had been ringing me around the town for it) and on reading it over, instinctively held out a hand for your assistance. This dependence! I shall be very pleased when we are together again. I trust you are standing up to the racket O.K.

Since returning to their home town, Les and Coral had been treated as *wunderkind* who had made their names across the seas. During the last few years, their columns, Coral's *London Woman's Diary* and Les's *London Lights*, had been devoured by the locals in Perth's daily paper, *The West Australian*. With this reputation came the weight of expectation. Les warned Coral:

> There's a tremendous responsibility on us two to do some big work in the future, since many people even now think we're geniuses. Whereas ... you know the rest.

Although he penned daily letters to Coral, Les did not factor in the haphazard nature of the mail service, or on some days the total absence of one. Then he realised that the mail would be travelling by the Trans, too; in fact, his letter would probably be on the same train as Coral so she wouldn't get it till she reached Sydney – damn!

Meanwhile Eileen and Coralie were about to arrive in Kalgoorlie, close to Eileen's family home in Boulder, for a jubilant welcome ceremony. The first leg of the journey had not gone well. They found they were separated from their luggage. The guard nonchalantly informed them: 'Probably in the luggage van – no chance of getting at it till Kal.' Then Eileen became bilious and blamed the water on the train. It was provided in a heavy glass carafe perched in a decorative wired cage up near the luggage racks. They watched it jostling between two glass tumblers of questionable cleanliness, the water inside sloshing around rhythmically with the rocking of the carriage. There was no toilet in the cabin, just one men's room and one ladies' room at the end of the corridor.

So the glamorous Eileen had no clean clothes to change into and wondered how she would combine a gastric attack with a very public welcome when the train pulled into her home town. Her mother, who had come to Perth for the reunion, warned her that the goldfields were planning big celebrations. The nuns from St Joseph's would be there too, the women who first recognised her prodigious musical talent. The idea of cheering crowds, her family and supporters waiting at the station weighed on Eileen's sick stomach and filled her with dread.

Then she would need to prepare for her performance at the Kalgoorlie Town Hall, a sumptuous edifice of baroque architecture with a real red carpet. That would also be an august occasion for the Australian Broadcasting Commission, a fledgling institution – the first concert to be broadcast, even though the radio waves did not carry very far. The Clarke and Rees families would be gluing their ears to the wireless in Perth, a few hundred kilometres to the west.

Les sent Coral a wistful message:

I shall be listening to the recital broadcast from Kal. and it will be some small link with you, dear. Pity you can't seize the microphone for a moment and whisper a message. You only need to whisper.

Give Eileen a chaste kiss for me. Keep beautiful, love, and please write.

Two days later he was on his way to Sydney by sea. On board the SS *Mongolia* he wrote:

This leaves me in the middle of the Great Australian Bight. I wonder how and where it will find you. The news of you has been so horribly sparse that I find it hard to grip the idea of your being in Sydney at all. But I suppose we must both put up with this business of not hearing from each other, not having time to write letters, missing letters, getting them whether they are stale and so on for some time. Certainly I shall be glad when it is over.

It has been a good trip – a cabin to myself, food excellent, accommodation luxurious by comparison with the 'Mortifying Bay'. In this cabin I have lights above bed with switch, bell to ring my steward, chest of drawers, electric fan with switch at bedhead. I am at the Captain's table, for the officers rarely condescend to eat with the vulgar passengers. The weather has been mostly bright and the sea quite calm. The dreaded Bight is a fiction.

Now, darling, you will say that this letter is all about me but I have no news from you on which to bite. Nor is this a complaint. I trust also that no he-men Australians have been wanting to run off with you and that, if so, you have stoutly denied them. You know how jealous I am.

While the ship was wallowing in the Southern Ocean, somewhere between Adelaide and Melbourne, Les found a passage in Hemingway that spoke to him deeply.

Darling one – Here I lie me down in my bunk and begin to write. (Actually just now the ship is giving some spectacular heaves and rolls. One of these has just smashed a kitchenful of crockery.)

Each day not only the time but the space between us lessens. I shall be glad to get off the ship tomorrow in Melbourne as it is getting rather dull. Nevertheless it has been a good rest. I have enjoyed a good deal of reading, both of English papers on board and of Hemingway's *A Farewell to Arms*. The novel has set me thinking a great deal about you, sweetheart. I think the love story is most affecting and beautiful by implication. How it all recaptures for me our slightly wistful but lovely early life in London. The expressed emotion, always given in dialogue, never in the prose, is beautiful. Hemingway should have been a playwright. I imagine his slightly affected simplicity of style, his deliberate naivety takes its cue from Gertrude Stein. […]

Yesterday we were at Adelaide. I went to lunch at a pub with several other journalists. I offered the Chief of Staff my carbon copy of 'Tension in the Mediterranean' (*The Daily News*) and he may take it.

Love to self and a little to Eileen

Meanwhile the concert party – Eileen with ABC Concerts Manager Leon White and Coralie – had arrived in Sydney. Coral set herself up at the Commodore, a guest house in Kings Cross. She made it clear she was disappointed in her husband's epistolary performance:

Well, of all the husbands! and of all the wives!

to start a love letter by nagging. But, darling, I haven't yet got over the disappointment of receiving only a brief rushed postcard by today's mail. You forgot my letter! And if you only knew how I was longing for it! […]

Darling, now that I know you're coming over to Sydney, I positively can't wait until you get here. Can't. Well just. Funny thing, but if I knew I was not going to see you and feel you for six months, I'd feel calm and resigned; but now that it's so much closer I could stamp my feet and scream. Come quickly; because I'm fit as a fiddle and ready … etc. Actually more ready than fit, so all the more reason why you should hurry. Get out and swim behind the boat and push it faster.

You said 'love to self and any that's left over to Eileen'! Well, there's none left over. So – Vitabrits!

Coral had sniffed out a possible job for Les on *The Sydney Morning Herald*. She tried to tone down his expectations:

> It's not first class so I hope you haven't been building too much on
> it or telling people about it in large capitals. You'll be second fiddle
> to the existing critic and knowing your temperament, I doubt
> whether you'll like that. He will naturally pick the plum shows in
> art, drama and films and leave you the rest. You won't have your
> name in *The Herald*, but you'll be able to write your best stuff. He
> murmured something about casual rates for a start, while you're
> on trial and then a permanency at about £8 a week.

The day after Eileen, Leon and Coralie arrived in Sydney,
Eileen was ready for a flurry of interviews. At noon she was in the
ballroom of the Wentworth Hotel, posing upon the grand piano
for the reporter and cameraman from *The Wireless Weekly*. The
meeting was published as 'An interview with the real Eileen Joyce':

> We observed the reason for the flowing dresses Miss Joyce wears
> in concerts; in her ordinary dresses she is as lithe as a tuning fork,
> not thin, but really well-developed, and, sitting at the piano, gives
> the impression of being a very special machine contrived for piano
> playing, compact of nervous and muscular energy [...] You can't
> be a nice little girl and a great pianist. She's an artist; you can see
> it in her face; she has thin features and thin arms, all freckled.
> She had little make-up, except blue stuff under and over her eyes,
> probably for the benefit of the cameraman; and she talks nervously
> and impulsively and no-nonsense.
>
> The reporter asked if she was travelling alone.
>
> 'I went away alone; but have come out with Coralie Clark-
> Rees [*sic*] and her husband; Coralie's a very old friend, and has
> been my secretary for some time. Always calm; the calmest person

I ever met; no matter what goes wrong, Coralie remains calm. Especially when I get temperamental.'

'Do you get temperamental?'

She smiled. 'So much happens. We got stuck in the desert near Port Augusta; the engine had consumption, burst one of its tubes. Two and a half hours. No one knew I was on the train coming over; every day I got up at four to practise.'

'Piano on the train?' the reporter queried.

'Yes. When the passengers heard, they said they wished they'd known.'

Coralie's duties apparently extended to getting up with Eileen for the daily practice. In a rose-coloured account, 'Sidelights on a Memorable Broadcasting Tour', she records:

Yawny and blear-eyed, I rose with her and watched the pale fingers of the dawn creep out over the Nullarbor Plain to the accompaniment of a Rachmaninoff concerto.

Just over a week later, Les arrived in Sydney and moved into Coral's room at the Commodore. But Coral was not there. She and Eileen had taken the train to Melbourne and then travelled by boat to Hobart. Nonetheless, Les got down to making connections and started work at the *Herald*. One of his first tasks was to report Hitler's May Day broadcast. Les, having just come from Europe where the awareness of rising fascism was on everyone's lips, knew it was critical.

I sat with pencil poised and heart aflutter for Hitler to begin his May Day broadcast from Berlin. I got most of it down (the translation). There was another chap from *The Telegraph* writing brilliant shorthand while I struggled with longhand. I felt very inferior until after the broadcast when *The Telegraph* man confessed that he couldn't read a word of his shorthand back, so I had to go through it with him. (Incidentally, I picked up a phrase or two from him). Moral: To hell with shorthand. Coming back to the office at 11.30 pm I found myself the man of the moment, all of them waiting on my Hitler hit. It is in the paper today and I hope Hitler will not send over a special envoy to shoot me.

Les was under the impression he would be hired as a critic on the *SMH* so it was a painful comedown to find he was required to do news reporting. Eventually he got his chance.

I find it difficult to impress the Chief of Staff with the fact that I have come 12,000 miles from the hub of the universe, the centre of civilisation, centuries' core, in order to report church services and RSL beer-gatherings.

However, I've got my first engagement as *SMH* dramatic critic!

And, at last, he had the possibility of some income.

I find that if I am put down to do five and a half days work a week at 35/- a day, that works out at nearly £10 a week, so not bad.

In Hobart for the concerts, Coral found the town disturbingly quiet.

I'm writing this in the concert studio of 7ZL Hobart. Eileen is practising on the grand here becos [*sic*] she got temperamental about the upright we hired for her at the pub. She's playing some lovely Bach. I find its ringing counterpoint very soothing. It's 8.15 pm. This must be the fourth time I've walked to and from this studio today. But what a prize awaited me. Your letter! I'd been longing for it.

121

Life is going smoothly, and much more quietly than hitherto. Almost too quietly. There's nowhere to make whoopee in this 1-horse village, if and when the mood's upon one. Hobart would be nice for a rustic holiday – with you – but stultifying to live in. The mentality seems very small town.

Devilish hard to get a moment to myself, living in the same hotel as Eileen. We haven't had time to go out much. Eileen sticks at the piano and I've had a lot of her letters to write and her Press Book to do. Yesterday afternoon there was a cocktail party for her. Wish we had time for walks and drives and river trips. Goodnight, loved one, sleep well and dream of

Your Coral xxx

Despite more than ten years' full-time newspaper experience under the belt, Les was still looking for professional reassurance on the quality of his work.

At the *Herald* I hear absolutely no comment on my work. I asked the Chief of Staff what he thought of it and he said: 'all right'. Nonplussed, I said 'No complaints?' and he said 'No'. How's that for caution. But it does not convey any criticism. I am put down regularly for work and sometimes my copy is a little cut. Space is very tight.

Now I must fly, Darling. At times I feel a terrible desolation here, which I know only your presence could dispel. So do hurry back. For God's sake don't fall in love with anyone else – or even begin to, will you? You'll never get anybody as good as me.

Till next time sweetheart, you fine girl, lovely girl, Hemingway girl – Les

Coral, writing from Launceston, had her own problems. She needed Les to offer some advice and sent a stop press:

Eileen has suddenly got in a panic about the amount my fares are costing her and wants to leave me in Melbourne while she goes to Adelaide. Ditto Sydney while she goes to Brisbane. What's your view – to encourage her to think she can do without me or to offer to forgo some salary or to contribute towards travelling expenses in order to stick with her? You see there were very small houses at the Tasmania concerts due to the small dead population. They were worthwhile every way but financially and she's starting to think she's not getting enough money out of the tour. White hates the thought of her being or travelling alone and thinks she is silly to dispense with me. Let me know your reactions to all this quickly. I feel a little tired of the whole business myself. If only you were here to talk it over.

Au'voir, sweet. Since you are complaining seriously about our separation just as this happens, perhaps we won't be separated for much longer ...

Les's job on the *Herald*, while not extending him, remained profitable.

A day's work yesterday was to see three films (one of them screened in a theatre specially for me & Josephine O'Neill of *The Telegraph*) and attend an Independent Theatre production of *Man with a Load of Mischief*. 35/- for that is jam, don't you think? Some days I have only half a day's work – 18/6. This consists of seeing one film.

Enough of money. You must not think that my mind naturally hangs on money-making all day, but if we are to settle here for a while we must do the best for ourselves. Meanwhile we ought to save a bit. Very soon I must be sending my mother her old 10/- a week, as when I was there, I found she had all kinds of debts.

It is lovely to be able to confide in you – pity you weren't here to discuss things while we cuddle in bed. Make those months scud by like storm clouds and come back to your ever-waiting Les.

Les was anxious to meet members of the literary community. He had already made a fortunate connection with Frank Dalby Davison who had swum into almost unbelievable success with his novel about a wild cow. Unable to find a publisher for *Man-Shy*, he had the novel printed and then hawked it from door to door. That book was becoming the talk of the town.

Davison took Les to meet Marjorie Barnard, a librarian, with whom he had a secret liaison. Marjorie was a writer of short stories and, with collaborator Flora Eldershaw, produced historical novels under the pseudonym M. Barnard Eldershaw. (The most famous is their first, *A House Is Built*.)

Yesterday I went to Marjorie Barnard's for lunch. Marjorie lives in a lovely spot up the Harbour. There are innumerable little bays and points and the Barnards live on the slope of a bay with gardens in front of them sloping down to the water and a complete view of the city. They live in some style, with a servant and a general English middle class atmosphere. We talked till about four and Davison and I caught the ferry back to Sydney together. He is a decent fellow, very young and simple with a slight embarrassment of manner. He says *Man-Shy* was the easiest thing he has written – wrote it almost without knowing it.

But Les was increasingly insecure about Coral's fidelity and desperate to talk to her.

I am very lonely when I am not actually working – sometimes even then. I hope your friend, living in the same hotel, is a gentleman.

Of course, you must have an outing and get some fun but I don't mind telling you that I am as jealous as hell. I'm certainly sorry for Leon but I'm glad he's flirting with Eileen and not with you.

It's lovely to know we're mutually yearning. I didn't see your photo in *The Australian Women's Weekly* but shall immediately buy same. About ringing me on Sunday. Yes, I'll make myself free at 1/4 to 1. It would be grand. I hope I can find a private place here to talk. The number is FL 2303.

Darling, this separation is ghastly: I really don't know how I'll stand another four and a half weeks of it and then another couple of months after a week together. I'm thinking, quite seriously, that we'll have to do something about it. It's not what we planned. We planned to go about Australia together.

We're both meeting with so much success that it's ungrateful to complain and yet too often it rings hollow in my ear. When you attempt to tell me how chronic you feel, I can complete your meaning out of my own experience before you are finished. I have found that the only way is to keep busy. But I positively dread having a night free. Loneliness would envelop me. This afternoon I imagined I was going to be free tonight and in a panic thought: 'I'll ring Nugget Coombs and go there.' I can see you are the same. I did not think that four months could be so bloody long! I don't like it. There's too much danger of it interfering with our permanent happiness.

The general atmosphere of the *Herald* office is not stimulating — precisely because it is so reminiscent of *The West Australian* — the dull-witted Chief of Staff poring over his engagement book, the rather nondescript collection of Cable men and sub-nibs takes me back a few years. Then there is a big bare reporters' room with chaps hanging on telephones and in shirtsleeves, also a notice board littered with unclaimed copies of *The Journalist* — how these newspaper 'daily' offices run to type. My position is still vague and expectant – they're a cautious lot of b—s, as the elfin Eileen would say. The new News Editor, who perused my Press Books with great interest, has quietly suggested that reorganisation of the staff is in the wind.

Meanwhile Coral had more worries with her contract. Eileen had 'turned snakey':

> Eileen is definitely leaving me in Melb. while she does her week in Adelaide. My fare to Adelaide would have cost her £7 and what with my salary she feels she can't afford it. I offered to suffer reductions to oblige her but she refused. Leon White tried very hard to get the ABC to pay my travelling expenses, but nothing doing. He says, however, he's going to insist on my going to Brisbane with her (worse luck!). At the present rate, it doesn't look as if she'll be wanting to take me back to Perth or even to Adelaide. This sudden craze of Eileen's to save money is alarming. She feels that other people are getting more out of the ABC than she is and has turned snakey.

Coral was also worried about their future. They had talked of eventually settling down to family life but she admitted to Les she was fearful of childbirth. Les immediately wrote to reassure her:

> Poor darling! How you are always meeting with people, reading books, hearing stories that make you fear having a child. Or is it that only the bad stories impress themselves on you! Well, look here, if you fear having kids, we simply won't have any damn kids. They're not worth it to us. You're everything and everyone to me and there's no need for anybody else. Family raising is largely a conventional habit. We're self-sufficient.

Coral wrote back:

You were a darling about the children, beloved. It's lifted a weight off me. Otherwise I feel there's an ordeal waiting ahead – like a visit to the dentist, which one is trying to put off, or like death which is inevitable but must be daily avoided. But I promise to be sensible, darling, if and when the time comes. In the meantime, to know that we are sufficient is heaven! It is more than one deserves; and that in itself is frightening. Oh, I'm mopey. I want your arms around me, that's all. Then I wouldn't care what happened, either way.

Shortly I must go to the station and see Eileen and Leon White off to Adelaide. He's taken her to his home for the afternoon. She's very moody and uncertain. There's nothing in their flirtation, of course.

Darling. I hate saying goodbye. Your letters are the only thing which makes life worthwhile. Life's going to be superlatively excellent when we are together again. In the meantime, love me every minute as I love you.

Les was consumed by loneliness, too.

Seldom have I felt so lonely for you in such a ghastly condition of dependence. I've had a quiet three days on the *Herald* – only half a day of work in three days. This wouldn't weary me financially, if only it doesn't let me down in other ways as well. You can't make arrangements to go out and see people at short notice. So I've been left on my own all this time, chafing at the bit and fed up with only a single ambition in life – to have you with me. At the same time, I am oppressed by my terrific and dangerous dependence on you – wonder if it is right for two persons to live in one another. Supposing you didn't come back, would life have any meaning or savour again?

And all sorts of small things have aggravated my emptiness.

No letter from you yesterday morning – I kept on looking in the box all day. Did you miss the post or has it gone astray? I tried to write an article and felt hopelessly restless. At night I went to a couple of concerts. Does that sound queer? However, that's the *Herald*'s doing. Friday afternoon I took Nugget Coombs to tea – life consists of taking people to meals or being taken – we have arranged to meet next week. I might stroll out there this afternoon.

Coming home last night I put through a call to you, feeling I must have a word with you. Now just where were you before midnight, big girl? I was bitterly disappointed, but they said, in any case, they didn't like taking calls after 11 pm at your end.

Sweet – I have been doing a bit of thinking about our future. If we can earn £15 a week, we ought to be able to get a good flat – a modern flat with the proper equipment for you. That means spending a couple of hundred quid on furniture, etc. then we want a car. And all we have now is £100 and some vases and pictures. So we'll have to work hard – just concentrate on raking in the cash for a while.

I also have other plans. I may as well set up as an authority on drama, if we are to stay in Australia. It might be an idea to rewrite that old thesis of mine and get my MA. I should like to make some contact with the University – there may be the opportunity of lecturing on drama as we once visioned.

At the Fellowship of Australian Writers Les met Mary Gilmore:

Mary Gilmore is a fine type of woman, rather aged and shaky but an obviously sterling person. She talked to me and I said I should like to call on her and she was delighted. Gave me her address, which happens to be across the road from here – in Darlinghurst Road. Isn't that decent? I want to get a series of interviews written with Davison, Mary Gilmore etc. – valuable in the future and more immediately for *The West Australian*. This introduction of me to the Fellowship in laudatory terms will be valuable. Davison and I have obviously 'clicked'. But I'm so used to you sharing every move of mine that I don't like going ahead with meetings on my own – I want you to join in.

Coral wrote from Melbourne:

I've been struggling with Eileen's enormous Press Book. Last night I felt so desolate here I walked down Collins Street and came to a big Hoyts Deluxe theatre with Fred Astaire and Ginger Rogers dancing on a 20ft hoarding outside. There were crowds pouring in and I feared I should be turned away. But 2/6 did the trick and I went up the imposing marble stairways. I let myself sink into the film, just like the thousands around me.

I'd like to ring you tonight if there were a faint hope that you'd be in and if I can find a private spot to speak – which is doubtful. Sydney and Melbourne seem so close compared with places like Perth and Hobart. We're a mere 600 miles apart. Must now force myself to say goodbye, darling. I'm sorry this is such a gloomy letter. I'll be cheerful again soon. Very much love and send some message every day, won't you.

And don't be jealous of me, dearest, I'm not letting anyone get within coo-ee of me.

Les wrote:

What do you think I've been doing today? Having lunch with Mary Gilmore. I received a letter from her yesterday asking me to call, as she wanted to ask my advice on London publishers and agents. Extraordinary. I called today – she's just across the road. Has a flat full of notes, notebooks, press-cuttings and pen drawings of herself around the wall. A rather rough practical-looking place. She brought me in – seems to be there on her own, though 70, and immediately began telling me about the 'New Australia' colony in Paraguay forty years ago – of which she was a leading member. Then she made me a cup of 'yerba mate', a South American beverage like china tea. Then lent me some of her books and took me out to lunch.

She's a remarkable woman. Has an extraordinary agility of mind, packed with ideas, beliefs, memories and anecdotes. I felt anaemic and colourless, not to mention inert, beside her. She claims a good bit for herself and seems to have been 'in' at the beginning of everything. For instance, she advised Henry Lawson on the publication of his first book, gave Dorothy Cottrell her first encouragement, and so on. She is a Communist-Socialist and reckons that the New Australia experiment gave the idea to Russia. You'll like her though she makes you feel just a bit limp. She has stacks of notebooks full of early reminiscences – stuff she realises should be set down. There may be a job for you or me. She said: 'I've got all the material but it's the hardest work writing it down. I need a collaborator.' This may have been a hint thrown in my direction. To help her with a book or two might not be worth much money but it would be vastly interesting. She has a mind as rich as a plum pudding. The smell of the pioneer is about her. I have an idea she won't last much longer. Mentioned that her heart gives her trouble – and she has a slightly blown-up look. [Dame Mary Gilmore lived on till 1962.]

Coral was finding Eileen a continuous challenge:

You're right about the fact that I'm not saving much money. Eileen is such a dilatory and uncertain payer. One can't roll up to her on a Friday and say Payday! She may be in tears, in bed, preparing for a concert, getting over a concert, being trainsick or seasick; and since great tact is necessary I have to be accommodating. If she were here to pay me today's fiver I should have £9 in hand. I could send you £5 if I didn't have to buy myself another warm dress and Mum's present and keep myself till the end of next week.

I'm glad to have your mature considerations on the Eileen question. I feel very sick about it at the moment – uncertain and foreboding – but the atmosphere must be cleared one way or the other when she returns next Tuesday.

Our separation has given me new insights into life and this week of aloneness has given me new insights into death. I tended to get so smug and cocksure when we were always together and always happy. Now I know what life must be like for people who are not together and not happy. I always thought I had enough inward resources to cope with any situation. Well, I can make a show of coping, but …

Les replied:

It is nice of you to refuse invitations out with men on my account. But you mustn't ask me for a decision what you should do, darling one. That's not fair. You must decide for yourself. Personally, the idea of taking other women out just bores me – like you, I prefer to go by myself. Apart from jobs of work, I'm afraid I'm frightfully tired about going anywhere without you. I've definitely turned down the invitation to the ball. Without you, it's just sheer hard work to be on special evening dress behaviour all night. I wish I wasn't so tired. I seem to have exhausted all my youthful enthusiasm and I can't find any sort of experience – here or in London – that excites me. Except the thought of reunion with you.

A week and a half till you arrive. People are getting excited about Eileen Joyce's return season – which for me means your return season. Nevertheless, can you get me any tickets for any of her concerts here? I'd like to hear the orchestral one particularly.

Sorry to hear you are still rather miserable – I can understand it exactly and sympathise to the last inward pang because I have been through it myself. I dread having a day alone. Chronic, isn't it, for two full-grown persons to go on thus.

Love and more love and yet more and more still till next time.

Coral reassured him by the next day's post:

Darling One, I'm in the middle of yet another struggle with Eileen's Press book, but I must just say at once that I love you madly and that I'm so lonely for you that I'm physically sick about it. It's like music in my ears to hear that you are worried about your dependence on me because that's just what's got me down. I don't and can't live apart from you. That's flat. I'm useless. I just don't function. And if anything's going to happen to you, let me know and I'll rush in on it, too. That's all I want.

The fact that I've been socially accepted by the more interesting element in this house did ease things a bit at first. It's better than brooding absolutely alone and left out. But you're my only panacea. And these are just a set of jolly people to smoke and talk and have a drink with, and when I've left them I feel as bad as ever. Sometimes even when I'm with them. We're in such a state about each other that the rest of the world simply has no bearing. I don't know how much longer we can bear this separation.

Tues 3 pm.

Eileen arrived this am and I haven't breathed since.

With Eileen back in Melbourne after the Adelaide concerts, Coral wanted a definite answer on her contract:

I've had to lay my cards on the table. She didn't make very much out of the Adelaide concerts, though they were judged successful. Still, Melbourne ought to be more lucrative. If she decides to dispense with me, I'll demand a month's salary, don't you think, to compensate for the *Moreton Bay* and messing up my stay in Perth etc, etc?

Outwardly the status quo seems to hold. It's almost as if we'd never been parted; which isn't so good in a way. White shouldn't have stayed with her so much in Adelaide, then she'd have felt the pinch. As it is, the only pinch she's feeling is my salary. I asked her to think about the future today and she was vague as usual. It nearly drives White and me mad trying to get anything definite out of her. He says she didn't discuss the future (a) with me or (b) without me, either way in Adelaide, much to his and my disgust. Still, I've told her to think it over. She said she'll see how the Melbourne concerts go.

Must now tear myself away from the delight of talking with you and on with the EJ junk.

Les was on the countdown for Coral's return to Sydney.

I have been wondering a lot about you over the weekend, my sweet, hoping you're not too lonely and desolate but also that you're not having such a good time that you've forgotten me.

Later the same day:

As expected, just got your two letters – sweetheart. Every word you write is lovely, delicious and I come too soon to the end and then the excitement is over – for 24 hrs at least. I'm still struggling with the Home article. I must go to it. Work on the *Herald* is not so prolific. I still have that *Manchester Guardian* chap in competition with me and what's more, the bounder has invited me to dinner at his home. Embarrassing!

It was crisis time for Coral in Melbourne:

I've just returned from a day spent by Eileen's bedside. Does that portend evilly to you? The fact is, she's cracking up. The concerts are proving too much for her. Last night – tho' it was a packed house and they applauded vociferously – she was in a frightfully depressed state – said her memory was going through mental and physical weariness, and that she forgot and messed up every piece she played. White and I and the audience could discern no difference in her playing but she retorted that the really musical people and the critics would! I pray the critics don't say frank things in tomorrow's papers. There are no Sunday papers (or trams) in this church-ridden village. She reckons that her performances are becoming more and more substandard, until last night's was 5th rate. Of course she's hypercritical and sensitive but the feeling of going downhill is getting on her nerves. Then she's worried about money and about the fact that when she does crack up – as she surely will at this rate – who is going to look after her and pay her nursing homes.

She tactfully asked me whether we intended to settle in Sydney – and began fumbling about my contract. I know it's been gnawing at her for some time and in all humanity I hate to add to her worries. She had a doctor in this morning and he said she ought to have a couple of months' rest. At one stage it looked as if she'd throw up the whole business from this moment. Anyhow, with regard to me, the upshot is that she cannot afford to keep me going. She did not intend to take me to Brisbane and after Bris, when the public concerts cease she'll only have her £25 a week, out of which she can definitely not afford to keep me. She's already decided not to go back to Perth herself – can't face the dreadful Trans trip. But she probably will go to New Zealand for a couple of months in the middle of August. We went into the business of taking me to New Zealand and the travelling expenses – £30 for boat alone – are far too heavy. So she'll go alone.

Coral suggested a compromise to Eileen, offering two weeks' notice so that she would finish up after the Sydney concerts. It had been a difficult brief – but there were compensations.

Taking all in all, I'm lucky to have got what I have out of it; she might have cracked up sooner. I doubt, too, whether I'd have made £5 every week in any other way. Of course, I wouldn't have spent it either. I bought myself a new winter dress – £3 – the other day. I think you'll like it. And a coat for Mother -£2/5/-. So that's something.

It's now Monday morning and Eileen's no better. I've lots of work to do too. I must get all her stuff absolutely up-to-date before I hand over. Do you know she even wants to save the postage stamps on fan mail now!

Goodbye for today, dearest dear. A week today I hope to be with you. The relief of being with you again will be almost more than I can bear.

PS It's true about Eileen's lapses on Saturday night. *The Argus* has given her a very cool and pernickety notice today. I haven't seen the other papers and I fear the worst. It's most upsetting.

Les was surprised to hear about Eileen. But it meant Coral was on the way back.

Darling – just got your serious letter with news about Eileen cracking up and about your contract. It's grand that you're coming up here next Monday – splendid. Two days less agony than expected. Bet your life I'll be waiting for you at the station on Monday morning with heart full of love and arms ready to enfold you.

13

On the Air

Only days into their long separation in 1936, Coral had written to Les about the possibility of a job at the ABC in Hobart. Nothing came of it but that was the start of them worming their way into a completely new world – the world of radio – or 'wireless', as it was called. This was a turning point in their careers, a move that would influence the direction of their lives for decades to come. How Coralie had heard about it, she did not elaborate, but from Adelaide sent a wire to Perth. It was the first communiqué Les received from the travellers and it lifted his gloom. He replied immediately.

The telegram cheered me like hell. Whether or not the ABC job is any good I shall not know till I hear from you but the idea of being offered a job before I reach Sydney appeals to me considerably. Always I have wanted someone to offer me a job instead of my seeking one. Now the impossible has happened – or so I like to believe.

Once Les had the details, he lost no time in writing off to the director of ABC Hobart to find out more information. He knew absolutely nothing about the ABC, broadcasting or Tasmania but he was out of work and short of money so had to take what he could find. The national broadcaster had only been established – by federal government proclamation – less than four years previously, its charter 'to provide information and entertainment, culture and gaiety'. It was also required 'to serve all sections and to satisfy the diversified tastes of the public'. My parents' arrival back in Australia happened to coincide with the setting up of federal offices to coordinate the work of the separate state departments. This move would allow for nationally broadcast material, including music, talks and drama.

I never heard or read anything more about the possibility of my father working in Hobart. Such an occurrence might have changed the course of all our lives.

So Les came to Sydney and worked as a freelance journalist for *The Sydney Morning Herald*, reviewing plays, films and art shows. But he wanted more. 'I knew I needed a more vigorous, innovative outlet.' Soon he was able to send word that he had scored an interview with William James Cleary, the ABC's second chairman. He wrote an excited letter to Coralie, who was in Launceston with Eileen Joyce.

I must tell you a little more about the ABC job, about which I sent you a stop press card yesterday. It's a clear case of their suggesting the job to me because I went in merely to see about talks. Cleary is a great talker and talked for an hour and a half about his drama plans. It was difficult for me to say much. He wanted to know about my history and whether I had any work to show him and then invited me to send in an application for the job – exactly what job I don't quite know. I went home and did this, working in a good bit about you, too, and giving a full account of myself. I also enclosed Nettie Palmer's article about me in *The Red Page*.

I had lugged in my Press Book – what a great treasure it's proving – and hurled it at Cleary's hand. Yesterday I said: 'In the event of your taking me on, what sort of salary?' He said 'Haven't the faintest idea'. I then told him of the *SMH* job. Today he said: 'Can you tell me what the *SMH* job is worth to you?' and I said '£500 a year at least.' He said 'Ha' and said he would think it over. At another time he said: 'Of course we have no fixed scales for salaries – we give a man what he's worth to us.' I gather he is anxious to have men of general culture in the ABC, no doubt following the BBC's idea. Let's hope he gets better ones than the BBC. He asked me if I was interested in music and what languages I could speak and seemed attracted by my general knowledge of art, literature etc.

As soon as my father returned to his digs, in a fever of post-interview elation, he set out the advantages an ABC job would offer:

1. There would be tremendous Australia-wide prestige resulting from the appointment, at least I imagine so.
2. Cleary talks as if the ABC has tons of money and can pay what it wants – might mean big rises in the future.
3. It would be a chance to do more creative, more practical work – reading and criticising and doctoring radio plays, arranging contents etc. with possibility of visits to other capitals and the country.
4. Cleary being keen on men with general culture, there might be various other chances within the Commission, such as taking over literary sections, or even the whole control of the

more serious programme arrangements. (You see, I am a man of vision).

5. The hours of work would be regular. Under the *Herald* arrangements, it seems impossible for me to know what I am doing for more than 24 hours ahead. Regular hours would give us opportunity of taking part in any other creative work, such as play production on the stage. In time I do not see why you and I should not get down to the business of writing and producing our own plays here, much more scope than in London I think.

But, interestingly, it was Coralie who made the first move into broadcasting. (This is something I would never have known if I had not discovered that pile of 1936 letters.) She was the one who first sold a 'talk' to the ABC to be delivered on national radio and then walked into a recording studio in Hobart and delivered it. It was a world in which she would eventually make her mark.

But there is a price for everything. She had to forgo her social life, as she reported:

Eileen and Leon went to the pictures last night. I felt like going but had to stay at the hotel and prepare my wireless talk and fell asleep doing so. Hope the listeners didn't fall asleep tonight when I was broadcasting it. I wonder if you were listening? I think it went well; the delivery might have been a trifle slow but it should have been clear. I didn't want to make your mistake of going too fast as you did in your voice test – and perhaps I erred on the other side. It is lovely to think that you were listening and might send me a telegram of encouragement??? I'm to get three guineas for it. It took lots of time to prepare.

Les did manage to hear the broadcast:

Firstly I must tell you I heard your voice on the wireless tonight. I discovered the *SM Herald* had a wireless set in its library. The librarian found the wireless correspondent and he spent about an hour tuning to get Tasmania for me. The atmospherics were crackling like a bushfire. It was chronic. However, I waited about till 6.30 and switched on and sure enough heard your sweet voice through the barrage of irrelevant ether-scraping noises. It was grand – though I contained my enthusiasm, not being sure that it was you, for the voice was so faint that I could not clearly distinguish. But then I heard the well-known paragraphs about the slim bamboo fingers of E.J. and knew it was you.

What a great pity I couldn't hear it better. From what I did hear, the broadcast was completely successful. Your voice is splendid, clear, bell-like, velvety and when we settle in Sydney we must do something about using it – either on the stage or on the radio.

Now, listen. Why not write to the Adelaide manager and try to arrange some broadcasts on the lines we have been dealing with – celebrities in Europe, women's life there, Eileen Joyce. Re the enclosed cuttings about Eileen, they are from *The Women's Weekly*, May 8 edition. There's quite a lot about you, too. I'll send one to your mother and father.

Leslie was not so successful.

The ABC has turned me down as I suspicioned by yesterday's letter. I don't think Bronner thought much of that broadcast on '200 Plays a Year' and, as I told you, he probably had some justification for I never felt less like broadcasting than at that moment. So when I saw him yesterday he said: 'We didn't get you into the national broadcasts. Your material is alright but the selectors of the programmes don't know enough about you, and feel you ought to have more experience broadcasting before putting you in the National bill. So we're arranging for you to give some NSW broadcasts.' It's a poor finish to all the spectacular interest they showed me and my suggestions at the beginning: but perhaps the fault lies with me.

Meanwhile, Coralie sent words of encouragement. While grateful, Leslie was at pains to water down her expectations.

Thanks, Love, for your congratulatory telegram about the Cleary job. Telegrams are so dramatic, final and clear-cut, like a climax in a stage play, but in life things are never like that. They are hedged with qualifications, doubts and compromises. So is the ABC job, as I have already explained. It is over-simplifying things to imagine that they will suddenly embrace me at a huge salary and with clarion calls of publicity.

I saw Charles Moses, the General Manager, today. I mentioned the play-reading job to him and he said: 'Nothing can be done for a few months.' When I mentioned to Moses the *SMH* work, he seemed relieved and said: 'Keep that. Meanwhile, perhaps we could give you a small weekly salary to read plays for us. This would probably develop into a full-time job.' This, though disappointing, is perhaps the best move.

Now that they saw the opportunity, both were separately planning broadcast talks. However, much of the material came from shared experiences so they had to negotiate who did what and then make sure they didn't encroach on each other's territory. Leslie reported some 'gratifying success'. He could see his future in the new world of radio:

Moses liked the ideas I submitted: all of them. Result: Federal Talks Director Bronner has ordered SEVEN National talks, to be broadcast all over Australia at FIVE GUINEAS a time. Think of it! But this isn't all. His is merely the Federal concern. I next went to the NSW Talks Director and arranged more talks with her. I am to give the first next week. Judging from general conversation, they seem starved for fresh first-hand talks and I should be able to give many of them. The directors seem more keen on literary talks.

This country is absolutely starved for European contacts: that's my dominant impression. I am desperately anxious to make a success of this broadcasting business because there seems so much future in it.

There was a future there – for both of them. Coralie would be 'on the air' for many years, making her name as a broadcaster. Leslie was appointed federal drama editor of the ABC in December 1936, and until his retirement in July 1966 he extended and enriched the role of radio drama. He could not have guessed that, by establishing his career in the ABC, he would have the opportunity to nurture and facilitate the literary careers of many other Australian writers, thus fulfilling that private resolution he made when trying to break into the bastions of London's newspaper world.

In 1936 Leslie's passionate belief that Australia must find its own voice in the arts, its own identity to replace slavish genuflection to British values and expression, was groundbreaking. As scriptwriter Eleanor Witcombe would declare:

The acceptance and recognition of an Australian literature and a truly Australian voice did not just happen. It has taken many generations of struggle. In the long history of the fight for existence, some names stand out: one of these is Leslie Rees.

Another legacy of my father's work was the profusion of Australians who developed their talents as playwrights under his guidance. One of those to benefit from that training was Witcombe, who went on to make a lifelong career as a dramatist. She played an important role in the birth of the Australian film industry, receiving accolades for her screenplay for the film *My Brilliant Career*. Of my father's contribution she wrote:

> Leslie Rees was well known for his generous support of new writers, particularly with practical advice, often with an introduction to radio writing – the only paying medium then available for would-be writers. 'Adapting plays,' he would say, 'will teach you structure.' It has been claimed that almost an entire post-war generation of scriptwriters and playwrights was influenced by him.

Looking back after decades, former chairman of the ABC Sir Charles Moses described Leslie as 'a man who has made a unique contribution to Australian drama and literature'.

14

Searchlights over Sydney

After the Eileen Joyce tour finished, my parents found themselves in Sydney. They fell in love with its physical beauty, its harbour, its mountains to the west, and its benign climate. And the life seemed to offer everything they valued.

As my father described it:

Sydney was indeed a smiling place to live. The beauties of the rocky inlets and points and coves, the pockets of virgin bushland, marvellous for weekend walks and so close to the built-up city streets, countless arcs of creamy or red gold beach along the near Pacific coasts, the unique vegetation and birds in wild, unsuspected gullies – all these riches were ours and we loved them.

My parents decided that here was the time and place to have their family. And of course, they intended to be writing. For this purpose, they found a spacious flat overlooking Shellcove, a little bay wedged between Neutral Bay and Mosman Bay on the northern shores of Port Jackson. It offered longed-for advantages:

water views from most of the windows and the hospitality of the landlord's harbour-fed pool. On top of that, it was just a short ferry ride to the city.

Leslie threw himself into his new role at the ABC and now, with a regular salary coming in, he and Coralie were able to buy a small car with a camping body and start procreating. On 30 August 1938 Megan Clarke Rees was born in the Saba Private Hospital at Neutral Bay Junction, an occasion my father remembered only too well.

> Shall I ever forget her arrival – me at home cleaning up and painting a pram that friends of ours had rescued from an old shed, my visiting mother complaining that I should have bought a new one, and then me passing out on the floor when the telephone at last told the news of a safe birth.

When her firstborn arrived, Coralie – despite earlier misgivings – embraced motherhood. She recalled one evening, looking down at her sleeping daughter and feeling 'such supreme happiness'.

> I felt that this was the fulfilment of my whole life. Although I'm very keen about my writing, my broadcasting, my travelling and all the other interesting experiences I've had, I would really give them all away – though I hope I don't have to – for this one, this common experience that every woman who has a child can feel.

At last there was progress on the writing front, too. My father's play *Lalor of Eureka* won first prize in a national competition and was produced by the Melbourne New Theatre. My parents took their second Australian camping trip, parking the baby with my mother's cousin Blanche and exploring Tasmania. Then, one Sunday evening, 3 September 1939, when both were taking part in a rehearsed reading of *Eureka* at the New Theatre in Sydney, world order collapsed.

> Just as one part ended, the newspaper boys down in Pitt Street were crying their wares – a special late edition of the Sunday papers. WAR DECLARED the boys intoned. BRITAIN HAS DECLARED WAR ON GERMANY.

Of course, being part of the British Empire meant that Australia was also at war. But even though men and women enlisted in large numbers, the theatres of war must have seemed so very far away and in places so foreign that most people would have had to look at an atlas to find them. Where were Libya, Cyrenaica, Syria? It never occurred to anyone that conflicts would come anywhere near the southern continent. So my parents decided to press on with building their family. Six months after World War II began, I was also on the way.

In September 1941 my parents took a trip to the Barrier Reef, leaving me (ten months) and my sister (three years) at home with our adult cousin Ailsa. This was the second time in Megan's short life, the first in mine, that our parents had gone away, leaving us with kind relatives. It was the beginning of a pattern that would continue throughout our childhoods. However, that adventure resulted in my father's first children's book, and very successful it was. So no doubt they would have felt their absence justified.

I was still a baby when the halcyon years ended, not just for my parents. All Australians were suddenly jolted out of their complacency. Those old enough to remember 'the war to end all wars' were frightened that the horrible experience, the chaos and waste of lives, was starting all over again. Those young enough to enlist had no idea what joining up would entail. They thought it would be an adventure. The country's isolation became not a boon but a threat, the miles of crenellated coastline no longer a proud boast but a very real hazard. Australia's population was only seven million, mostly scattered in the cities around the eastern and southern fringes of the continent.

After Japan bombed Pearl Harbor and declared war on Britain and the United States, the battle lines moved south. When Singapore fell, thousands of Australians were taken as prisoners of war. Then the Japanese established a major base in New Guinea, an Australian territory, meaning the enemy air force was now in comfortable flying range of the continent itself.

Of course Australians had taken part in other conflicts. But they always happened overseas. It had been unthinkable that Australia would be attacked, but on 19 February 1942 two hundred and forty-two Japanese aircraft bombed Darwin, killing military personnel and civilians. Ships in Darwin Harbour were scuttled and flying boats bringing refugees from other countries shelled. My uncle Max, my mother's younger brother, spent his twenty-first birthday burying the bodies that washed ashore. Japanese air attacks continued along the undefended coastline in the Northern Territory, far north Queensland and northern Western Australia. Indigenous people still lived their aeons-old traditional lifestyle in the remote regions of the north. To the south were thousands of square kilometres of desert and sparsely populated grazing lands, all remote and mainly inaccessible, making the southern cities particularly vulnerable to surprise air attack.

Most of Australia's available fighting force was engaged in overseas theatres of war. My father had not been called up. He was of the 'tween wars' generation: too young for World War I, too old for World War II. But he was requisitioned for duties as an air-raid warden and a precautions officer. There was a yellow metal sign with large black letters on our front gate: WARDEN. It had a contact phone number on it. As soon as darkness fell, Leslie was required to patrol the streets of our neighbourhood and make sure everyone had their lights low, blackout curtains drawn. During the day, he was at the ABC, which was striving to keep services going despite wartime austerities.

But Sydney Harbour's wide heads open to the Pacific Ocean made the city an easy target. Sydney would be the next port of call for the invading Japanese.

Only a few months after the bombing of Darwin, three Japanese miniature submarines sleuthed their way through the heads. One mistakenly torpedoed the HMAS *Kuttabul* (a requisitioned ferry), with the loss of twenty-one sailors. Their sights had been fixed on two Allied warships anchored in the harbour but the subs were detected and fired upon. They were eventually scuttled by their own crews in an act of suicide.

Sydney was a small city curving around a glittering harbour that, with criss-crossing ferries, was both a transport hub and a playground for weekend activities. So when the enemy came unbelievably close, slipping through the not-yet-completed anti-submarine barrier across the heads, my parents like all Sydneysiders would have been terrified. The rising slopes of the harbour and its bays were encrusted with houses and low-rise blocks of flats, the outer suburbs a development of the future. The Sydney Harbour Bridge had only been completed a decade before, linking the northern and southern shores.

After the assault of the mini-subs, Japanese submarines began attacking merchant shipping in the waters off eastern Australia. Three ships were sunk, others attacked, the ports of Sydney and Newcastle bombarded. The climate of fear was escalating: the very real fear that Japan was about to invade Australia.

I clearly remember the searchlights that criss-crossed the night skies over Sydney. These long trailing beams of light that were seeking out enemy aircraft seemed to us children something mysterious and other-worldly, the only illumination in the dark cavern of sky above the blacked-out city. Our windows were brown-papered over to prevent them shattering from bomb blasts or shelling. As soon as evening came, blackout curtains and blinds were drawn. It was advised that where possible, women and children should be evacuated to relatives and friends in safer places. We were among those in the city who had to take shelter when air-raid sirens sounded.

There were two air-raid shelters in the garden of our Neutral Bay flats. They were dank rooms quarried out from under the two garages that opened onto the street. Because the land sloped down steeply, there was space for two roomy chambers with sandy floors, the sides substantial blocks of Hawkesbury sandstone. One of my earliest memories is of huddling in there by a dim light while the air-raid sirens screamed, my sister and I closely held by our mother, squashed in beside the other tenants of our building. Fear was written on the silent faces of our neighbours.

Most families faced the loneliness of separation, either through having loved ones away in fighting zones or through evacuation. As the anxiety escalated, my mother, Megan and I were evacuated to the Blue Mountains to share a house with another family – friends of our parents with four children of their own. After that we went to Young, a small country town 270 kilometres south-west of Sydney, to stay with my mother's cousin Blanche Purchas and her family.

In late 1942 my parents decided to risk taking us to Western Australia to meet our grandparents, aunts, uncles and cousins. During the war, there was only one way to get across to the west – by merchant ship in a convoy escorted by naval vessels. I was too young to remember this trip but my parents later described how terrifying it was, fearing the ship would be torpedoed and us all blown to smithereens.

It was during World War II that Coralie volunteered for the Women's Land Army. It informed her ABC radio documentary,

Land Army Ho!, broadcast nationally in 1945. In this work, she describes the shiver of panic that went through the country in 1942.

> Malaya was overrun by the Japanese, Singapore falls! Bombs over Darwin and Broome! The hordes of Nippon advancing on Australia and – so it seems – nothing to stop them. There was only one thought in all our minds – mobilise our manpower ... the cry was all for guns, guns and men to man them. Recruit, recruit, call up for the Army, the Navy, the Air Force, the munition factories, the Civil Construction Corps.

The government propaganda that induced and sustained widespread fear led to men from all walks of life rushing to enlist or work in munitions. This included one-third of rural workers, which left farms struggling for lack of labour – even after bringing daughters home from boarding schools to work on the properties. But food production had to go on. It was desperately needed, not only in Australia but, as Coralie wrote, for further afield:

> [...] for the men who are recapturing the oil fields of Borneo, for the men who are bombing Tokyo, for the sailors who are sweeping the Japanese from the Pacific, for the people of the British Isles with reduced ration cards, for the starving peoples of Europe who have been liberated from German guns [...]

The concept of a Women's Land Army was raised by Mrs Aileen Lynch, head of a voluntary training organisation, and by September 1942 recruitment of women between sixteen and fifty years of age had begun. In New South Wales the recruits were trained on the job, picking and packing fruit and vegetables, planting and harvesting crops, raising poultry, shearing sheep, and even classing wool. In October 1944 the deputy director-general of manpower announced that volunteers were needed to harvest the cherry crop at Young and would be billeted in the showground. Coralie put up her hand. This was one of the rare times she went off adventuring on her own though it was to a place she already knew well.

Meanwhile, in the city, conditions were spartan. Luxury goods were unobtainable and basics like petrol, clothing and food rationed. Every family was given a number of food coupons, depending on how many were to be fed. Tea, sugar, butter and meat – you had to produce your coupon book to purchase them. Milk and eggs were later added to the list.

There was no refrigeration; the iceman delivered huge translucent cubes of ice every few days. My mother had a secret stock of a few tinned goods (camp pie, sardines, powdered milk) hidden away in a top shelf of the kitchen 'for an emergency'. They loitered there until after the war when she decided to bring down a small can of Atlantic salmon for a treat. Alas, the tin had rusted beyond recognition.

Obesity was not a health issue. Kids were skinny by default and childhood illnesses were rampant. Measles, mumps, chicken pox were inescapable – we had them all. 'School sores' (impetigo) were highly contagious and highly unattractive. Whooping cough and diphtheria were feared, infantile paralysis (later known as polio) a scourge. Children who contracted polio were placed in an 'iron lung' for months on end. There were no antibiotics, few patent medicines. Hot water and salt was a cure-all and Condy's crystals, which turned water pink, could be gargled to avoid getting infantile paralysis (but don't swallow!) or could be put on a snake bite in crystalline form to hopefully prevent death. Clothes and shoes were mended, not bought, and always passed down through the family. With an older sister, I could count on one hand the brand-new items of clothing I had as a child. My father had a bootmaker's last he would set up on the kitchen table at night, repairing our shoes by gluing a black rubbery substance to the soles with Tarzan's Grip.

As children born into these conditions we absorbed the blackouts, the rationing, the limited resources, even the air-raid shelters as our normality. The worry and distress did not invade our small world, did not dent our wonder at the ribbons of light that criss-crossed the night skies, our excitement when we were packed off to the country. Megan and I were luckier than many of our age-mates who had absent fathers for their formative years, fathers who – if they did return – reappeared as strangers, immeasurably changed by their experiences.

Strangely enough it was during this period of unimagined foreboding, of austerity, of isolation, that Leslie had his first three books accepted for publication. This despite the shortages of paper, ink and manpower.

Coralie, meanwhile, wrote her book-length elegy and protest to war. It welled up out of the depths of her dismay and grief.

15

Two Writers – One Typewriter

So I was born into a world at war. Nonetheless, 'the race that stops a nation' still took place. My mother said it worried her that she was in labour during the running of the Melbourne Cup. Were the medical team concentrating? Apparently they were, because she woke from a fog of anaesthesia to hear Dr Toohig say: 'Another little girl, Mrs Rees. And this one's like you.' My official name was Stella Dymphna Clarke Rees, and I grew to be proud of it, that gift from my literary godmothers.

Some forty years later my father was getting ready to publish his autobiography and asked me to restore the photographs he wanted included in it. At that time I lived with my own family on the steep side of Elvina Bay, a tiny water-access-only community on the western shores of Sydney's Pittwater backed by the dark sandstone ridges and hidden streams of the Ku-ring-gai National Park.

To do the photographic work I had to use an old shed which doubled as an outdoor laundry as my makeshift darkroom. Even with the heavy swathes of black cotton I strung over the window and door I couldn't make it light-tight, so could only use it on moonless nights.

My father would stand beside me in the red glow of the safety lamp, watching as each picture came out of the developing fluid. I was working on a tiny faded black-and-white print from our family photo album showing Miles Franklin in one of her flowery hats sitting beside my mother who was dandling a baby on her knee. Dymphna Cusack with her coronet plait was standing beside her. Although you could not see the baby's face in the picture, I knew very well it was my sister Megan. But I had always wished it was me. After all, I was the one who inherited their names. So I pushed for a slight deception: 'Dad, do you think we could cheat a bit with the caption for this one? Couldn't we call it "Stella Miles Franklin and Dymphna Cusack with baby Stella Dymphna"?' It is a measure of my father's probity that he replied firmly, 'No, we could not.' And that was the end of that.

Of course Miles would have nursed me as a baby and taken an interest in my progress. She had plenty of experience with youngsters, as the eldest of a large brood of siblings. My parents were among those she called 'my congenials' – those who were both friend and colleague in sharing her passionate crusade for an authentic Australian literature. Miles was more than a generation older than my father. He said she displayed 'a motherly attitude' towards him. In his autobiography, *Hold Fast to Dreams*, he describes one of his visits to 'her little old-fashioned workman's cottage' in an outer Sydney suburb.

Thinking of her (as most of us did) as an impoverished elder in need of all kinds of help, and gradually getting to know and like her, I volunteered to come to her home after ABC work and do odd garden jobs like digging out a tree stump and hacking firewood. Miles accepted. She cooked me a homely roast dinner with five vegetables and a cup of tea.

On another of his visits, Miles showed some true country hospitality:

> As night drew on and conditions outside were cold and drear, with Coralie away in the country, Miles said 'You're not going home tonight.' She then produced a pair of male pyjamas and led me to an old-fashioned double bed – while she retired elsewhere.

I've always thought it an irony, one Miles would have appreciated, that with the exception of *My Brilliant Career*, a work she detested and which brought her much pain, her novels are rarely read. She is seldom acknowledged for the *Brent of Bin Bin* series or for her memoir *Childhood at Brindabella: My first ten years* (published posthumously) into which she poured her passion for the bush and its people. Instead, her name lives on for endowing Australia's most prestigious literary prize.

It is also a sad fact that Miles lived in penury, secretly scrimping and saving, a lonely and embittered woman during her last years and in failing health. Towards the end of her life she had moments of deep despair as this diary entry of January 1950 reveals:

> Feeling terribly discouraged & as if I had better give it all up & die. I've struggled so long for nothing – long enough to prove over & over again that I have no talent for writing. Could have made a success & helped my family if I had set to something else. There's not a soul alive to whom I'm of any consequence, none to care a pin how soon I die. Failure & Desolation indeed.

But I cannot rid my mind of the diary entry, one of her last, when she recorded she had nothing to eat and was feeling too weak to go out so she went into the garden and rescued a piece of bread her neighbour had thrown over the fence for the chooks.

For Miles, Dymphna Cusack was more than one of her congenials – she valued her more like a literary daughter. For Dymphna, Miles was her dear friend and mentor. They were both novelists of the soil, Miles preoccupied with her deep experience of country living and Dymphna with a passion for social justice. Both were devout pilgrims in the quest for an Australian literature.

Miles died when I was barely a teenager but I knew Dymphna well into my adult years. She wrote warm letters to us from Russia where she and Norman, her Communist partner, lived in a writers' retreat. When she came back to Australia, we shared some happy occasions and one not so happy when I sat beside her hospital bed after she suffered a devastating stroke. As far as she was concerned there were only three Dymphnas in the world worth acknowledging – she was Dymphna I, her niece was Dymphna II and I was Dymphna III. Like my parents, she made it clear she hoped I'd be a writer. They all expected me to carry on the tradition they had worked so hard to establish. This could have been Miles Franklin's intention, too, in bestowing her intimate name Stella on me. Just to keep me reminded of this, Dymphna Cusack inscribed one of her books: *To Dymphna III, the coming generation of literary Dymphnas*.

I went along with this expectation at first. I wrote a short novel, *One-Eye Williams*, when I was at primary school and illustrated it, too, though I have not the slightest ability for drawing. As I had no personal experience of boys at that stage, I leaned heavily on books I had recently read – adventures starring unattractive sub-adolescent English schoolboys in glasses. (Why didn't *I* think of Harry Potter?) I was egged on by my father who enthusiastically typed up my handwritten manuscript and then included himself as co-author.

As a young child, there was no doubt in my mind that I was part of a literary production line. My father's first children's book was published when I was two – a milestone of which I was unaware, though I was posed for a photograph on the front lawn, peering at a copy as if I was an amazingly precocious reader.

In his oral history for the National Library of Australia, Leslie described how surprised *he* was with this aspect of his career.

It had never occurred to me to try to write a children's book until I acquired some children of my own. When my elder daughter, Megan, was three Coralie and I went off to the Barrier Reef on a long-desired holiday. We had been invited to join a party led by Frank McNeill, curator of marine invertebrates at the Australia Museum and an acknowledged authority in his field. I absorbed not only the charm and colour and visions of teeming sea life but its factual background through colleagues from the Museum who shared the trip.

Coming back home I found Megan eager to know every detail about the fertile and enchanting life of the Reef so I began to tell her a story of a little boy, no bigger than his mother's big toe, who got himself by hook or by crook to 'Sunshine Island'. He had all sorts of adventures with the animals, fishes and birds there – the green turtle, the whale, the crabs and coral fishes, the trochus shell, Miss Nautilus, the spider shell, bêche-de-mer and the octopus who blacked out Mr Crab's party. The villain of the piece was Mr Shark. Megan liked the story so much that I wrote it out and submitted it for publication. The artist Walter Cunningham made the most delightful drawings, creating a loveable character. When the book was published it sold 40,000 copies. The *Digit Dick* jigsaw puzzles and a board game called *Digit Dick's Walkabout* helped the popularity and soon there wasn't a copy to be had. I couldn't even get one myself.

A sequel, *Digit Dick and the Tasmanian Devil*, was written for my second daughter, Dymphna. About the same time *Gecko the Lizard Who Lost His Tail* was published and also very successful. My relationship and collaboration with the illustrator of these books, Walter Cunningham, was one of the most rewarding experiences of my life.

In my first twelve years, my father brought out ten more titles. No wonder I was badged as Leslie Rees's daughter. All my contemporaries were growing up with his books. Teachers read them out in class. Excerpts would appear in the New South Wales Department of Education's *School Magazine*. At my school, Neutral Bay Public, my father was lionised. Miss Clifford, our headmistress, adored him. 'Mr Rees is such a darling!' she cooed as I delivered an inscribed copy of the latest title. She immediately sent back a thank you with an invitation for him to address an assembly. During Book Week he traipsed round schools making appearances like a member of some children's literature aristocracy.

Meanwhile Coralie Clarke Rees was exercising her own literary skills.

I've always loved writing poetry. A little of it had been published but not a lot of it had been written: there are special things which need to be said in poetry and special emotions. In 1944 my younger brother Max, an airman in the Second World War, was killed in Canada as he was about to go on operations over Germany. Hearing the news had great impact on me, the personal grief and what it meant, the whole feeling about the war at that time, young men dying needlessly. Losing Max was just our particular loss. Thousands of people were having losses like this. Thousands of mothers, fathers, sisters and brothers, wives and girlfriends were grieving. Max had stayed with us in Sydney before sailing off to Canada. I was the eldest of six, he was the youngest and there was such a bond between us. I felt keenly for my mother. She'd loved us all but for him, her last born, I felt she had a special love.

Max was only 22 when he was killed. The night I heard the news, I sat up all night by the window at Shellcove. I couldn't sleep at all. I just sat there looking out on the harbour and gradually as the dawn started to break, I began to write this elegy, a long poem called *Silent His Wings* which was published as a book a year or two later.

Morning dawns, silver, silent, bare
Empty the sea, empty the sky
And in our hearts black bottomless despair.
He was too young to die, too taut with the thrill of living
Others are ripe for death's iron glove to maul
Without our giving him,
So tall, so lithe, so gay, so full of love.

Despite the continuous weight of domestic life, Coralie pushed ahead with a range of projects. Her talent was versatile. She could, and did, write in whatever genre she could see possibilities.

One of my earliest memories is sitting on the floor between her feet under the table, the typewriter over my head clattering away.

From the time the children were young I kept up as much freelance writing and broadcasting as I could. I reviewed novels. I wrote a series for the ABC on current topics using a sort of fictional dialogue. As a broadcaster, I did a lot of talks for the ABC *Women's Session* and regularly anchored the sessions myself. I wrote and broadcast on literary subjects, on travel, on whatever was of interest at the time. I also wrote short stories and had some of them published in magazines and journals.

While Les was bringing out what equated to one new book a year, he was also pouring his energies into drama, overseeing a steady diet of radio plays and serials for an ABC national audience that was fast developing a taste for them. Households all over the country were being organised around their daily dose of Gwen Meredith's serial *The Lawsons*, the precursor to *Blue Hills*. Just like we now look forward to our favourite television series, families would gather around the wireless for a regular treat – a broadcast play or the next sequel of a drama, packed with familiar characters.

To allow for the prodigious flow of words emanating from our household, my parents had to negotiate a way of supporting each other's writing time – not to mention getting a turn at their shared typewriter, which balanced on a rickety camping table at the far end of their bedroom. My father explained their arrangement:

> For many years we had a system whereby Coralie had Saturday for her writing and I took over the household and children. Sunday was my day at the typewriter. This was quite a satisfactory modus operandi. Coralie would stay working in our bedroom study for 10 or 15 hours – I don't know how she did it. We'd ferry in trays of food. My method of working was in bursts. I'd think it out and I could write 1,000 words quickly in rough form. Then I'd say to the kids: 'Come on, we're going for a walk – or a swim' and start to breathe outside. I always found it very necessary to get out in the open air.

As small children, we became very aware of this regimen. Weekends were our parents' work time and we knew not to interrupt the one holed up behind a closed door. It did not occur to me at the time but on reflection it is clear our parents were decidedly unconventional. In the 1940s and 1950s they continually challenged aspects of the widespread conservatism. On our mother's writing day, our father would get stuck into the chores. He used to hang out and bring in the weekly wash and fold the clothes. He always ironed his own shirts. He was not a cook but was quick at producing simple and nutritious snacks: bread and cheese, salads and fruit. After dinner during the week, he would often volunteer to wash up (relieving Megan and me) so he could listen to particular broadcasts through the kitchen wireless speaker.

My parents did not subscribe to the Anglophile diet of meat and overcooked veg that most families ate nightly. Probably influenced by Bernard Shaw's vegetarianism, with which his longevity and vigour were widely credited, both my parents placed importance on healthy eating and my father on exercise. Wholemeal bread was specially ordered from the shop; cakes, sweet biscuits and lollies were only for special occasions. Rather than the Northern Hemisphere tradition of a hot carnivorous Christmas feast ('the boar's head in hand bear I') for which someone female had to spend hours in the kitchen, they invented the Shellcove version of Christmas Day, which was largely spent relaxing by the pool *en famille*, with a mid-afternoon cold meal of salads and the treats of tinned sockeye salmon and asparagus spears, followed by various sweet indulgences.

Our parents had not owned a car since I was a baby. They used to joke that they could not afford to keep both it and me – so they decided on me. My mother once said in a press interview that writers should not own cars as they would be tempted to go out when they should be getting on with their writing. Instead there were regular afternoon walks. Our father would take us along the bush path of the Cremorne Reserve, and sometimes round the point as far as Mosman Bay, sometimes even to Sirius Cove. There, we would comb through the harbour flotsam and jetsam which would usually deliver up an old tennis ball and a slat from a wooden packing case, perfect for a game of beach cricket.

If our parents were otherwise occupied, we had plenty of liberty to follow our own pursuits. As long as we had tidied our rooms on the weekend, we were free to go off by ourselves, up to the swings on Kurraba Point, down by the waterfront, or, if invited, to the home of one of our friends. Our parents would eagerly give permission to any reasonable request, only too happy for us to be out of their hair for an hour or two – preferably more – so they could get on with their real preoccupation: writing.

16

My First and Second Mothers

Photos of me taken by my father with a Kodak Box Brownie reveal a skinny nut-brown will-o'-the-wisp, barefoot and peering out with round sombre grey eyes from under a mop of light-brown hair. The writer D'Arcy Niland described me as 'the elfin Dymphna'. I was nine years old and it was the time that my mother began coming home late from town, for what seemed weeks on end.

'Town' was the Sydney CBD. All it took was an eleven-minute ferry ride from Kurraba Wharf to Circular Quay and then a ten-minute ride up George Street in a green and yellow tram. 'Town' was where my mother went when she went out. In town she broadcast at the ABC studios, met with publishers, shopped at the department stores – Farmer's, David Jones and Mark Foy's – socialised with her women friends, withdrew money from the Commonwealth Bank in Martin Place to pay the household accounts, and did whatever other business or entertainment her life required. When my mother went to town, she would always be formally dressed in thoughtfully toned fabrics: a frock or suit, jaunty or elegant hat, gloved hands clutching a leather handbag, nylon stockinged legs in high heels. 'Our legs have been admired for fifty years,' she assured me conspiratorially when I got legs myself worthy of a few admiring glances.

Mostly, my mother would go to town during the day when we were at school – but sometimes she would say, as we skipped out the door in the morning, always running late for the tram, 'I might not be home this afternoon – I'll leave the key out.' Such warnings would fill me with a heavy dread I carried around all day. I hated to go home from school knowing I would not have my familiar comforts. When I rang the bell on the heavy front door I expected it to be opened by my mother's smiling face and welcoming kiss. Then the ritual of afternoon tea at the kitchen table: a slice of Big Sister fruit cake and a glass of Milo. If my own big sister was not with me (from the time I was in Year Three she was at a different school) I had to let myself in by taking the key from its secret hiding place. I would creep in and the flat would seem full of echoey silences and threatening shadows. I would go into each room by turn, looking behind the doors and under the beds, even in the wardrobes, gloomy built-in cupboards big enough to hide an assailant. Then would begin the long miserable wait for my mother's return. Every half hour I would go round the corner to Kurraba Wharf. I'd skip down the long stairway between the angophoras to meet each ferry as it pulled into the wharf. If she was there I'd greet her with a cheery, 'Hello, Mummy. I've come to carry your shopping home.' I thought that was sure to please her.

Then a mysterious change in this patterning took place. For some weeks, my mother was home late every day of the week. What's more, when she came home, instead of gathering us up with her warmth and enthusiasm, she went straight to her bedroom. Weak and ashen faced, she undressed out of her town clothes, carefully put them away in the wardrobe and then climbed into bed. 'Make me a cup of tea, darling,' she would request and then lie back wanly on her pillows. I had never seen my mother like this. I was mystified. After a while she would say: 'You'll have to start getting the dinner so something will be ready when Daddy gets home. Go and start by shelling the peas.'

My father usually burst through the door at 6.30 or 6.45 pm, rarely earlier or later. This was because, after his day's work at the ABC office, he and his Drama and Features Department colleagues had a nightly meeting 'in Studio 19'. This non-existent studio was code for their time to talk together over a drink and chew over the day's problems. After a beer or two, Les would leave the discussion and stride down Pitt Street to Circular Quay, then hop on the Neutral Bay ferry. By the time he was home, he was ravenous. So, under my mother's instructions from her bed, I would start to prepare whatever we were having for dinner by cutting up or peeling vegetables. When my father arrived, he would go straight in to see her, his face full of concern. Then, together with my sister, we would get dinner on the table and take a morsel in to my mother on a tray.

By whatever strength and skills Coralie acknowledged and coped with the full implications of her diagnosis – that she had a rare and incurable degenerative disease that would eventually affect every aspect of her life – she appeared not to let it disrupt or impinge on her lifestyle and relationships. I did not understand until years later the reason for her regular trips to town and her sick, exhausted returns: she had been enduring a program of radiation therapy on her lower spine and pelvis, intended to stop her disease. This treatment, which fried all her reproductive organs and whatever else lay in its path, was supposedly successful in four out of five cases. For my mother it made not a whit of difference.

It seems incredible that when my mother's condition was eventually diagnosed as ankylosing spondylitis (also known as AS), little connection was made to the fact that her own mother, Sylvia Clarke, had suffered an acute attack of rheumatoid arthritis in her late twenties. It had left her hands and feet severely affected, the joints of her fingers and toes misshapen and enlarged, the digits themselves lying at an oblique angle. Sylvia's upper spine was also permanently damaged so that she had a marked curvature. As in AS, once the disease had ravaged the joints there was less pain from inflammation but the joints had lost flexibility and their function was, to some degree, impaired. While my indomitable grandmother could no longer play the piano with her damaged hands, she went on cooking and caring for her large family, was famously hospitable and also an invincible correspondent, not only penning reams of long detailed letters but also transcribing them. When my mother sent letters to her family from London and later Sydney, Sylvia would copy them out word for word by hand and send them around the more far-flung members of the tribe to keep them in the loop.

No doubt my grandmother's attitude of seeming to disregard physical impediments set an example for her eldest daughter. At forty-one, my mother's beauty was in full bloom. Her waves of fine blonde hair crowned a wide brow. Her deep-set grey eyes shone with intelligence, her full mouth and spontaneous smile always ready to dazzle. At her full height she was five feet six inches (one hundred and sixty-eight centimetres) with a strong frame. But as the effects of her spinal disease increased, she became shorter and shorter, further and further physically reduced. Strangely, I failed to notice this or any of the challenges that ravaged her wellbeing. Throughout my growing years, I never regarded my mother as ill or impaired in any way. This was easy; although her body was deteriorating, her spirit – her essential self – remained unassailable.

My mother's ready warmth and empathy, her easy ability to make a quick connection by giving her listener absolute engagement, her wit and fiery intellect, her love of language and wordplay: these were all part of who she was and what made her my mother. From a child's viewpoint, she had the sort of personal strength that you didn't mess with, commanding and forthright, but also a ready vulnerability that could reduce her to tears. When she castigated me for a serious misdemeanour – most memorably for being light-fingered with the housekeeping purse – she was so moved at my tears of remorse that she'd taken me on her lap and cried with me. But generally, the tears that rolled down her cheeks were from laughter. Laughter was ever-present: laughter and an unselfconscious physical connectedness. Her radiant warmth combined with her beauty, vivacity, intelligence and wit made her a positively alluring woman.

Indeed, Coralie Clarke Rees had a swag of natural attributes – but a domestic goddess she was not, nor did she aspire to be. Domesticity had been dumped on her through marriage and motherhood and by her commitment to create a generous home for her children, partner and guests. She considered herself not a 'cook' but an 'organiser'. She ordered all our food by phone and it was brought to the back door by the providors themselves. She charmed and conversed with the men as they made their deliveries. There was George Groves, who carried a splintery wooden packing case of fresh fruits and vegetables on his leather shoulder pad and then gently placed it on the kitchen table twice a week. My father would tease her about Groves, a darkly handsome if slightly sweaty man, inquiring at the dinner table, 'Has Groves been again today? And what did you talk about this time?' Then there was Horton, who had the small grocery shop on Ben Boyd Road opposite my school. Mr Horton, as I addressed him when slinking into his shop to buy a rainbow ball (two for a penny), took a phone order from my mother once a week and brought us everything from triangular blocks of cheese to Mudgee honey in a colourful tin, Schweppes lime cordial and a refill for the soda syphon. In later years, some grocers had a licence to sell alcohol so bottles of Penfolds dry sherry, Chateau Tanunda brandy, Dalwood Hermitage and Ben Ean moselle would be delivered as well, ready for the next dinner party. Every morning, milk would be placed on the back step by Bob Harris, the milkman, and the butcher, father of one of my schoolmates, would deliver the meat.

My mother made sure everyone ate well and nutritiously. She *could* cook, however reluctantly, and on Sunday there might be a leg of lamb with roast vegetables – but it usually didn't appear until one was ready to eat the legs of the chair as well. It was not unusual for lunch to be served at 3.00 pm. It seems that from the time she was first married, Coralie displayed a certain tardiness in getting meals to the table. By the time she had children, she had developed this tardiness into an art form. When we complained she would protest, 'I started getting the meal ready – but I got sidetracked.' The kitchen scraps and detritus were always wrapped in newspaper (plastic bags were an invention of the future) and one of my mother's favourite 'sidetracks' was to find an interesting article she had missed reading in *The Sydney Morning Herald* just as she was about to wrap the rubbish in it. She would stop and pore over the piece, then carefully cut it out – to be kept, passed on or included in a letter. If you happened to enter the kitchen at this time to tactfully inquire when the meal might be ready, she would discuss the item with you. This practice endlessly delayed the passage of food to the table.

Another of my mother's characteristic reluctances was in making the bed. We were required to make our own as soon as we could. But my mother had a particular hesitancy about tidying up what she called 'the CC' ('the connubial couch'). Yet she seemed to consider it a mandatory part of her responsibilities. One evening at about 6.00 pm we were chatting in her bedroom when she glanced at the clock: 'Quick, darling, give us a hand to make the bed before Les gets home.' More memorable still is the time my parents left for an overseas trip of ten months, firmly closing their bedroom door on the unmade bed.

So much for domestic imperatives.

Relief from housewife's purgatory arrived in the person of Aunt Averil who moved over from Western Australia to be nearer her daughter. Ailsa lived, at the time, in a tiny artistic flat in the inner city. Averil's contributions to our ménage had benefits all round, including for Megan and me. We were young teenagers at the time. For Averil *was* a domestic goddess, and not only in the kitchen. A talented dressmaker who could design and create anything from a beaded wedding gown to upholstery, bedspreads, cushions and curtains, she was also a stunning cook. After moving to Sydney, Averil needed to support herself financially and by then my mother could patently do with some help. So they established a mutually agreeable arrangement.

Averil came at least two days a week, cooking up potfuls of glorious food. Her signature dishes were beef bourguignon, savoury rice and vegetable casserole. 'Veg. cass.' was a baked mixture of shredded cabbage, carrots, celery and onion with a cheese topping, which my parents introduced to dinner guests as 'Russell Drysdale' because the colours resembled one of his landscapes. And of course there was that Shellcove specialty, a meatloaf we called 'Bungarra' (an Aboriginal word for a type of goanna, as the meatloaf was vaguely shaped like a small perentie). Averil also briskly wielded the Electrolux, made our clothes, and whenever our parents were entertaining on a large scale, oversaw the catering. On such occasions I used to help her in the kitchen, making asparagus rolls with soft white bread, Jatz biscuits decorated with green and red cocktail onions on a bed of cream cheese, savoury eggs and tiny meatballs to go on a toothpick. Being shy, I was more comfortable working with my aunt in the kitchen than mingling with the guests. She taught me much, encouraging my already enthusiastic culinary skills. After we'd finished preparing the party food, I'd pour her a brandy and we'd perch on kitchen stools and talk while she smoked a cigarette.

My parents were gregarious by nature and endlessly hospitable. When people were staying, my sister Megan had to shift out of her room and share mine, a regular relocation over which she simmered with resentment to the end of her days. Her bedroom was more private as it was off the lounge room and closer to the bathroom so it functioned well as the guest quarters. As well as the house guests and regular Friday night dinner parties, a new book published would be welcomed by a party with twenty or thirty people. Public book launches supported by publishers were unknown – writers provided any celebration for themselves and their supporters in their own homes. For these celebrations Averil's catering was a necessary ingredient. My mother's role was to 'organise' everything – ordering in luxurious food and drinks and setting out the lounge room in great style with boxes of cigarettes, china ashtrays strategically positioned and vases of blue hydrangeas from the garden, specially requested from the landlord. My sister and I were to meet the guests and hand round platters. As teenagers, we were also required to do the washing up in the cramped kitchen sink.

I once revealed to my mother how much I admired her easeful knack of entertaining. She looked me in the eye and expounded her doctrine of hospitality: 'This is the recipe for success: you bring together the people who should be brought together and in the right place, you provide them with the best food and drink you can afford – and after that, my darling, it's up to the guests to make it happen.'

My mother's wisdom is something I have treasured over the years and passed on to other grateful recipients. She could deliver an aphorism with convincing power, her broadcaster's deep voice and perfectly articulated diction making it stick in the mind so that when it is recalled, it is spoken in *her* voice. My sister and I enjoyed the benefits of her mandate, 'Never economise on health or education.' 'All men are contra-suggestive' had me puzzled for a while – I thought it had something to do with 'contraceptive': a word rarely heard before the pill reached our shores in the 1960s. ('Birth control' was the preferred term to refer to the various devices and unguents that were optimistically dedicated to that purpose.) My mother responded to a worried inquiry about her inherited illness with: 'In our genetic inheritance, we get the good as well as the bad.'

~

In my sixteenth year, my childhood innocence came to an abrupt close. I was thrust into a messy adult world but, because I was still regarded as a youngster, I was never told the awkward truths that lay behind all the tensions, the sadness of it. When I did find out, accidentally and through a third party, I felt deceived and found the reality shattering. But that was months after.

On the night itself, the end of July 1956, cold and stormy, I relayed urgent messages by phone from Aunt Averil's neighbour, asking my parents 'to come straight away' to their flat at Chatswood as Averil's daughter Ailsa was 'very ill'. My parents called a taxi and disappeared into the night. Megan and I were left perplexed. At about midnight my parents arrived home with a silent Aunt Averil. My mother took me quietly into her bedroom and said: 'Ailsa has died.'

I was stunned, never having been confronted with death at such close quarters. Besides, I had no idea that Ailsa was ill. We hadn't seen much of her in the last few years. I wasn't sure why. But she was invited to dinner later that week to celebrate her birthday.

The night of her death, my mother said I could sleep in her bed. I think she wanted the comfort of me, too, as my father was sleeping on the lounge to be near his sister in the night.

A few days later, my parents told me I was to stay home from school and look after my aunt while they went to Ailsa's funeral, which my father had arranged. Aunt Averil was adamant: she had avoided funerals all her life and was not going to break this practice with her own daughter's. So I stayed with her, my heavy responsibility to confront the distraught grieving of a bereaved mother. My aunt wept inconsolably between endless cups of tea and cigarettes and I tried to do what I imagined was appropriate, though I had no idea what that was.

Over the next few months, as strange and inexplicable as it might seem, a close bond developed between a grieving woman in her sixties and an oversensitive and self-absorbed teenager. We discovered a connection, a harmony, a friendship. She found in me a consolation, a protégée who could assuage her grief. I found in her a repository of surprises, a surreptitious peek at family ghosts long gone and glimpses into a world I would otherwise never have discovered. She also allowed me the odd cigarette.

As our relationship grew in trust and affection, Averil began to call herself my 'second mother'. I don't know how my 'first mother' reacted to this – did she feel a little threatened by her sister-in-law's poaching some of my filial loyalty, particularly as she was the one left with the difficult job of bringing me into line? I now wish I had told my mother she needn't have worried; there was no contest. She was 'my mum' from the alpha to the omega. A generation younger than Averil, Coralie was expressive, open and frank. You knew where you stood. My aunt couldn't have been more different. She had a tightly controlled mien, a dignified reticence as neat and stitched as her appearance, all suggesting smoky secretive pockets that would never be revealed, even to me.

Averil was born in Queensland in 1891, the second child and only girl in the family. After her father was sacked from his teaching job in Queensland, the family moved to Tasmania to live with Harry's parents.

Her kind grandparents could not always protect Averil and her brothers from their father's bursts of irrational anger, resulting from his alcoholism. It was many years before Averil would tell me how, on one occasion, her father had chased her wielding an axe. On another, he beat her savagely with a belt in front of the class he was teaching. The violence of their childhood was to leave irrevocable scars on all the children, including my father.

For Averil, assaults from a drunken father were only the start of many hurdles. Though she was emerging as a twentieth-century woman, it was not surprising that her social values reflected the Victorian era from which she and her parents had come. She was unshakeably inhibited about all aspects of the body and its functions, 'sex' was a nasty word and she displayed a cagey cynicism about men and marriage. She alluded darkly to the miseries of childbirth but never mentioned the details, just warning me, 'You'll find out.' Averil never went anywhere without her corsets – indeed, she told me her former husband had never seen her without them! (Did she wear them to bed?) When leaving the house, her formal attire included a hat, either a finely tailored suit she called 'a costume' or a skirt and twinset, hosiery, court shoes, pearl necklace and earrings, gloves and handbag. A summertime concession would be a coat of some light fabric over a frock. But the accessories didn't change.

Averil married the evening before the Anzacs landed on the beaches of Gallipoli: 24 April 1915. Like her mother, she made an unfortunate choice of husband, also falling for a musically gifted charmer. After having her daughter, Ailsa, Averil divorced her husband for 'sowing his wild oats around town', divorce being considered so shocking in the early 1920s that, even decades after, my father admonished us never to mention it. So, like her mother, she began the life of a single parent in times when the condition was considered shameful and there was not an inkling of social or financial support for women in such circumstances.

Averil was deprived of a secondary education through her family situation. But after the breakdown of her marriage, she had to find a way of earning a living. She established a stylish dressmaking studio in the upmarket Bon Marché centre of Perth. Later, she managed the box office for the iconic His Majesty's Theatre. Clearly an indomitable woman, Averil triumphed over many challenges in her life, the greatest losing her beloved daughter.

When I was young, it seemed to me that my cousin Ailsa had it all: beauty, intelligence and artistic skills. What I didn't understand was that her dreams and her stability had been shattered by two failed love affairs. Until it was explained to me in graphic terms by a medical woman who knew my aunt, I had no idea that Ailsa had for many years suffered a hopeless addiction to alcohol and that was what caused her death, just before her thirty-eighth birthday.

17

Patience Rewarded

'Dad, Dad, I've found a boat.' Bashing away at the Remington, my father paused. He was mid-sentence and none too pleased. I was fully aware that I had transgressed. It was one of the golden rules of our household that you did not interrupt the parent whose designated writing day it was – you should address your concerns to the other parent on domestic duties. However, I knew that my father was my best chance of success in this cause.

'Dad, I've found a boat.'

My father seemed tempted to hear more, then shook his head. 'I've got to finish this chapter before dinner. We can discuss it later. Now,' (in a cross voice) 'clear out!'

When we went for our usual walk in the late afternoon I put forward my proposal, listing all the arguments I could invent about how owning a boat would increase the quality of our lives. He listened but was noncommittal. Having grown up in poverty and lived through tough times, he was reluctant to part with a hard-earned penny for anything but the necessities of life.

After school during the week I would skip down to the

waterfront, pad along the swimming pool walls and across the splintery wooden ramps to Mr Morgan's boatshed. On tiptoe I would peer through the cobwebbed window at the object of my dreams, lying face down on planks, its beams shrunken and warped, its paintwork cracked and crusty with neglect. Then on weekends I would continue my campaign.

One miraculous day, out of the blue, my father asked: 'Is that old rowing boat still for sale?' My heart leapt. He then went to the box where my parents kept their private financial papers and took out a cheque book. He wrote in it, tore off the cheque and then showed me the cheque butt on which he had written 'ONE BOAT' and underneath that '25 POUNDS'.

I was almost too excited to speak. Almost.

'What shall we call it, Dad?'

'I think we should call it *PR*.'

'But what that does that stand for?'

'*Patience Rewarded*,' he said sternly.

I beamed with gratitude.

'Okay, you scallywag. Perhaps it should stand for *Persistent Rees*.'

~

Our family home, a roomy three-bedroom flat, was perched on the steep side of Shellcove, a crenellated inlet that fits tightly between two narrow fingers of land jutting into the water, both culminating in rocky promontories covered with low scrub. The incline on which our block was built is so acute that there were three flats on the road side, but room for a fourth flat on the waterfront side, butted into the rocky slope behind it. That was Flat 1, which we called home. Below our windows, the garden fell away to the waterfront in a series of rocky terraces and ferny paths. You wound down through overhanging greenery until the final drop, by steep wooden ladder, to the saltwater pool and boatshed. From there you could step – or slip – into the deep cool shadowy water of Sydney Harbour. Whether it was frolicking in the saltwater pool, playing Perry-Race-Winkles with my friends (a slow game we invented where you line up the small shellfish in a row and wait for them to make their competitive progress along a rock), dangling my legs over the Kurraba ferry wharf while fishing in the school holidays or rowing my three-metre boat around the bays – the harbour was the centre of my world, making my childhood glow with light and with small adventures.

We were not allowed to play in the front garden of our building. Our landlord, Mr Chapman, was a cranky Yorkshireman who lived in the flat above ours with his wife and her sister, two grey ladies who smiled at us but never spoke. He wore pince-nez and had a wired-up knee of which he was proud (the 1880s precursor to the knee replacement). When he wore long shorts you could see filaments of wire holding his kneecap in place under his pellucid skin. Chappie, as we called him, was a devout gardener. He manicured the sloping lawns and continuous displays of flowers – phlox, pansies, snapdragons, zinnias – in colour-coordinated tiers leading up to the street frontage. He did not like us to play in that garden. It was purely for display.

Chappie made it clear that he did not approve of children, though he always remembered my birthday on Guy Fawkes Day. He would solemnly present me with a ten-shilling note and an unlabelled bottle of port – to reward my parents for their endurance, no doubt. When they bought an old piano for us to learn music, he made a rule we must not play it after 7.00 pm. He used to watch the time carefully. If it was five past seven and one of us was still practising our scales, he would thump on the floor above with his walking stick until we stopped.

Most of the occupants in the six other flats were elderly couples. As the only children in the building for many years we made the waterfront our own domain. Our parents taught us to swim soon after we could walk – a necessary precaution when bringing up children on the edge of deep water. By the age of two I was confident when out of my depth.

My capacity for self-lifesaving was proved one bleak day when I was eight. I went down to the waterfront by myself, dressed in layers of clothes including a woollen overcoat and lace-up shoes. The swimming pool was covered in its winter mantle of yellow-green seaweed. We used to call it the Sargasso Sea. I must have been peering in and tripped, for the next thing I knew I was in the water struggling to bring my head up from under the heavy carpet of weed. Despite the sodden overcoat and my own surprise, I swam my way to the steps and eventually dragged myself out.

Up the ladder and along the paths I trudged and squelched. I stood in a puddle at the front door and called my mother. 'I fell in,' I announced matter-of-factly. It must have been the shock for she was speechless. She stripped off my clothing right there and marched me into the bathroom for a warm bath.

Nobody used the boatshed and ramp next to the saltwater pool so my father arranged to pay a few more shillings a week in rent to use it. The boatshed was built out over the shoreline and had a floor of wooden slats through which you could see the tide washing against the tawny oyster-encrusted rocks. At low tide there were small black crabs skittering about among tufts of sea lettuce.

When my cousin Rose was staying for the holidays, we devised a plan to camp in the boatshed. This could be our own version of *Five Go to Smuggler's Top* (we were both hooked on Enid Blyton). There was a wooden bench along one wall that we agreed was strong enough for us to sleep on, toe to toe. My father, always one for an adventure, supported the idea. He dug out some decrepit camping gear including a little spirit stove. He fixed the side door of the boatshed with a nail and wire hook so we could lock ourselves in and told us we had to think of a password. My mother provided some old blankets and a hurricane lantern.

The night of our camp was cold and blowy. We descended to the boatshed before dark and ate our provisions. The lamp was flickering, making spooky shadows on the walls. A southerly had sprung up and the strong wind, combined with a high tide, was making the water surge up and down under the floor slats and occasionally send up a spume of spray. We crawled under our blankets on the uncomfortable shelf and tried to sleep. About ten o'clock there was a knocking on the side door.

In tremulous voices we called out, 'What's the password?'

'Bungarra,' came the reply. My father had come down in his maroon dressing-gown to check on us. Should we capitulate, admit defeat and go straggling up to our warm beds? What would the Famous Five do? Before we could even consider such a question, my father shone his torch around and said enviously: 'This looks very cosy. See you in the morning.' With that he closed the door and was off to his own bed.

Another of our maritime adventures took place in *Patience Rewarded* with the enthusiasm and support of Charles Maclurcan who lived next door. He was a visionary character. Although his family owned the Wentworth, one of Sydney's well-known hotels, he preferred to spend his time on the top floor of his house where he had installed a radio transmitter and receiver. From there, in the middle of the night, he would speak to other amateur radio enthusiasts on selected short-wave frequencies. Mr Maclurcan, as I knew him, had been a yachtsman in his younger days. He appointed himself my honorary grandfather and took great pleasure in aiding and abetting any waterfront enterprise. In his workshop under the house he secretly created a pair of oars for *PR* made of balsa wood, that lightest of timbers used in the Kon-Tiki expedition, to replace the heavy oars that had come with the boat, which I could hardly carry. The new ones were the right size for a ten-year-old and he painted them cerulean blue, which my father explained was the colour of the sky.

My father hatched a plan that we should row *PR* all the way up the harbour, under the Harbour Bridge and then down the Lane Cove River. This was a long way for oar power to propel a heavy clinker-built dinghy with an adult and two children aboard. It would require an overnight stay. Mr Maclurcan, who had a facility for tools and timber (my father was limited in that capacity), created a system of interleaving planks to fit between the thwarts so that we could sleep in the boat. He then drew up plans for a system of interlocking pipes to make a superstructure to support a light tarp for keeping out moisture or – heaven forbid – a downpour.

These were the halcyon days on the harbour before outboard motors and other speedy devices came and shattered the peace. Our expedition was relying upon our rowing power and faith in our father's judgement. We did, in fact, make it to the shallow end of the Lane Cove River by nightfall. What our father's judgement had not accommodated was the movements of a tidal river. Three of us stretching ourselves out on planks in a three-metre boat already seemed the height of discomfort but when the tide receded, the boat lurched to an ungainly angle and sat there on her beam, happily wedged in the mud. What was a romantic idea turned into the longest night of our lives.

Our flat was chilly and shadowy in winter as it faced due south. From the lounge room windows, through the angophoras, you could see diagonally across to Cremorne Point and the cottagey outline of its roofed ferry wharf, moving up and down with the tide or rocking slightly in a swell. But from the waterfront below, on a still morning and at spring tides, a swimmer could look across the water to Double Bay and Rose Bay on the other side of the harbour. In between, the line of vision was crossed by the wake of passenger ferries chugging back and forth or tugs or fishing boats or steamers with spurts of black smoke rising from their stacks.

From our flat we looked across to the other side of Shellcove where native bush rose from the foreshore of tumbled rocks to halfway up the slopes: a tangle of grasses, ferns and understorey shrubs among the casuarinas and angophoras. Above the tree line was a row of gentrified two- and three-storey boxes, blocks of flats that backed into the hillside and nestled below the road above. Their front windows would have been in direct sight of the Sydney Opera House on Bennelong Point – had it been built. But that was still decades away, unthinkable in wartime and postwar days. At that time opera was not part of the Sydney arts menu; it was considered to belong in Europe whence it came.

Directly opposite our waterfront sat Old Mother Rock, a giant rounded explosion of Hawkesbury sandstone that in some faraway aeon must have come cascading down the hill and landed, plop, in the shallows. Now settled in her place OMR formed a regular part of our outdoor living. My father embraced the rock as a setting for publicity photos. We would row over and he would perch on some craggy protuberance, casually displaying a typed manuscript or published copy of his latest book while Megan and I were required to look engrossed in one of his works as if we had never seen it before. All this was staged to take in the background of the harbour. After all, his books were all about celebrating the glories of nature.

Looking at her from our side of the bay, Old Mother Rock sat golden and welcoming. Some winter Sundays, my parents would walk round the bay to her or row over in *PR*, complete with wooden fruit cases to sit on and piles of manuscripts and some cheese and chutney sandwiches. Thus set up, they would get on with their collaborative writing, enjoying shafts of winter sun while our side of the bay was in gloomy shadows.

To mount Old Mother Rock's lacy indents from the bush track on the other side, you had to leap across a number of smaller rocks, some crowned with periwinkles and jagged oysters or, at a higher tide, fringed with swaying green seaweed. This passage could be tricky and slippery. In this context, my father introduced us to the tongue-twister: 'Round the rugged rocks, the ragged rascals rambled' though 'scrambled' would be a more appropriate verb and many a slip resulted in a shoeful of water or waterlogged trousers. To avoid this, I preferred to row over in *Patience Rewarded*. My proud boast was that I could reach OMR's outer side in eleven strokes of my oars – with a small glide in between with oars shipped. This was only possible when the water was glassy. If a strong southerly was blowing or there was even a slight chop, the boat would take the swell on the broadside and shipping the oars would see me blown down to the narrow shallows in no time.

Given the right weather, I would sometimes ferry Aunt Averil across the water after she had been visiting us. She lived in one of the flats on the eastern side, almost directly opposite. Going by boat saved her the long walk round the head of the bay and along the other side by the bush path. For Aunt Averil there was no such thing as 'smart casual', even when climbing into a small boat. In her high heels and stockings, twinset and pearls, she would make the leap from my rocking dinghy onto Old Mother Rock, climbing up and over in a sprightly fashion. With a degree of trepidation, I would watch her corsetted figure negotiate the jump across small encrusted rocks exposed by the lapping water before she scrambled up through the bushes towards her home.

Scrambling through bush or hopping across submerged rocks to get around what are now inner suburbs of Sydney might seem far-fetched to a modern reader but my parents did not own a car. Very few people of our acquaintance did. There were three common means of transport: walking, trams or ferries. Walking was not considered exercise – that was calisthenics. Walking was just how you got to school or work or the shops, sometimes coupled with a tram or ferry ride. My father took the ferry to Circular Quay and then walked up to the ABC offices in Market Street, later Pitt Street. To get to school Megan and I walked about two kilometres to the tram stop. The green and yellow 'toast-rack' – so called because of its rows of narrow transverse compartments – would rattle slowly up the steep hill to Neutral Bay Junction, its wheels screeching and slithering on the iron rails. My mother caught the ferry into town for shopping, business or meeting friends.

My parents did not own a house either. They lived for nearly three decades in their waterfront flat overlooking Shellcove. They rightly argued that they could never afford to live in such a beautiful area with luscious water views and only a ten-minute ferry ride to town if they had to buy it. However, there was absolutely no stigma attached to living in rented accommodation. Most of the people I knew did. The concept of a mortgage in the suburbs was unheard of.

The privations of wartime followed by a decade of austerity and recovery meant that living was simple and spare. Most families only had one breadwinner (invariably male) and his responsibility was to put food on the table and pay for a roof over their heads. Maybe in other parts of the country home ownership was more the norm but where I grew up, the streets were stacked with blocks of flats, usually no more than three storeys. I'm not sure how the term 'flat' originated, but it was common terminology for a rented home. This was before the Americanisation of Australian English. The glitzier word 'apartment' had never been heard of. My mother always referred to our home as either 'Shellcove' or 'the flat'. 'I haven't been out of the flat in a fortnight' was her familiar lament.

When recording her oral history towards the end of her life, my mother spoke wistfully about 'the lovely flat at Shellcove where we lived for thirty years and the girls were born, brought up, educated and married'.

Shellcove burrowed itself into our psyches and became a part of each of us. It permeated our dreaming like no other place ever has.

'What a privilege,' my mother declared, 'to bring up our children in that beautiful environment!'

And how lucky were we that our parents made that choice.

18

A Writer for a Father

I was fortunate enough to have two mothers, both of whom influenced my formation, contributing their accrued wisdom, their grace and style, their determination and resilience to my template of Essential Womanhood. But what was it like having a writer for a father? What was his part in my growing years, my golden Shellcove childhood?

I remember his smiling face bearing a plate of Vegemite toast fingers to tempt me when I was a little girl, sick in bed. I remember him patiently rising from sleep every time I called out insistently in the middle of the night: 'Daddy, I need to go to the LAV-TREE!' He would escort me through the darkened rooms, so full of sinister shapes, to what seemed like the faraway bathroom. He did not hesitate or complain. He would wait outside in the hall then escort me back to bed, tuck me in and return to his own bed and my sound-asleep mother who made it quite plain that night duty was his call.

I remember him striding along the bush paths of Cremorne Point on our regular weekend walks, calling out quiz questions or throwing nuts in their shells so we could race ahead on our scooters and pick them up. As a child, I could never keep up with my father's walking pace so if I wasn't on my green scooter, I had to more or less lope alongside.

I remember my father bearing trays of food for each of us as we sat around in our lounge room, the wireless tuned to the ABC's *Sunday Night Theatre*. It was part of his ABC work to maintain the broadcast radio drama repertoire of at least three plays a week, each of at least an hour's duration, some much longer. While he would have selected and edited the scripts – indeed, often been part of the writing process itself – he needed to review the final broadcast work to assess the quality of performances and production. For family Sunday night play-listening Dad would serve his standard fare, what he called 'Welsh rarebit' (for years I thought it was 'Welsh rabbit'), a slab of grilled cheese on toast, decorated with Holbrooks chutney and served with a few stalks of celery and raw carrot, followed by a cup of tea. After that we would settle down, often with a pile of mending, sewing on buttons or darning socks. We listened to radio plays as quietly and with as much discipline as if we were in a theatre or a church, giving our utmost concentration to every word and never, ever speaking – that is until after the broadcast, when there would be a burst of energetic discussion and critique. Our opinions were always taken seriously, as if we were adults. Without knowing it, we learnt to analyse and evaluate, and to articulate our responses.

Indivisible from my father was his passion for swimming. In summer, when he came home from the office, Dad would swing in the door and yell, 'Who's coming for a swim?' We would drop everything, get into our togs and troop down to the waterfront. If our mother had started cooking dinner, Dad would implore: 'Leave that, Coral.' After swimming, cold water from a rusty shower plumbed against the rock shelf was used to wash off the salt. Dad insisted we dry ourselves by the 'George Bernard Shaw method'. This entailed using one's hands to slick water off the body, creating a friction which, if combined with standing in the sun, obviated the need for towels.

The self-appointed chief custodian and curator of the harbour pool, Dad would think nothing of setting the alarm to get up in the middle of the night when the tide reached its zenith and going down the dark steps to the pool 'to put the plug in'. The pool was substantial. Made of whitewashed concrete, it was ten metres long and, when full of water, two and a half metres deep. Seawater entered through an ingenious arrangement: there was a small round aperture in one bottom corner of the outer wall with a sand-filled India rubber ball which would be pushed just out of the way by the incoming tide. The theory was that when the pool was full and the outside seawater lower than the inside water level, the pressure of the water would roll the ball back into position to cover the hole. While the physics of this were convincing, the system was not infallible. So there was a back-up apparatus: a vertical plug hole of about a hand-width's circumference just above the ball. The plug itself was a heavy pewter disc with a ring on top onto which was fixed a long wire. A person could perch on the outside wall of the pool (about thirty centimetres wide) and juggle the plug in or out of its casing. Dad would work by the tide chart to ensure the plug was out for the incoming tide. However, to keep the maximum height of water in the pool, the plug had to be put back as soon as the tide was on the ebb. Dad would rise from sleep to do this if it happened in the middle of the night but if by day, we might get a call from the ABC office: 'Could you go down and put the plug in?'

One might hesitate to swim in the waters of Sydney Harbour today, but in my childhood the water was so clear I could stand on the edge of the pool and gaze down the steep descent of the harbour walls to the dark green depths below. The sides of the harbour drop away like those of a fjord but in the shallows the brown kelp waved to and fro and fish darted in and out. You might catch sight of a brown-and-yellow-striped Port Jackson leatherjohnny mouthing a floating morsel.

By four years of age both Megan and I could swim the length of the pool and we would spend hours in the water. One of our favourite activities was 'turtle rides'. One of us would climb onto Dad's back and he would breaststroke along, then suddenly plunge underwater and continue swimming until the passenger fell off. Great hilarity! As we got older we had races, up and down the pool. Dad borrowed a silver stopwatch from work (it had 'Property of the Australian Broadcasting Commission' engraved on the back). He timed us and gave us tips on improving our style. This training became more intensive in the lead-up to school swimming events. Although my parents were not remotely interested in competitive sport, they encouraged our swimming prowess. As a point of honour, each year my father advised his head of department he needed to take a day off work to attend our school swimming carnival at North Sydney pool, under the northern end of the Harbour Bridge. Our mother and Aunt Averil would be there, too, to cheer us along.

Dad also took a great interest in our schoolwork – some subjects more than others. A lacklustre performance in maths or science was acceptable, even expected. My mother called it 'the inherited family weakness'. But where it came to language, particularly the English language, we were expected to excel. After all, it was in our genes. Not only in our genes but in our daily lives.

During our early years, our father was churning out books. Between bringing out new children's book titles, he was preoccupied with producing several on Australian drama. But it was the series about what he called 'the natural indigenous creature life of our continent' that cemented his reputation. After the success of the early *Digit Dick* books, he was asked by his publisher to produce a new work, not of fantasy but based on the authentic life cycles of animals within their own environment, so that children, increasingly receding into urban lifestyles, might develop a richer and more compassionate relationship with the natural world.

When *Shy the Platypus* was published, a book my father described as 'a biography of a platypus from its own point of view', it opened his eyes to a world of possibilities, not only literary. 'The whole Australian ecology came under my continuing gaze,' he later recounted.

> I learned the habits of scrubby mountain wallaroos and euros, of rock wallabies, of red kangaroos of the inland plains with their blue flyer mates by their sides. I learned of different snakes and goannas and crocodiles, of many birds from our eight hundred species, birds of the lakes and swamps, high trees and open skies. I learned of other furred creatures both familiar and rare, ringtailed possums and phalangers, bilbies and numbats, rat kangaroos and upside-down flying foxes and of Tasmanian devils. The potential of this great wealth of natural endowment seemed endless.

This rapture for the Australian environment and its wildlife became what he called his 'intoxicating faith'.

But dedication was also required. For each of the books there was research, months of it. As all the writing and background work had to be done on the weekend, we were often taken along to zoos, nature reserves and natural history museums. Without even realising it, Megan and I were drinking in not only a deep and continuing delight in the natural world but also the imperatives of conservation, a message embedded in the Rees nature stories.

My father's enthusiasm for the process of writing his children's books was contagious and so a cooperative effort in the family.

He said in interviews that Megan and I, as small children, were his initial inspiration, and we were certainly his first readers as he'd try out various drafts to gauge our responses. My sister recalled him reading her *Mates of the Kurlalong* on Sundays after he'd written his two or three thousand words for the day. If you happened to be the designate taking in a tray of food or cup of tea and biscuit to him on his writing day, he'd pause over the typewriter and persuade you to stop and hear the latest sentences. The names of his characters were also discussed with us and he would gravely consider our feedback.

When the National Library of Australia produced a heritage edition of *Shy the Platypus* in 2012, Jackie French (who launched the book) asked me in our on-stage conversation whether I was ever jealous of the characters in my father's children's books. Jealous? An incongruous concept. The characters, particularly those that reappeared in a series like the *Digit Dick* titles, were as much a legitimate part of the family as we were. The main characters of the animal biographies like *Kurri Kurri the Kookaburra* or *Sarli the Turtle* were too. They were part of the family lexicon, indivisible from the fabric of day-to-day living, slipping in and out of conversations by name without any need for additional explanation. Because of the way our parents included us in their writing process, we shared in the development, the progress of each of the works so that its final success was a triumph we all celebrated. (The occasional failure was not discussed.)

We were involved in the steps to publication, too. Our opinion would be sought on the roughs of illustrations and we were always lined up to read the proofs. If we picked up a mistake, the going rate was sixpence. Megan always scored more handsomely on this task as she was definitely the superior speller. However, I had other discernments. I once found an egregious error – the gender of a subsidiary character changed halfway through the story. For uncovering this blunder, I received 2/-, unthinkable riches when one considers that most of my indulgences at the time – rainbow balls or a threepenny ice cream – only cost a fraction of that figure. On one memorable occasion, Dad arranged for us to leave school early so he could take us to see one of his books rolling off the presses at the John Sands printing house.

All the book writing and production were sidelines to my father's daily occupation: drama. We had opportunities to taste that, too. When we were quite young our parents offered us up for a season in *A Midsummer Night's Dream* at the Metropolitan Theatre, one of Sydney's small semi-professional theatres. Our father had to spend evenings at the Mitchell Library doing research for the first volume of his history of Australian drama, so he would drop us at the theatre, go off to the library and pick us up after the performance. I was cast as Peaseblossom, first of the four fairies in Queen Titania's train. It did not take me long to determine that the footlights were not for me. I have spent the rest of my life relishing the theatre but only from the other side of the curtain.

We also often went into the ABC studios in Sydney. As well as mentoring writers, editing plays and arranging the programs for national radio, Dad enjoyed producing radio dramas, choosing only the choicest scripts, sometimes a new work but often classics like Greek tragedies in modern translations, Shaw's plays or Shakespeare's. He had a firm commitment to the educative role of the ABC and made sure that important plays from the world's great writers were available to the listening audience. Because of the relatively low cost of radio compared with stage production, he could present plays that most people would never have the opportunity to see, choosing lesser-known works such as Shakespeare's history plays, the social-conscience plays of Ibsen, or verse dramas such as TS Eliot's *Murder in the Cathedral*. Alongside the international fare, he commissioned a steady diet of new Australian plays specially written for radio. He considered them as good as any written in other parts of the world.

The play productions used top professional actors and were broadcast live nationally, being up to two hours long, depending on the work. And much preparation went into them. If not written for radio, they first had to be adapted. This task would be handed out to a freelance writer. Then, after my father as drama editor had approved it, the script would be sent to the typing pool (a group of glamorous women with racehorse typing speeds) to be typed and then roneoed off on foolscap paper. The ABC producer would then appoint a cast of actors and arrange several full rehearsals. At performance time, the producer would sit in the control room with a soundproof glass wall separating him from the cast standing around the mike in the studio. He used hand signals to cue in different roles, or for silence while music was used. The sound effects man sat next to him in the control room using a turntable to fade in music or other recorded effects. If we were invited, we sat there too and did not breathe a word.

Besides their entertainment role, radio dramas had another important function: they provided an income stream for writers and actors. Most people of literary ambition produced material for radio, even if they went on to be novelists, like Ruth Park, or poets, like Douglas Stewart, or academics, like Coral Lansbury, mother of former prime minister Malcolm Turnbull. She was one of my father's protégés. He privately considered her a stunning woman and declared her gifted as a writer.

I suppose I took for granted the interesting nature of my father's job. He explained to me when I was quite young that he counted himself lucky as he loved his work. It came as a shock to me when I went out into the wider world to find how many people have no choice but to struggle through their days in dangerous, repetitive or boring occupations. I'd grown up instilled with the notion that it's the nature of the work that counts, not what it provides. The ethos was if you can spend your days in work that excites, fulfils or pleasantly extends, you've found gold.

But even gold had its disadvantages. When my mother said, 'You don't know how lucky you are to have your own room. I have to share mine with Leslie Rees,' I did not appreciate why a certain venom crept into her tone. No doubt she was seething with the frustration of not having any personal space – let alone 'a room of one's own'. My parents' bedroom was not only where they slept and dressed but where, apart from occasional incursions onto the dining room table, they did all their literary production. As my mother worked from home, the bedroom had to function as her office as well. It was from here that she organised all the complex itineraries and correspondence for their outback expeditions.

I can't help smiling when I see a photo of some writer, posed in their study beside a desk of glowing timber, the background an impressive wall of volumes in matching bookcases. I think of my parents, the old Remington their only technology, the dressing table and any other flat surface strewn with papers. It was just a bedroom, but light flooded in. A bay of three large windows with ledges deep enough to sit on looked out over Shellcove and gave it a sense of space. There was a double bed, a painted wardrobe for my mother's clothes, a lowboy for my father's. (Whenever my father had a disappointment with a literary project, he worked out his angst by repainting the furniture.) The floor was carpeted with brown Feltex, thin in places, the holes covered over with 'druggets', cheap fringed rugs of a coarse material.

My bedroom was opposite my parents' room so I could hear the murmur of their voices, even when their door was closed. I found this comforting, as I was frightened of the dark. When going to bed I would plead, 'Don't close the door.' My parents would leave their door open to humour me but my father would often get up quietly in the morning and firmly shut their door – even lock it. Why was that, I wondered? He was an early riser, my mother an inveterate night owl. She used to say, 'We're like ships that pass in the night.' Small children think they own their parents. Parents quickly discover that small children are the best method of contraception. Sometimes one just has to lock the door.

My room was oddly shaped with high ceilings, dingy despite having three windows with wide timbered ledges. The biggest window looked out onto the courtyard where I used to play hopscotch. A holland blind had to be drawn on this vista otherwise anyone who came to the front door could see right in. The side window overlooked a narrow shadowy path down to the waterfront. There was a small casement window with a triangular ledge that my father converted into bookshelves.

The flat had several built-in cupboards and I had one in my room. I found it cavernous and scary. Even now that wardrobe lurks in my subconscious. I would always open it carefully, fearful of what I might find. Whenever a brown dusty moth the size of my hand flew out into my face, I'd panic. I'd yell, 'There's a dirty butterfly in my room!' and refuse to go back until someone captured the moth and put it outside.

Beside my bed was a door that had six glass panes covered with the sticky opaque paper used in the war to prevent glass from shattering in a bomb blast. I spent untold hours trying to prise off little strips of that material to let chinks of comforting light from the dining room shine through. This door was never opened. On the other side of it were high wobbly piles of *Meanjin*, *Southerly* and *Walkabout*, the journals my parents subscribed to and for which they sometimes wrote articles.

I spent my first twenty years in that room and, though I haven't been into it since the mid-1960s, it is frequently the setting of my dreams.

It seemed to me, and still seems, that my father had an equable temperament, a sunny nature that made loving him easy. But a child never sees the parent as a whole, instead drawing conclusions from aspects of his or her own relationship, so the result can be markedly different for other members of the family. My father must have had his darker side because at one stage, after they had been married over twenty years, my mother dubbed him 'Heathcliffe', a final 'e' added to Bronte's noir hero to no doubt give an extra dimension of Gothic gloom. As a lifelong devotee of *Wuthering Heights*, I fail to see any likeness of Heathcliff's dark and restless passions in my buoyant male parent. But my mother would have known. She would have chosen this title with her usual perspicacity.

My father seemed amazingly balanced to me, perhaps because of his unremitting positivity. Certainly his mandate 'Never lose the bump of wonder!' influenced my own perspective, a glow cast on new experiences or discoveries, whether small or overwhelming. The bump of wonder was his gift, his way of seeing the world. His facility with words let him share that wonder: with readers and listeners, family members and the world at large.

When I discovered the letters between my parents from 1936, after they came back to Australia, I have to admit a chill went through me as I came across my father's words:

> Well, look here, if you fear having kids, we simply won't have any damn kids. They're not worth it to us. You're everything and everyone to me and there's no need for anybody else.

That's not the father I knew, the father who welcomed us into his world, treasured us, encouraged us, delighted in our every achievement, who included us in almost every aspect of his life and work, the father who produced more than twenty-five books of children's literature and became 'one of Australia's best loved children's authors'.

Still, in a close partnership based not only on reciprocal love and respect but on the sharing of work and passionate interests, the prospect of children might have seemed a threatening intrusion. When he wrote those words, my parents had been tightly bound for six years, living their twenties on the other side of the world in an alien environment. They had become utterly dependent on one another.

As the unit of 'Coral & Les' they were self-sufficient, feeling themselves 'alone against the world'. But as they both grew in maturity, wisdom and experience, the writing team widened its boundaries to become a family-raising team. And what a loss to the world of children's literature if that hadn't come to pass – not to mention the significant fact that I wouldn't be here to tell their story.

19

An Outback Explorer

Though enjoying all the benefits of their waterfront life at Shellcove, my parents still had itchy feet. It was always their plan to see as much of Australia as possible, but they had been encumbered by small children and the austerity of wartime, not to mention their writing projects. Nonetheless, they managed to get away on their own for short exploratory trips – to Victoria, Tasmania and northern Queensland – gathering material for my father's children's books. And of course they'd taken us on that perilous sea journey to the West to show us off to their families.

Then, in 1946, Coralie's cousin Blanche passed on to her a precious diary written by Benjamin Clarke, their grandfather. The posts and telegraphs officer of Kapunda in South Australia, Ben Clarke had in 1871 been co-opted to join the party laying the Overland Telegraph Line between Port Augusta and Tennant Creek, 500 kilometres north of Alice Springs. He was officer-in-charge of the first telegraph operators who installed instruments and sent messages along the thin wire line that was pushed, repaired and defended for 3000 kilometres through the very centre of Australia.

No doubt Blanche had thought their grandfather's diary would be a source of inspiration for her literary cousin. What she had not foreseen was how significant it would be to both my parents, instigating a new direction for their writing: adventures in remote parts of Australia. Of even wider consequence, the overwhelming open beauty of the outback – the big sky country – would captivate their hearts, energise them and inspire a spate of books, drawing them back again and again over the next twenty years.

Today the luxurious Ghan overland train crosses Australia from south to north through a still remote and sparsely inhabited landscape. It's one of the country's iconic rail journeys. My parents rode its predecessor, the original Ghan – by reputation neither luxurious nor reliable. It used to rattle alongside the old route of the Overland Telegraph Line.

My mother recorded that journey in a two-page article, 'Trail of the Overland Telegraph', featured the following year in *The Sydney Morning Herald*'s weekend magazine, accompanied by dramatic pen drawings. Here is an extract:

My grandfather left Port Augusta at the end of September 1871. When I followed his trail 75 years later his diary lay on my knee. The trains chug beside the OT line almost all the way from Port Augusta to Alice Springs, first beside the Flinders Ranges country which is like a succession of Hans Heysen canvases: sun-splashed rocks and huge dappled gums set against jagged blue untameable peaks. But grandfather Ben Clarke wasted no words on the beauty of this country. He was too busy grappling with practical problems, as his diary records:

> *5th Oct: ... The back axle of the heavy waggon broke ... We had to send back to the nearest blacksmith's about 50 miles to get it repaired ... Camped at a well ... water very good.*

13th Oct: ... Camped at Blindman spelling horses ... Good
supply of water in creek. Feed good.

The telegraph line and the train march through the Lake Eyre
basin within sight of Lake Eyre South, its salt-encrusted surface
glittering blue with the illusion of water. There is great beauty
of colour in this dry, treeless region – terracotta and dusty pink
sandhills, and in the hollows between them tufted bushes in pale
yellows and sage greys, pastels, greens and browns. But Ben Clarke
kept his eye on the job in hand:

25th Oct: Had some heavy pulling through the sandhills, and had
to use extra horses, with heavy waggon.
7th Nov. Some of the waggon horses getting done up.
9th Nov. The Peake. Made arrangements for an earth wire being
laid in readiness for opening line ... horses being shod.
14th Nov: Left The Peake and went as far as Neales. Mr Kraegen
joined the party here ...

As far as Charlotte Waters my grandfather's diary had been
surprisingly void of drama. And then there was an incident which
reveals starkly the accepted risks of the assignment. To speed up
the job, three telegraph masters (Kraegen, Mueller and Watson)
were sent ahead to prepare for installing batteries and instruments
at the prospective telegraph stations at Alice Springs and Barrow
Creek. They took three saddle and two pack horses and written
directions to the various waterholes along the route. Eleven days
later my grandfather found them doubling back on their tracks:

15th Dec. The Old Depot. About 2.30 pm Mueller and Watson
arrived back with one horse and the pack saddle. They reported they
could not find water at the places they expected, and that in the

evening Kraegen went ahead, taking his own and Mueller's horses, to try and find water and bring some back as they had none since 8 am and were quite exhausted from having exerted themselves, it being a very hot day. In consequence of Kraegen not returning at the time they expected, they tried to get along towards him, but were unable to go far that night. The following day they looked for water in all directions but not finding any, they were obliged to kill one of the horses to save their lives by drinking the animal's blood which revived them sufficiently to make another effort to find water, which they succeeded in doing after they had been without water for 54 hours. They found Kraegen's tracks leading towards the water but could not see anything of him. ... It is greatly feared that poor Kraegen did not find it and may have perished as he had no food with him.

20th Dec. Rocky Camp Waterhole. Young followed line today. He found the remains of poor Kraegen lying near the line about three miles SE from this camp, his revolver and belt and spurs lying at his feet, quart pot, pannican and three empty water cans at his side. We dug a grave near the spot and buried him.

January 1, 1872 was the contract date for the opening of the telegraph line and there were still hundreds of miles to be covered. So Benjamin Clarke pressed on and opened the Telegraph Station at Barrow Creek on January 19, 1872. He decided to make his personal push from there, taking two men and packhorses.

23rd Jan: The road was fearfully boggy. We had to lead our horses, and could scarcely get through it.

24th Jan: Today we came upon some blacks who made a great row calling out. We could see them walking between the trees and all armed. Shortly after meeting them, part of pack came loose and the horse made a bolt, kicking and plunging, and two other packhorses after him. Fortunately they did not get far away.

4th Feb: Tennant's Creek – we have travelled 1,284 miles from Port Augusta by road. Our rations are nearly out: no meat or sugar left, and only a small quantity of tea and flour.
8th Feb: Attack Creek. Met Mr Harvey and party at camp.

That was then the most northerly camp of the Central Australian section of the OT line. In fact the line was wired only as far as Tennant's Creek, so the party returned there to look for current, but getting none had to ride south along the line inspecting for breaks.

Ben Clarke stayed on as telegraph master at Tennant Creek until August 1872, replacing the officer who had died of thirst on the expedition. Meanwhile, as his diary reveals, the thin feeler wire was being extended north to meet the feeler wire being pushed vigorously south from Daly Waters. Clarke began receiving messages from Adelaide for transmission to England and one lot of messages were received from England and speeded on their way by horsemen and telegraph to Adelaide.

The two ends of the overland wire were joined on August 22 of that year amid great rejoicings and congratulation. The ambitious work, notwithstanding challenges and disasters, had been accomplished within two years, thus linking Australia to Asia and Europe by wire and breaking the isolation of the southern continent. But it achieved more than that. It opened up the red heart of the continent. The lonely telegraph stations, two hundred miles apart, such as Alice Springs, Barrow Creek, the Tennant and Powell Creek, were the first centres of white settlement in the Northern Territory. When pastoralists galloped up to take advantage of all the spade work of the explorers and the telegraph pioneers, the telegraph track became a stock route with, in due course, Government wells or bores along it. If it had not been for the telegraph line and the cable station, the now strategically vital town of Darwin might have languished and died as had other attempted settlements in that region.

After my mother's article had been published, her father Guildford Clarke – one of Ben Clarke's nine children – wrote to her from Western Australia:

I was very impressed with your article on the OT odyssey published in the *Herald*. Dear old Benno, as Mother always called him, little guessed that he would figure prominently in a description of the laying of the line, 75 years later and written by his granddaughter. The other members of the Clarke clan will be thrilled to read about the exploits of the dear old man who, by the way, was one of the retiring modest type and beloved by all who knew him. Charles Todd was Post Master General when I started as a messenger at the Kapunda Post Office where our father was Master of Posts and Telegraphs. I received 10/- a week and Father gave me three pence pocket money from it which I promptly exchanged for a meat pie at the pastry cook's shop.

Benjamin Clarke had sent the first morse code message from the Old Telegraph Station at Alice Springs. In 1962 a street in the town was named in his honour and the information in his diary acknowledged for adding to the history of the telegraph station at Alice Springs. An extract from the diary referring to the death of Kraegen, the telegraph operator who died of thirst, was included in a permanent exhibition in Adelaide's GPO, preserving and honouring the expedition that had linked Australia to overseas for the first time.

The Overland Telegraph line between Adelaide and Darwin is a tribute to the foresight, enterprise, courage and tenacity of the Postmaster-General and Superintendent of Telegraphs in South Australia at the time, Sir Charles Todd, and a willing band of colleagues. It stretched over a distance of nearly 2,000 miles through inhospitable country, much of it without water, food or settlements and inhabited by hostile, nomadic tribes of aborigines, totally unfamiliar with the white man. Five deaths occurred during the erection of the line, and occasional outbreaks of hostilities accounted for other casualties after the line was opened for traffic.

My mother donated Ben Clarke's diary to the Mitchell Library. It is an important record of the Overland Telegraph expedition of 1871 and her grandfather's part in what has been called 'the greatest engineering feat carried out in nineteenth century Australia'.

20

Peripatetic Parents

My parents labelled themselves 'peripatetic parents', the alliteration and reference to ancient Greece giving an extra layer of gravitas to their role as travelling writers collecting material for broadcasts, books and articles. They even used this title when inscribing our copies of their travel books, as if to make up for leaving us behind.

> With warmest love from us
> Mum & Dad
> Peripatetic Parents

Perhaps it was a form of self-justification. At any rate it had a better ring to it than 'absentee parents'.

Gathering material is an essential part of any writer's life and work. Some only mine their resources from other texts. Before the electronic age, that meant physically delving into libraries and stacks of documents. But as Coralie's and Leslie's curiosity about travel writing grew, it became imperative for them to gather firsthand experiences. This type of work must, by definition, involve intrepid travel, remote places and fascinating people. That is what attracts and holds the audience and the readership.

The ABC documentaries that resulted from their travels were known as radio features. Coralie and Leslie, as narrators, gave the factual information and background and a cast of actors played different people, some real, some imaginary. Background music was used, much as it is today in film and television drama. Inventive sound effects (such as cutting through a cabbage to make the sound of ice shattering) were used in the studio to create the sense of place and action. Putting all these together with an engaging script re-created real places, people and events. It was a means for the medium of radio to both inform and entertain, long before the age of audiovisual equipment.

Without tape recorders or video cameras, writers of documentaries had to use their written notes of face-to-face interviews to reconstruct conversations and then craft the material into dramatic dialogue. The dialogue was interspersed with blocks of explanatory text called 'continuity', which was spoken by the narrators. The continuity was written in sentences and paragraphs, so was more formal in style than the colloquial language spoken by the various characters. The listening audience could detect who was talking by the different voices and the tone of language used.

As well as writing the scripts, Coralie and Leslie took part in the production, usually as narrators, sometimes in brief character roles. ABC radio features were broadcast nationally and a wide audience all over the country lapped them up as fascinating listening. But it was a long and labour-intensive process to produce thirty minutes of listening infotainment and sadly, after it went to air, there was often nothing left of the feature but a pile of scripts roneoed on foolscap paper. However, these did not go to waste. My parents wrote many of their notes and drafts on the back of used ABC scripts, thus recycling resources.

As travel writers, Coral and Les faced a challenge both practical and ethical: how to balance doing their work while bringing up two young children – for they were also deeply committed to parenthood. My mother was determined not to be the sacrificial domestic lamb, keeping the home fires burning while her collaborator went off adventuring. This did not fit with her belief that critical to the balance of their research were both male and female perspectives. She also did all the legwork of preparation and planning: background research, writing polite letters to request meetings and interviews, investigating means and costs of travel and putting the whole itinerary together. Travel agents are a more recent invention. In Australia during the postwar years, a time of financial austerity, very few people journeyed far from home and even fewer went to remote regions, or 'off the beaten track'.

My father also had to confront the problem of getting leave from his job at the ABC. His practice was to save up his three weeks' annual leave over several years and then take it in bigger chunks. For some of the longer trips, he took leave without pay, making it even more necessary for them to produce books and documentaries on their return to pay for their travel and keep up with the household expenses.

So, intermittently, our parents would take off on one of their working trips together, and sometimes were away for months. For Megan and me, this became the routine of our childhoods. We would be sent to stay with other families, sometimes related, sometimes not, sometimes together, sometimes separately. We didn't have any say in the matter.

Not everyone agreed that such a lifestyle was justified. Was it self-indulgent or, worse, irresponsible? Was it sound or legitimate parenting? And how do long parental absences affect children in their formative years? Both our parents defended this practice when they were interviewed about their writing, as when one questioner asked, 'How did you work in the daughters with the travel?':

> 'Ah' Coralie said, as if thereby hung a tale. 'That first came up when the girls were six and eight. Leslie wanted to go hitchhiking to Alice Springs and see the North. He wanted me with him and I wanted to go. BUT – what about the girls?
>
> 'I had to make a decision. I could let him go alone or I could go with him, sure that the girls were left in good hands. I decided then and there that my husband came first. That's been my philosophy of marriage. And the girls haven't been deprived. They've told us they had a wonderful childhood and learnt to appreciate what home means.'

Leslie explained it differently, reflecting many years later on their collaboration in travel writing:

> Now the third part of my writing was in conjunction with Coralie, my wife, who was a great partner with me, although she was never a robust person, but she had a tremendous wish to go along with it, and be in everything. Instead of leaving her at home, we left the children at home. We managed to find satisfactory care for them and we went off on many trips around the world to different countries but her greatest interest was in going into parts of Australia that were hardly known at that time, off the beaten track.

I now contemplate my parents' attitudes on this with some ambivalence. I definitely had some tough experiences while they were away and always felt a great sense of dread as the moment came for them to depart. But many children have to deal with worse and come out the stronger for it. And what were the alternatives? Our country cousins were sent off to boarding school for their secondary education. We soundly rejected that prospect. It sounded like incarceration. Anyway, our parents could not have afforded the fees.

On reflection, I can see that the arrangement had definite benefits. Our parents' absences widened our experiences. Early on we became flexible to different patterns and ways of living, later we became self-assured, adventurous and independent. Although a naturally shy child, I learnt to live in other people's homes, eat different foods, play by different rules, accept other authority figures, survive at different schools, and to express myself appropriately in whatever company I found myself. More importantly, I learnt that love and respect could be given and received outside of the close family network. I also stumbled on a few dangers, which are part of any exploration.

When I was eight years old, we travelled as a family to Western Australia again, this time overland. To cross the continent by train was a tedious and uncomfortable journey, taking five or six days. At that time, each state in Australia had a different railway gauge so every time we came to a border we had to change trains. Because the four of us were going to be away for many months, we had thirteen pieces of luggage, including the aforementioned Five Bob Case (a leather strap round its belly to prevent disgorging), the Alwyn (presented to my mother on her departure for London in 1930 and bearing a little engraved plate to say so), our Globite school cases, my mother's red hatbox, and a string bag. I carried my life-sized doll, Baby Pam, close to my chest. Every time we had to change to another train (usually at some inhospitable hour), our raggedy collection of luggage had to be arranged along the station, checked, counted and recounted, only to be reloaded into the overhead wire racks of another bulging compartment.

This was not a joyous homecoming for our parents. It was a journey of sadness. Between January and April, both had lost a parent in faraway Perth. The day after New Year, my mother received a telegram to say that her father had suddenly dropped dead of a heart attack. She was stunned by the news and frustrated at being so distant from her grieving mother and siblings. Then, after Easter, my father received the news that his beloved mother had died. My father was too grief-stricken to talk to us. It was the first time I saw him cry, which made more of an impression on me than the passing of a grandmother I barely knew.

This 1949 journey was special in that for once my sister and I were included – if only in the first part. We were to visit all our relatives, the Clarke and Rees families. But then our parents were taking off up the coast for the six-month outback odyssey that would culminate in their bestseller *Spinifex Walkabout*. Our mother's sister Jess had offered to mind us for the duration. Her only child, Malcolm, was my age so perhaps my aunt welcomed the idea of some cousinly company for him.

The family lived in the tall-treed southwest in a little town where Uncle Cooee was a stock auctioneer. The name fitted perfectly. On the days he was operating at the sales yards, his voice could be heard echoing over the town and through the wooded hills and orchards. In the crisp mornings, I walked through the bush with my cousin to a tiny school with a composite class and a male teacher. I still remember the first time I bit into a green apple off the tree. It tasted like no apple ever has before or since. One day my cousin told me, conspiratorially, that his father kept a dead man in a box under the bed. Everything was so new and strange to me that anything was possible.

Then disaster struck. I developed a very serious illness called 'virus pneumonia'. Fortunately for me, the new wonder drug penicillin had become available, otherwise I probably would not have come out alive from the cramped hospital room I shared with a few old ladies. Despite my aunt and sister visiting daily and doing their best to cheer me, I cried and cried into my pillow, longing for my mother's tender words and touch, as any sick child does. My parents, meanwhile, were uncontactable somewhere in the Kimberley and none the wiser until I was well out of hospital and beginning a long convalescence.

When I was in Year Five, my parents went off to New Guinea (then an Australian protectorate) for three months. They stayed in the Highlands, learning about the life and work of patrol officers, meeting the indigenous people (some groups then reputedly still headhunters), and examining the recently erupted Mt Lamington volcano at close range. This adventure resulted in my father's novel for young people, *Danger Patrol*, as well as the creation of a series of radio documentaries in which they both performed. Blanche invited me to stay for the duration at the HP.

The Purchases lived in a sprawling Federation house that stands at the end of the wide tawny-gravelled main street in Young and is still used as a medical practice. In the time of my visits, the property was also the family home where Blanche and Maurice raised their five children and gave so much hospitality the place was known affectionately as 'the HP': the Hotel Purchas. Maurice Purchas was the town's multitasking family doctor. His work covered the entire medical spectrum from general practice to surgery, pathology, radiography, obstetrics: a birth–to–death line of responsibility. This was the scope and challenge of a country practice.

While growing up I had a number of sojourns in Young. I always felt very at home there because my mother and Blanche were so alike – not in appearance but in personality. They had grown up on opposite sides of Australia so they didn't meet until my parents came back from London and settled in Sydney. Once they did meet, these two granddaughters of the feisty Anna Wilhelmina

Schlinke (who ran down the streets of Tanunda in her petticoats and shocked the little German-speaking Barossa Valley town by marrying an Englishman), found that they had more in common than their genes.

Both vibrant, expressive and 'vaguely contemporaneous', as my mother would say (Blanche was older by several years), the two women quickly developed a delicious friendship and rapport, a talent particular to women when they find their passions and values reflected in another. There was distance separating them as well as busy lives so their friendship was largely expressed in writing. Using their shared delight in language and characteristically self-deprecating humour, letters beginning *Dear One* or *My Love* and brimful of spicy revelations encrusted in their equally baroque handwriting flew back and forth between 9 Shellcove Road, Neutral Bay, and 12 Boorowa Street, Young. Whenever I retrieved one of these missives from our letterbox, I would deliver it to my mother with the solemn announcement: 'There's a letter from My Love.' My mother would drop everything, swipe the envelope from my hand and immediately disappear into some private space to devour its contents.

The two cousins had grown up not only separated by a continent but with very different influences. Blanche came from a prestigious medical background. Her father, Dr Guy Prior, had made his name in psychiatric medicine as superintendent of first Ryde and then Parramatta mental hospitals in Sydney. Blanche's mother, Blanche Clarke, had trained as a nurse in Adelaide and travelled to the Western Australian goldfields in the 1890s, caring for prospectors in a tent hospital during the typhoid epidemic. She'd gone on to nurse in Fiji and was engaged four times – all to doctors. She was reputedly a beautiful young woman with 'topaz eyes'. My mother's father, Guildford (the younger brother of Blanche's mother), also left the family homeland in the Barossa Valley of South Australia and travelled to Western Australia to find work and later settle.

On my visit to the country in 1951 there was no need to interrupt my education: I went off to Young public school with my cousin Rose. For the second time in my schooling, I had a man teacher. This one I found unpleasant. He used a long ruler to whack children who misbehaved. He didn't whack me because, as he sneered in front of the class, my uncle was the town doctor (he had also been the mayor). A whack would have been preferable to exclusion.

At the age of eleven my whole vision of school and domestic life was extended by staying in a home that was also a busy medical practice, riding a bike to school, and coming home at lunchtime to a formal hot dinner, my uncle sitting sternly at the head of the table in a white coat. The rousing final chords of *Blue Hills* were our signal to be back on the bikes and up the hill to school for the afternoon. This was as far removed from the battering typewriters and haphazard mealtimes of Shellcove as one could imagine!

When I was thirteen, my parents went adventuring across the Indian Ocean, to Cocos Island, Mauritius and South Africa, then up the east coast of Africa to Zanzibar and Mombasa, then on to Europe. They could easily have disappeared off the face of the earth but I had faith and waited patiently for the blue aerogrammes that intermittently brought tightly written accounts of their adventures. Their travel book *Westward from Cocos* was the outcome of the first part of their journey.

For this absence, there were no kindly relatives available or willing. Some indeed were openly critical of the whole plan, particularly the leaving of two vulnerable teenagers for nearly nine months. Separate living arrangements were made for each of us. As we were both at North Sydney Girls' High, my parents reasoned we could see each other at school. I was to board at the Villa Peculia, a rambling sandstone house at Hunters Hill with a chaotic garden going right down to the Parramatta River, a couple of recalcitrant goats expected to keep the undergrowth manageable.

The Villa Peculia was home to two stylish sisters and their teenage children as well as an eclectic mix of people (hence the name of the property). The women rented out rooms in this expansive but fashionably decrepit estate, doubtless to defray the costs of maintaining it. Both proprietors were widowed and in high-profile jobs: one a senior newspaper journalist, the other a publicist. I was aware that each of the sisters had a spectral lover somewhere in the background, too. The other residents were a young couple called Rene and Bob who drove a red MG sports car, and a man called Barney about whom we teenagers knew little. We once discovered him lying on the pavement at Circular Quay in a drunken stupor. This was the first time I had ever seen a person I recognised in such a condition and I was horrified.

There is no need to go into detail about how the experiences of living at the Villa Peculia for six months broadened the mind of a naive thirteen-year-old, but positive opportunities included learning to sail a VJ skiff on the shark-infested Parramatta River, going for a wild ride in a sports car and having my first hamburger and Coca-Cola 'spider' at a milk bar. For my fourteenth birthday, I was escorted to the Borovansky Ballet by a handsome seventeen-year-old, son of the proprietor. For this I was adorned in a borrowed white dress – ballerina-length with a swirling skirt – which the owner had worn to her graduation. I had nothing remotely suitable in my own meagre wardrobe. This was effectively my first date, though whether the boy was dragooned into it by his mother or volunteered, I would never know. Less romantic was my usual afternoon chore of repositioning the uncompromising goats after chasing them through half an acre of perilously inclined shrubbery.

Of course, during these adventures, I had my moments of self-doubt, a jabbing sense of isolation and intermittent longings for my parents' return – when there would be small presents from exotic sources, endless excited exchanges and slideshows of my father's Kodachromes projected onto the lounge room wallpaper, showing us where they'd been and what they'd done. I never doubted they would return and that our life at Shellcove would get back to its own normality. I now see that confidence as my innocence, the essence of childish faith, but also as a measure of how securely we felt we were loved.

21

Collaborating: A dicey business

'My idea of living,' said Leslie Rees, 'is not to own anything.'

'Spend it all on travel,' cut in wife Coralie.

'The world as your oyster is much more available if you don't own anything,' said Leslie.

'I believe,' Coralie allowed, 'in owning a toothbrush.'

They burst out laughing. It was highly infectious. So was the zest for living that has taken this lively literary pair round the world and up and down the remotest parts of Australia, and produced a spate of books either in collaboration or apart.

So wrote Kay Keavney in a feature article in *The Australian Women's Weekly*. It was 1970. Les and Coralie's latest travel book, *People of the Big Sky Country*, had just been published, following the success of *Spinifex Walkabout* (1953), *Westward from Cocos* (1956) and *Coasts of Cape York* (1960). In all these works, they collaborated – a new experience for them as writers and one that Coralie publicly admitted nearly wrecked their marriage. She termed the painful process of working out a way of writing together 'battling and bashing out a book'.

On another occasion Coralie explained why collaboration was, for them, such a fraught procedure:

We had not written a travel book, either of us, neither had we collaborated over anything. We had gone our separate ways while criticising each other and supplying encouragement. However this business of collaboration was a very difficult thing. How do people collaborate?

We made many false starts, sort of pooling our personalities and writing 'We did this' and 'we did that' but it didn't satisfy us because we're very different people really, with different outlooks, and after a lot of arguing and quarrelling we came to the conclusion that the only workable way for us to collaborate was to write separate chapters and write them under our own initials so the reader knows who's writing what. Then you can be really free and frank – you can be personal to the reader.

Each person would rough out a separate chapter, we would agree on a plan of the book, we would divide up the material, decide who was to tell which. Some experiences Leslie would go off with men and I would stay behind and talk to the women and it would divide naturally.

The one who wrote each chapter would have to submit to the other for frank criticism before the final draft was made and this was when the sparks would fly. We would be devastatingly frank with each other on each other's finer points of style.

About our method of writing for these travel books. We did find that an excellent way to organise these trips was to discipline ourselves by arranging, in the first place, to write documentary features for the ABC about certain aspects of outback life. That is a help in that it gives you an entrée and an introduction to people.

You are semi-official, you have got permission from the ABC to write about the subject and that helps you to get in and get a lot of material. It also disciplines you in that it means while you're there, you can't get lackadaisical on the job, you have a commitment to gather material on certain subjects; you must be conscientious about it, you must get the facts, you must meet the people, you must interview them, you've got to get that material.

All that cannot be contained in one broadcast and while you're on the job you get so much more material that you have what you need for a book as well.

It is clear from Coralie and Leslie's adventure writing that they could only have written their books and documentaries of outback adventure by being free, fearless and unencumbered. They had to get to the stories by whatever means were available – trucks, small aircraft, mission boats, even by tractor or on foot. Their method of transport was a central part of their adventure. Commercial options were limited – non-existent in most of the places they wanted to go. 'Seeing the country through other people's windscreens' became their signature explanation. It was a way of being more accessible to meeting people. This was what their readers and audiences demanded – colourful accounts of people and places they themselves would never have a chance to experience.

Both Coralie and Leslie were unendingly interested in other people, their work, their challenges, their triumphs. Since their journalist days in London when they interviewed some of the century's literary greats in their own drawing rooms, both had developed the art of question and answer, of showing that necessary mixture of interest and respect while probing into the sensitivities they wanted to explore and which would capture the imaginations of their readership. At the same time, they had the self-assurance and relaxed sophistication not to be daunted by these exchanges but to be natural, gracious and without pretension. Their methods could not be farther removed from the crass, intrusive and combative styles some media interviewers use today.

As collaborators on books and documentaries about their intrepid adventures, they used those same skills, meeting and talking with people in far-flung locations. Les couldn't be more delighted than when camping out with Aboriginal men in the Western Desert or being presented with an Indigenous breakfast of baked goanna eggs in the wilds of Cape York. They recorded these accounts in books, articles and documentaries. Our lounge room mantelpiece at Shellcove housed a collection of artefacts they had been given: firesticks, carved emu eggs, samples of different ochres, a woomera. On the wall were original watercolours they had bought from the artists of the Hermannsburg School, the Pareroultja brothers. Staying there in 1949, they had taken a picture of Albert Namatjira with his paintings in a hessian sack at his feet.

Of particular interest was visiting missions. Using an investigative approach, they talked to missionaries and to the people living there and were not afraid to raise difficult questions about the policies of assimilation that were widely practised. At the time of their second trip to central and northern parts of the continent, there were about fifty missions scattered throughout Queensland, the Northern Territory and northern Western Australia. Mostly run by the welfare arm of church bodies, they were the direct result of the cruel governmental policy of separating children from their families. But missions also housed whole Aboriginal and Torres Strait Islander communities who had been deprived of their country, which was appropriated without their consent to be farmed or mined.

The process of writing separate chapters gave Coralie and Les the opportunity to exploit their different styles and preoccupations. My father's forte was narrative writing, a skill he used extensively in his young adult adventure novels like *Quokka Island*, which were popular books, often chosen for high school reading. *Danger Patrol*, about the lives of patrol officers in the highlands of Papua New Guinea, was used as a text in all Queensland public schools for a number of years. (I was recently contacted by a former patrol officer who told me the book was the inspiration for him and many of the young men who eventually joined the patrol officer service in Papua New Guinea.) My father's focus was always on the sensory experiences rather than the emotional ones. He could bring action and atmosphere alive with the use of precise physical detail.

Of course, as Les often confessed, at heart he was still a boy who was always on the lookout for adventure. Sometimes my mother thought he pushed his luck too far, such as when he went down into the throat of a recently erupted volcano with a vulcanologist in Papua New Guinea. He had a few close encounters, once on Cocos Island being chased by a school of sharks when searching for crayfish on a distant reef, another when he was carried out by a rip on a deserted Queensland beach. On that occasion, his life was saved by George Landen Dann, the playwright whom he was visiting at the time. But the trip on a mission boat in the shark- and crocodile-infested Gulf of Carpentaria waters with the Bishop of Carpentaria was perhaps the closest shave; though, as Les was honest enough to admit, it provided excellent material for their travel books.

In 1957, Coralie and Leslie set off to explore Carpentaria, pursuing their interest in the missions that were dotted about both sides of Cape York. After some weeks Coralie had flown home as Les was joining a party travelling down the Gulf of Carpentaria by boat to take supplies to Mapoon, Weipa, Aurukun, Mitchell and Edward River missions and to allow the Anglican bishop to tour this part of his far-flung diocese. (They had been warned in a letter from the bishop that the trip would not be appropriate for

Mrs Rees 'as there is no proper toilet facility and little privacy'.)
The Anglicans' own boat was out of commission so the *Reliance*, a
sturdy if basic seventeen-metre two-masted ketch, was borrowed
from the Presbyterians. On board were a local crew, a skipper new
to the boat, an engineer called Flag, an Aboriginal woman and her
baby catching a ride home to Mitchell River, an Anglican priest
and the bishop.

This extract is from a chapter that appeared in two different
travel books, *Coasts of Cape York* and *People of the Big Sky Country.*

Mission Boat in Peril – LR

The morning wore on. Although the seas were high and the winds
strong from the inevitable south-east, the winter sunshine was
soothing and we all sat about on boxes on the edge of the hatch
cover. Just after eleven o'clock, Flag Ayre pricked his ears, jumped
up and ran to the stern of the ship, calling Horace of the crew to
follow him. He disappeared down the steps leading into the hold,
where the twenty tons of cargo were lying thick-piled.

The rest of us took little notice until suddenly a mass of lifebelts
was thrown up on the deck from below. Flag's head appeared,
demanding of Horace, 'Is that enough to go round?' The words
hardly registered with us at first, then the Bishop turned to Father
Sutherland.

'You heard what he said?'

'He said, "Is that enough to go round?"'

'Lifebelts,' I said. '*Lifebelts.*'

The idea gradually clarified. Something must be wrong. But
what? Nothing that was discernible to the three landlubbers. Flag
had gone below again: now he was back. His movements were
quick and economical.

'She's filling up!' he said.

220

'I beg your pardon?' said the Bishop.

'The water's rising. She's filling up.'

'Is it dangerous?'

'I'll tell you. Did you hear a noise?' We hadn't. 'Well, the propeller shaft has parted in the middle. There's a gap of nine inches. Propeller can't turn. If it can't turn, it can't push us along.'

We looked around the horizon.

'We don't seem to be moving forward,' Father Sutherland remarked.

'And yet,' said the Bishop, 'the engine's running.'

'The engine's OK,' said Flag Ayre. 'It's the shaft that joins the engine to the propeller. Like a broken axle in a car. Like a man with a broken back. What's more the shock of the fracture has pushed the stern end of the shaft through the gland backward and that's our real trouble, the gland has opened up.'

'That's right ... and the water is coming in.'

'Fast?'

'Slowly, but it won't take long to flood a ship of this size. Not with all that cargo sitting on it.'

'What can we do?' said the Bishop.

'Find a pump. Must be one somewhere.' Flag called, 'Hey Horace, where pump?'

A voice came up from below. 'Pump on deck. Near wheelhouse.'

Father Sutherland found it. 'Hand pump. Fixed in the deck.'

Flag yelled from the stern. 'Try it.'

I joined Father Sutherland. We lifted and dropped the handle of the pump, vigorously, many times. Only a dry metallic sound issued.

Flag called to the crew. 'Better get those two dinghies over the side.'

The Bishop looked at the heaving water. 'It's very rough. Do you think they can be launched?'

'Have to be, Bishop.'

The skipper was calling to the ship's crew. Father Sutherland and I kept on at the so far ineffective pump, while the rest moved to the stern to try pushing overboard a very heavy dinghy that we had only just managed to drag on board at Aurukun.

'Careful,' warned Flag. 'It may swamp. Bishop, would you help on the bows. Smart!'

The Bishop, Father Sutherland and I all helped but the solid dinghy was reluctant.

'Another shove.'

'Swivel her this way.'

'Now ready. Push.'

With a roaring plunge she slid back into the yellowing sea. Twenty or thirty gallons came over the edge, but no more.

'Good,' said Flag. 'Tie her up, William. Fast. Now for the other. She's lighter.'

We got the second boat over without much trouble. But in these seas, would they survive when full of passengers?

'I shouldn't like to try them,' said the Bishop.

'Not with my weight in one,' said Father Sutherland.

The dinghies bounced astern, ready for emergencies. Flag came back to the wheelhouse.

'So the pump doesn't work. How about the sails, Tumena? Could you get any sails up?'

Tumena had never sailed on this boat. In a booming voice he appealed to the regular crew. While tension tightened, the heavy sails at the foot of the two masts were laboriously hauled up, all hands tugging at the halyards and steadying the unpredictably swinging booms. But, lacking a jib – there was one but it was badly damaged – the deeply laden ship failed to make any movement in the direction we wished. The resistless south-easterly trade wind, the wind that blew Captain Bligh for a couple of thousand miles in an open boat across the Pacific, refused entirely to trade with us;

in fact was tearing wildly at us from the shore. It seemed we were drifting from the coast towards some dangerous-looking shoals. Flag gave the order to drop anchor. In spite of wind and wave it held, in two and a half fathoms.

Flag turned his attention to the underdeck. 'Get men to bring up some cargo on deck. All that flour, sugar. We might have to ditch it.'

As the boys moved to help, the Bishop said quietly, 'Ditch it? I hope not. Edward River needs that food. Needs it badly.'

'The water's still rising,' said Flag. 'It might be the food or us. Anyway, we've got to get it out of the way of that propeller shaft to see what we're doing. And for hand bailing.'

'I see.'

'Our only hope is to get on the sked. Hope the set works.'

Since boarding the *Reliance*, I'd hardly noticed that we had a set. But there it was, with various knobs, placed inconspicuously under the canopy. I knew that the five missions of the Gulf coast, Presbyterian or Anglican, were linked with the Queensland Government's shortwave service based on TI [Thursday Island], two hundred and eighty miles north. By a bit of sheer luck, the *Reliance* was the one ketch so linked. If Flag could raise TI on the ship's transceiver, someone there might be able to help us. Contact could be made only at certain hours. So we waited: while the Aboriginal mother sat quietly on deck feeding her baby from a bottle. Neither had uttered a sound.

At last the transceiver whirred. The four white men gathered around.

'Coming on now.'

'Good.'

'Listen.'

A little furred, with liberal crackle, a voice came to us. We recognised it immediately as that of Ian Mullins of the TI base station.

'The sked's open and in a minute I'll be calling you all in turn. I've a couple of telegrams for Mitchell River and three for Mapoon and four for Weipa. But before I start are there any urgent medical calls? Over.'

Flag was in charge of the switches, once again the only one among us with know-how. The Bishop said, 'Now's your chance!'

'*Reliance* to TI. Emergency call! Emergency call!' Flag spoke, tense and low. 'This is the *Reliance* on the Gulf coast. Are you receiving me? Over.'

A fractional pause and then, mixing in with the howl of the wind around the ship, 'Receiving you loud and clear, *Reliance*. What's the trouble? Over.'

'We're off the coast about sixteen miles north of Edward River. We have a busted propeller shaft and water coming in from the stern. We can't move. We're filling up, repeat filling up, slowly but definitely. Are you receiving me? Over.'

It seemed to my ears that Ian Mullins gulped, before replying, 'Ye..es, go ahead, *Reliance*. Go ahead.'

At least a few dozen ears up and down the coast, on TI and in Torres Strait, must have been eagerly awaiting Flag's answer …

'Looks like we might have to abandon ship and row ashore in dinghies, but we don't want to do this if there's any chance of saving her and the cargo. Anyway we don't know if we'd make the shore. It's very rough. If we reached the shore we'd have to try walking to Edward River and there's rivers to cross and they say they're full of crocs. Are you receiving me? Over.'

'Receiving you, *Reliance*. Go ahead.'

'Before I ask you for suggestions as to rescue, I'll give you details about what happened. Ready? Over.'

'OK, *Reliance*. I'm alerting the Anglican and Presbyterian offices here at once. All missions down the coast will listen and they'll suggest what they can. Over.'

'About 11 am we were ...' As Flag searched for words, I looked at the faces of the Bishop, Father Sutherland and the young mother. In their various unemotional ways they reflected relief at this measure of contact with the outside world. The miracle of voice reception and voice transmission had at least let other people know of our plight.

~

Actually the news travelled further and fast. At Shellcove we were in the kitchen getting our breakfast when the ABC's 8.00 am news bulletin reported: 'A supply boat carrying the Anglican bishop is in danger of sinking in the Gulf of Carpentaria. There are grave fears for the safety of the people on board.' Before my mother hurried off to ring the ABC newsroom for more details, she turned to me, grim-faced. 'There's no end to the lengths Les will go to for a good story.'

~

Coralie's natural skills of empathy and gentle diplomacy came to the fore when she met people who might feel threatened or shy in responding to an interviewer's questions. She was interested in creating psychological depth by sensitively probing the actions, reactions and interactions of people she met. 'Queer Night on Quintell Beach' was a favourite piece of hers. She never forgot the romance of meeting the phantom horseman by moonlight and no doubt he fell victim to her charm and ease, as many people did. She wrote of that encounter more fully in *People of the Big Sky Country* and then contracted the story for a radio talk she narrated herself. The following text is from a radio script she broadcast on the ABC.

Queer Night on Quintell Beach – CCR

Perhaps you've never heard of Quintell Beach. It could be described as one of the loneliest beaches in Australia and among the most inaccessible. To get to it you must first go to Cairns and then take the plane that runs north to Thursday Island. Your first set down is Cooktown. Next stop is Coen, a handful of people on the map, deep in the cattle country of Cape York Peninsula. Third stop is Iron Range, just a hundred and fifty miles south of the northern most tip of Australia. And that's where you alight for Quintell Beach.

Iron Range has a permanent population of one – the keeper of the aerodrome who is also the post and telegram master, the radio telephonist, meteorologist, bridge mender and transport consultant to all who set out for Quintell Beach.

'You'll find the track pretty rough,' he told us. He went on to say it was seven miles down to the beach and all badly gutted by recent floods. As for transport, there was an old tractor belonging to the mission we were about to visit and there were some mission boys to drive it. He would lend us a trailer and Les and I would have to sit on the floor, clutching our luggage and be jolted along through the bush behind the tractor. At the beach a little engine-driven mission boat would be waiting, or should be waiting, the aerodrome keeper said ... The scepticism in his voice was a little disturbing.

Anyhow we trundled down the rough track to the coast, through stringy-bark or messmate trees and shoulder-high blade grass. It was late afternoon when we arrived at Quintell Beach and a more eerie desolate stretch of coast I've never seen. The southeast trade winds were blowing straight onshore at gale force, lashing the sea into angry muddy waves, whipping up the sand into a spray of spiteful needles and contorting the pandanus palms until they looked like souls in torment. Out in the waves, the little mission boat was tossing and bouncing and straining at her anchor like a mad dolphin on a leash. Quite frankly, the prospect of boarding her and clinging in her open cockpit, drenched with spray, through twelve long hours of a storm-savage night caused me to hesitate.

We asked the mission boys: shouldn't we wait until daylight tomorrow to see if the storm blows itself out? Their faces were polite but deadpan.

One of them spoke:'That boat sink a few month ago right over there!' He pointed to the murky distance then added cheerfully: 'We got boat up two week later.'

While we were considering this information, out of the tangled scrub that grew right down to the beach, rode a horseman – tall and lean as a stockwhip. His hair was grey and his horse was grey – both so ghostly grey we wondered whether he was a phantom. We had been told there were no white men for miles around.

'The Don Quixote of Quintell Beach,' murmured Les, 'riding Rosinante.' The horseman wore a battered felt hat, frayed pants and boots laced up with string. But when he spoke, the voice that came from under the hedge of grey stubbly whiskers was unexpectedly warm, rich and courtly.

'Madam,' he addressed me, 'do you intend crossing to the mission tonight?' He stroked his grey chin doubtfully and added: 'If I were you I wouldn't set out, not tonight …'

What was the alternative? We looked again at Quintell Beach. Great grey shoulders of rock lurched drunkenly through the sand, bearing down on us. But spending the night on Quintell Beach would be definitely preferable to breasting out into that snarling sea. The horseman pointed. 'Madam, there's a rough bough shelter over yonder between the swamp and the creek. You could doss down there. Have you any food?'

'Very little. Only some bacon and coffee we were taking to the mission. We expected we'd be there tonight.'

'I'll see you at moonrise.' And the strange horseman dug his heels into his horse and melted into the scrub.

Darkness stalked up on us with a flail of pricking rain as we made a damp little fire in our bleak nook. The mission boys brought us a billy of water from the soak and we shared coffee with them. We had a feeling we would never see the phantom horseman again so we decided to try and sleep. The night was pitch black with no sign of a moon. We'd been asleep some hours when a rustling in the bushes startled us awake. A great yellow pancake moon had risen and silhouetted against its light was our horseman with a sack slung over his shoulder.

'Here's your bread, Madam,' he announced as if it were the most natural thing in the world for fresh bread to be delivered to a bough shelter near Taipan Creek. He dismounted and handed us the sack. 'I ran you up a batch of scones too and brought you a drop of spare boy – golden syrup – to spread on them. All I had in the shack.'

We built up the fire and made more coffee and sat on our haunches and yarned with him while we munched scone after scone until the stars turned pale. Then, as suddenly as he had appeared, he swung into the saddle and wheeled away towards the scrub. 'I've got to round up my horses at daylight. But it's been very enjoyable talking to you both. A man gets hungry for a bit of conversation when he's been in the bush most of his life. Well, so long …' And as he spoke, his shadow was swallowed up by the dark mass of the trees.

We dozed till sunrise then walked down to the turbulent beach to signal the little mission boat. She was gone! The grey horizon was bare. Both boat and crew had disappeared. We waited for hours, till well past midday. Then we decided to make it back to

Iron Range. At last we arrived at the lonely airstrip and started to explain to the lone occupant and caretaker.

'Are you sure you saw the boat when you first arrived? I've just received a radio message from the mission saying *Boat broken down. Tell Mr and Mrs Rees to proceed to Thursday Island.*'

We protested loudly. Of course we saw the boat. It was just as real as the horseman we had seen.

'What horseman?' the aerodrome keeper asked cynically.

'Don Quixote on Rosinante. Look, he baked us a loaf of bread.' And we delved into the sack and brought forth the remains of a perfectly baked loaf to prove the truth of our queer night on Quintell Beach.

~

22

The Perils of Literary Coupledom

Coral and Les were not the only renowned literary couple of their era in Australia. There were two other notable partnerships that, like the Rees duo, combined love, travel, family and literary endeavour in one heady and challenging mix. Ruth Park and D'Arcy Niland were both born in 1917 and Charmian Clift and George Johnston were born in 1923 and 1912 respectively.

Of the six writers, the eldest three would be deeply affected by World War I. While Leslie was growing up, two of his brothers were away at the Front; one lost an eye and was injured by shrapnel in the trench warfare of the Somme when he was just seventeen. George Johnston's father survived Gallipoli, only to be sent on to France for three years. Coralie had a young relative killed at Bullecourt in France at the age of twenty-six. As with the rest of their generation, their worlds were shaky: they were 'acquainted with grief'.

Most of them struggled to find work in the Depression at an age when they were ready to establish themselves. They then faced another period of war, this time closer to home.

All six writers made their start as journalists, although only Leslie and George completed cadetships. Ruth Park was editor of the children's page of *The Auckland Star* before becoming the first woman promoted to the newsroom, not without 'blood on the floor', as she recorded in her autobiography. George was a war correspondent for the Melbourne *Argus*, the same paper Coralie's grandfather had worked for at the end of the previous century. Charmian Clift did a brief stint on *The Argus* before she and George left – or were asked to leave – to start their life together. D'Arcy Niland started as a copyboy on the Sydney *Sun* and was sacked when he turned seventeen because he required higher wages. It was the 1930s, the height of the Depression.

It seems that the inducement of sharing 'a vocation as well as love' is what catapulted each of the three women into their marriages. None was typical of her time. Each was forthright, independent and determined. Few women in general, including their mothers, worked outside their roles as wives and child rearers. Having a career generally meant refusing marriage to earn the unenviable title of 'old maid'. If marriage intervened, the career had to go. Coralie, Ruth and Charmian were not interested in that sort of marriage. The last thing they were looking for was a meal ticket in trousers. They were bent on their own ambitions, their own individual shining goals of becoming writers. They were all also stunning young women.

Les and D'Arcy were of similar age to their girls and were talented, charming and interesting, while George had the undeniable éclat of being a published writer before he and Charmian met, an experienced journalist who had travelled the world. So the irrepressible mating instinct had its way despite Coralie's feminist pretensions, Ruth's determination not to get married and Charmian's obvious challenge in that her man was already married to someone else.

Of course when starting out, none of them had any idea how hard it would be to make a career as a writer earning enough to provide a reasonable living. All worked prodigiously and all struggled financially. All eventually had families to support. Ruth, D'Arcy, Charmian and George took the courageous step of freelancing as journalists and producing novels – a risky and uncertain source of income. In her autobiography, Ruth tells of the complicated financial side of a freelance writer's life – in reality, total insecurity. Charmian and George in Greece were endlessly trying to wrangle advances out of their publishers to tide them over and were devastated when large portions of their meagre royalty cheques were deducted for income tax.

The Rees family enjoyed a little more financial security thanks to Les's tenured position. His regular if unprincely salary allowed us to live not lavishly but well, in salubrious surroundings with plenty of food and avalanches of books. Our parents were able to indulge their passion for travel of an unluxurious type: what Coralie acidly described as 'round the world second class with Leslie Rees'.

Because of my father's position, Coralie was able to work mostly from home at her various writing and broadcasting projects. But there were obvious disadvantages to this. She regarded all domestic chores as an imposition and resented the fact they ate up her time and energy. What she loathed most was 'culinary responsibility', a burden shared by many of her kind. Elizabeth Jolley was known to complain that she couldn't write a word until she had worked out what they would eat for dinner that evening.

Les was endowed with abundant vitality and health, a gift that, along with his determined efforts at the typewriter, allowed him to produce an impressive body of work while maintaining a full-time career and his voluntary position as chair of the Playwrights Advisory Board. But not all were as blessed. In each of the families, one of the partners was struck by a major life-threatening illness: George with tuberculosis and other lung disease, D'Arcy with a congenital heart problem, and my mother with ankylosing spondylitis. For these three, the burden of ill health was a constant and determining factor of their output. So Les, Charmian and Ruth had partners who for large chunks of their marriage were not invalids but less than robust, struggling with conditions that, in each case, brought premature death.

Despite the difficulties they all faced, their combined literary output totals well over a hundred published works: novels, plays, poetry, children's literature, travel books, autobiography and literary criticism – plus a cartload of first-class journalism and scriptwriting for radio and television. The old adage that 'success as a writer is achieved by applying the seat of the pants to the seat of the chair' was proudly upheld.

But what effect does a two-writers-in-one-family set-up have on intimate relationships? Does the dream of a marriage of true minds survive the rigours of family life? From the lives of these three literary duos it seems clear that if literary partnerships are to survive, one partner needs to make greater sacrifices than the other, and in each of these cases it fell to the female partner to make them. It was almost the duty of the female partner to make them, being as she was of her time and place. Many creative people avoid having committed relationships; many more choose not to have children because of the added burden of responsibility parenthood imposes. But each of these Australian literary couples launched into procreation.

Like everything, such a decision came with a cost. Especially for Coralie. Despite growing up as the eldest of six children and seeing how hard her own mother worked, she was stunned by the domestic turmoil the first little person would bring into their lives. Coralie Clarke Rees was beginning to make a name for herself as a writer and broadcaster. By choosing to settle in Sydney, my parents had physically isolated themselves from their large extended families in faraway Perth. There were no doting grandmothers to call on and there was no such thing as childcare as we know it today. And there were no refrigerators, washing machines, dryers, dishwashers, even hot water systems. Domestic life was highly labour-intensive and endlessly time-consuming.

My mother was suddenly faced with the question of when she would ever find the time or energy to do her writing. When I was born two years after my sister, she was again boiling cloth nappies in an outdoor copper and winding them through a hand wringer instead of addressing herself to the typewriter. When she did get to write, it was to fire off short stories about the role of women and the dreadful choices they have to make: children or a career. Meanwhile her consort was flourishing, striding through the heart of the Sydney world like a literary lion while basking in the glow of a beautiful wife and two small daughters at home.

When Coralie was offered the full-time job of anchoring the ABC *Women's Session*, a role made for her, she had to turn it down 'because there is no-one to mind Dymphna'. Since I discovered that sentence in one of her letters, I have carried a mixture of guilt and sadness while being secretly reassured that she put my welfare first. There is no doubt she made that choice with much heartache and disappointment. A similar thing happened to Ruth Park a few years later when offered a salaried job on *The Sydney Morning Herald* immediately after winning the *Herald* prize for *The Harp in the South*. Though the pay was, in her estimation, 'the stuff of fantasy', Ruth demurred faintly: 'But I have two little children.'

It is clear that my mother struggled to balance the demands of her family life with her literary career. She must have written of her frustrations to her writer friend Frank Dalby Davison because he wrote back to her saying:

Sorry to hear that the B.B.'s are still interfering with your career, Coralie; and I don't know what to do about it [...] I know that you can make resolutions about setting aside even a little bit of time each day, and holding that sacrosanct – but when the bit of time comes round you may be feeling too tired, or upset, or if not that, then some demand is made on you that can't be disregarded. It's a hard world for women, Coralie, if they want to do something.

When I came across two typed letters from Frank written at the beginning of 1946, I found my mother was sharing her disappointments with him and that he was writing back to her, and her alone. Some years before, she had dramatised his *Children of the Dark People*, a delightful children's book about two Aboriginal children lost in the bush. Coralie had adapted it into a series of twenty-four episodes for radio. No doubt she and Frank had their heads together on this project. My father told me that Frank had once been in love with her. Although he had remarried by the time he wrote that letter, I was surprised by its intimate tone and the depth of empathy and support he offered, more than one would expect from a male colleague who was having his own literary success. There seemed nothing covert or even particularly affectionate in his letters but it made me question whether Frank was showing her more understanding than Leslie was. Then there was that sepia studio portrait of Frank, inscribed 'To Coralie from Frank, 1946' that set me wondering. Perhaps, he wanted to remind her there was still some lingering tenderness there. (I also pondered long and hard about what 'B.B.'s' might stand for, since it referred partly to me. Was it Frank's term or my mother's? I came to the conclusion that the second initial stood for 'brats' – a common name at the time for the irritating young, and one my mother was prone to use and with her usual emphasis. But the first B? It could be 'blasted' or it could be something else.

This is one of the prices of peeping into your parent's private correspondence!)

One of the perils of being a literary wife was to be cast into the role of sounding board. Apparently George ran everything past Charmian, even handing over each page as it came out of the typewriter for her critique and praise. The time and energy spent doing this would have markedly reduced Charmian's own output, which in turn resulted in her being seen as the lesser writer. Coralie suffered to the same degree. She was an intuitive listener, empathic and instantly engaged. My father once told me that was why he fell in love with her. In his earliest letters when they were separated by oceans, he kept mentioning how he missed her listening to his ideas. Ruth, who admitted to being 'darkly secretive' about her own work, revealed that D'Arcy never read any of her novels, though she was his perennial sounding board.

Sounding boards are rarely acknowledged by their sounders. In my father's books of drama history, the dedications read: 'To Coralie, who has always sat at my right hand, both within the theatre and without.' When I commented to my mother that this was a lovely tribute to her, she said: 'Yes, it is lovely. I wrote it myself, that's why.'

Ruth and D'Arcy first met Leslie in his capacity as the ABC's drama editor. They had submitted a play to one of the play competitions my father was running. Whatever their play, it didn't stand a chance against the winner. But the competition had a very helpful long-term consequence for Ruth and D'Arcy: with Leslie's encouragement, it started them off writing for radio, something Ruth would continue in the years after D'Arcy's death with her long-running serial for children *The Muddle-Headed Wombat*.

Play competitions were one of my father's innovations for drawing out hitherto undiscovered talent. This particular competition for verse drama (a form in vogue in England and America at the time) had discovered a real jewel. Leslie was to declare he was prepared to burn his boats that *The Fire on the Snow* was 'the finest-written play to come out of Australia and among the finest half-dozen from anywhere'. His judgement was vindicated, of course. Not only did the play divert Douglas Stewart from his desk on 'The Red Page' of *The Bulletin* and push him into the world of playwriting, but *The Fire on the Snow* had an illustrious career of its own. When I sat for the Leaving Certificate in 1957 it was a set text for English in New South Wales – an embarrassment for a schoolgirl as my father featured in the dedication and had also written a lengthy appendix published with it. Even worse, another of our set texts was my father's *Modern Short Plays* collection.

Douglas Stewart was at first reluctant to have his verse drama produced on radio but he came to be grateful.

> I owe Les a great personal debt as he put me on the map as a playwright by insisting on performing *The Fire on the Snow*, and steadily supported my work thereafter. But, apart from that, I think he has done more for the Australian playwright than anyone else, ever.

In the Sydney literary milieu of the 1940s, Coralie and Les and Ruth and D'Arcy had much in common, including small children of about the same age. The couples became friends. Ruth inscribed a lavish gift, a Phaidon edition of Van Gogh reproductions, with this rhyming couplet:

> To Leslie Rees and Coralie Clarke
> From D'Arcy Niland and Ruthy Park

For many years I treasured a little china hippopotamus with an impossible grin that Ruth had given me for my birthday. Such ornaments were scarce and probably expensive in the postwar years, making it all the more precious. The gift spoke of Ruth's easy capacity to connect with children. I remember her as a shy person who once retreated from one of my parents' noisy literary parties to sit on the end of my bed and tell me stories.

Some years later, Ruth and Leslie collaborated on turning *The Harp in the South* into a stage play. Les described the process thus:

> Ruth had no experience of stage writing and evidenced very little interest in it. She was a practical worker, applying herself to specific markets, and the theatre certainly didn't qualify. But she allowed herself to be persuaded by me. I mapped out a detailed scenario; and while (like Mary Gilmore) peeling potatoes or washing dishes in the Nilands' tiny flat, Ruth shaped line after line of agile dialogue, some of it very different from the printed novel's version. She gave me scene by scene on odd bits of paper. I brought my knowledge of theatre craft to trimming or adjusting; she added one or two extra bits of scene; I added extra shreds of dialogue; and so at last the play was formed.

First produced by Doris Fitton at the Independent Theatre, North Sydney, the play has remained a favourite with amateur theatre companies over the decades since.

In the mutual back-slapping way of literary people, D'Arcy at one time published an article titled 'Kids Are His Business' in a small journal targeting commercial interests, the article's subject Leslie Rees, author of popular children's books. When my father brought a copy home and read it out to us, there were hoots of laughter. Just the irony that a story about a writer was included in a magazine about making money was reason enough for our mirth. But we all howled at D'Arcy's luxuriant epithets describing each member of the family. There was Leslie with 'hair like a silver fox', Coralie 'his beautiful honey blonde wife' and daughters 'the golden-braided Megan and the elfin Dymphna'. These descriptions were quickly absorbed into our family lexicon. Although we were used to getting publicity in the print media, never before had we been described in such lavish terms.

At the time of this friendship, Charmian and George were still living overseas. However, they visited Shellcove on several social occasions when they returned from Hydra. As Leslie was planning to retire from the ABC in 1965 to get on with his writing, he was not involved in working with George and Charmian on the television adaptation of Johnston's novel *My Brother Jack*. A young ABC producer named Storry Walton who had been his protégé in the Drama Department took a key role in the production. The series was hailed as a success, due as much to Charmian's scriptwriting abilities as to the novel itself.

My mother used to say, 'No-one knows what goes on in marriage except the two people involved.' True in some cases, but two of these six writers wrote autobiographies, and two wrote novels that were undisguisedly autobiographical. So there is some evidence from their own pens about how these literary unions played out.

Coralie did not publish any work about herself but several years before she died, she recorded her oral history with Hazel de Berg for the National Library of Australia. She chose to open her life story with this statement:

This is Coralie Rees, wife of Leslie Rees. And therein lies the story of our marriage: I call [pronounce] it 'Reece' and he calls it 'Reeze'. Nevertheless, we recently celebrated our thirty-seventh wedding anniversary, and on that day I said to him, – 'Well, the fairest thing I can say is that if I had my time over again, I'd like to make the same mistake twice.'

Coralie did not harbour any romantic illusions about the institution of marriage. In the early 1960s, the buzzword for gauging the potential success of a relationship was the degree of 'compatibility' between the parties. When I met my future husband, in my dewy-eyed state I beseeched my mother, 'Do you think we're compatible?' She turned on me like a blowtorch: 'I very much hope so because even if you are, it can be pure hell much of the time.' Maybe she was having a bad day and feeling particularly disenchanted with her side of the arrangement, despite her pragmatic and unsentimental attitude. Besides, my mother's dynamic pronouncements were always underscored by hyperbole.

In her short story 'The One Week-End Plan' she tells the tale of a man vacillating between two very different women – a dazzling flibbertigibbet who raises his blood pressure and a girl 'with a sensible face' who shares his tastes and interests. The tale ends with an ironic observation when he asks his housekeeper:

'What are you laughing at, Mrs Williams?' The old girl was splitting her sides.

'Bless you, Mr Pope,' and she wiped her eyes on the duster. 'I was only thinkin' of the fairy tales, you know. And they lived happily ever after.'

And so they did, despite Mrs Williams. More or less happily; as happy as most of us, in the ratio of one-tenth bliss, six-tenths compromise and three-tenths sedimentary contentment.

I was *in utero* when my mother wrote that cagey summary of married life. Despite her tone of resignation (or was it realism?), it seemed to me as a daily observer of my parents' interactions that they had happened upon that magic potion for a fulfilling lifelong relationship. Alongside their commitment to the literary life, they had harmony, honesty and respect, affection and tenderness, well-oiled teamwork, shared responsibilities, debate that was serious and forceful, and exchanges that were lively and colourful. Conversations, even the most mundane, were facilitated by laughter, an ever-present luminescence. Pettiness, meanness, anger and resentment seemed not to show their heads. Or not often.

When I was nineteen years old, I characterised my parents' union in my prize-winning poem as

> the blended two of my beginning
> treasuring each a boundless sharing
> if acrimonious over detail.

My earnestly considered phrase 'acrimonious over detail' produced such hilarity in the subjects to which it referred that the words went immediately into the family vocabulary, being applied to all sorts of relationships and situations from then on.

Coralie was always modest – almost self-effacing – about her achievements. She was not one for airing her knowledge, though she had a fine intellect. However, one night the four of us were gathered round the radiogram, carefully listening to a radio production of one of Ibsen's plays, *An Enemy of the People*. It was a long play and towards the end, my mother had her eyes closed as if she had dozed off in her armchair. At the time Megan and I were both doing English majors at Sydney University and were bursting with intellectual hubris. After the play finished, we were discussing it with our father in our usual opinionated fashion and laughing among ourselves. Then someone remarked: 'Ibsen was too much for poor old Mum. She's passed out.'

To this, my mother opened one eye and then the other and glowered at the three of us. She lowered her brows and let forth a tirade. 'Listen, you pusillanimous blobs! You think you know about Ibsen. *I* was the one who spent a whole year studying his plays. And as a postgraduate student. Now, let me correct you.' And with this, we were stunned into submission and politely listened to a small extempore lecture on social realist drama and Ibsen's part in that movement. Needless to say, we did not forget 'pusillanimous blobs'.

My parents usually presented a united front. Nonetheless, I sometimes remember the time my mother turned to me and uttered in a harsh tone, 'Les is *so* domineering.' I was in my mid-twenties and could see she was finding her life much more challenging through the increasing deterioration of her spine. But her words shocked me, not only because they were uncharacteristic but because of their vehemence. I could sense the frustration that she lived with, the painful transition she was negotiating. At that point my mother walked with a stick and had shrunk to the height of an eight-year-old child. She could no longer stand for any length of time, could not dandle a grandchild on her knee and found the simplest tasks of daily living, like getting dressed, a time-consuming battle. The result was that the equity of my parents' strong partnership – which she had always insisted on – was out of balance. As my father once confided to me, her agile mind and her intellect were livelier than ever, but her body and its limitations demanded that he now carry more and more of the load. How agonising this realisation must have been for her and how dispiriting. The truth was that her condition meant their relationship had entered a new zone – an alien territory – and both were finding the adjustment harrowing.

Charmian and George fought out their conflicts through their alter egos – characters in their novels that were recognisably autobiographical, if not always accurately so. It seems from these writings that their marriage, though at times tumultuous and eventually mutually destructive, was central to their lives. They remained almost indivisible unto death, dying within just over a year of each other.

And Ruth mourned her lost love long and hard, as she describes in the second volume of her autobiography. She called this book *Fishing in the Styx*, a title indicative of her misery.

Looking back on their marriage, my father said: 'We were friends, lovers but friends.' In his autobiography he wrote: 'On the writing front, we were of one approach and each other's best critics and "word-friends". The two-writers-under-one-roof plan had worked, at least to our satisfaction.'

23

Valentine's Day, 1972

Valentine's Day – 1972

When the phone call came
to hurry with fresh clothing
I sensed that this was not
a night for garments and
felt fear; I found you
legs dangling, on the side of
your bed, wearing a childish nightie
I'd made for you one Mother's Day.

'I'm glad you're here, Darling,'
you said, taking my desperate hand
in your chill fingers which
death had reached already, your
tender eyes dull and distended
in their gaze. And so I made
you comfortable with pillows,

caressing the cold hands, reading
– sometimes aloud – the Brennan
you so loved: this being
the night for journeying.

When, on the midnight stroke,
the heart valves closed you shut
with a shocking sigh, I had to tell them.
Stunned, we sat around you drinking tea
then kissed your white-cold face
and closed the door.

A man in a flat black suit
who used to be a bus driver
came in answer to our call
offering 'Condolences!' as if
they were the Compliments
of the Season.

Down the cold morning stairs
he carried your bird-frail shell
strapped on an unlikely pallet
to a waiting unmarked van.
But then and now – through all
my grieving years – I've found
his oily greeting inappropriate.

– Dymphna Stella Rees

So I wrote one Valentine's Day. Time and again, especially on
the anniversary, I relive that hot February evening in 1972. But it
took many years before I could bear to dig into the soft tissue of

my sadness to articulate the details of that night and my part in its drama.

My mother had been ailing for less than a week, the doctor coming every day. Although he hadn't said it in so many words, she had bronchopneumonia. Because of her spinal curvature, her lungs were tightly constricted. They were tucked away inside her pelvis with all her other soft organs. So there would be a struggle to beat it, despite the heavy doses of antibiotics. His way of saying it to her was: 'It's a shame we can't hang you from the ceiling by the ankles and give your chest a chance to drain.'

At the time I lived with my own family in a rural area northwest of Sydney, about fifty kilometres from my parents' home at Balmoral Beach. During my mother's brief illness, I drove to see her most days in the few hours I could find minding for my smaller children while the elder two were at school.

My mother had some prescience of doom – as I did. In the few days beforehand, she had been discussing with me and my father some rearrangements for a dentist's appointment and theatre tickets for that week. She said, 'Les, cancel the dentist. As for the theatre: I won't be going. Why don't you take Thelma?' (Thelma was the widow of Les's old ABC colleague and friend, Max Afford.)

My father, however, was battling a heavy summer cold and was preoccupied with that. Although concerned about Coralie's current illness, he seemed to have not confronted the seriousness of its progression.

It was a steamy humid Sydney February day. I had been to see her the day before. My father rang me in the afternoon to say that she was not eating anything. When I came the following day, could I bring some little treats to tempt her appetite, please?

Some hours later, I had just fed my children and was getting them ready for bed when my father rang again, this time with some urgency in his voice. Could I come straight away and bring some clean nighties? She seemed to be very hot and damp. My friend Margaret Molt came immediately through the dark bush to mind the children. David and I took off into the night, my stomach already tight with apprehension.

I wished my husband would drive faster, such was my sense of urgency on the long hour's journey. When we got there, my mother looked up at me, her large grey eyes seeming to swim in her face. 'I'm glad you're here, darling. You'll be moral support for Les.' My father was pottering about in his dressing-gown, obviously relieved we were there. I bathed my mother's face and hands and helped her into a clean light cotton nightie. Then I rang the doctor's home number. His teenage son answered the phone and said his father was out but he would give him the message.

I settled my mother back on her pillows and soon she was drifting in and out of sleep. Looking in and seeing me sitting beside her and that all was quiet, my father went off to bed in the room next door. He was obviously exhausted. I sat quietly reading from a volume of Christopher Brennan's collected poetry, which my mother had beside the bed. *The Wanderer* series was a favourite of hers and mine. These verses spoke to the moment:

I know I am
the wanderer of the ways of all the worlds,
to whom the sunshine and the rain are one
and one to stay or hasten, because he knows
no ending of the way, no home, no goal,
and phantom night and the grey day alike
withhold the heart where all my dreams and days
might faint in soft fire and delicious death:
and saying this to myself as a simple thing
I feel a peace fall in the heart of the winds
and a clear dusk settle, somewhere, far in me.

About 10.30 pm my mother opened her eyes and looked at me with a dreamy gaze.

'Is there anything I can get you, Mum?'

'No, darling,' she murmured softly. 'Everything's just perfect.' She closed her eyes.

I reached over and took off her glasses to make her more comfortable. Towards midnight her quiet breathing became more irregular. When her heart stopped with a shudder, I had to wake my father.

As in most people's life journey, I have climbed a few mountains. I look back at sharing in my mother's death as an immense experience: both a privilege and a challenge. It was an inexpressibly beautiful gift to sit with my mother as she journeyed towards her earthly end, to share in her confidence and grace, to learn that dying is not always harsh and terrible but can be a serene experience, a graceful passing between realms. My mother's faith allowed her to cope with excruciating physical deterioration without self-pity. For so long, her courage had been a shining example.

In all this I was truly blessed. But to have to waken my father from sleep and tell him that she had died, his life's companion, his friend and collaborator, his Great Love, the woman with whom he had shared almost every day for over forty years – this was unquestionably the hardest task I have ever had to face.

I went into his room and tried to rouse him from sleep. Strangely, I called him by a term I had not used since childhood.

'Daddy, Daddy, she's gone.'

'What? What are you saying?' When I spoke the words, the dismay on his face was terrible. 'She's gone? But I didn't realise she was so sick. If I'd known I wouldn't have gone to bed and left her.'

The doctor never did ring back. His son had forgotten to give him the message. It didn't matter. Nothing could have been achieved by taking her off in an ambulance to struggle to the end in some alien hospital ward. She died in her own bed, in her own dignified way, assured by the presence of those she loved.

24

Sheer Gallantry of Spirit

At the time my mother died, she had battled an insidious incurable disease for more than half her lifetime. Ankylosing spondylitis primarily affects the spine, but it can also affect other joints and organs. It is one of the autoimmune diseases where the immune system attacks the body's own tissue. It is also an inflammatory disease. Beginning at the base of the backbone, the vertebrae become inflamed and, in severe cases like my mother's, go on to create new bone so the spine becomes fused and immobile. The associated pain is then reduced but other problems escalate as the body loses its ability to remain upright. The weight of the head causes the upper body to fall forward, creating a stooped position, which in turn affects the space and movement of the internal organs. It also causes the eyes and facial features to be tilted downwards, which can make swallowing, sitting, walking and sleeping all difficult. Breathing issues can result from the chest's inability to expand.

Ankylosing spondylitis is hard to diagnose, even today. In the first half of the twentieth century there was little known about it, little recognition of autoimmune diseases or of genetic markers that can assist in their diagnosis. Now it is generally diagnosed in the sufferer's second or third decade, though it might be active in a less severe form for many years before. From her twenty-first year, when she was working as editor of *The Dawn*, Coralie recorded in her letters and diaries how she was forever plagued by what was commonly called 'rheumatism', 'lumbago' or 'neuralgia', or she was just plain 'tired'. Doubtless the inflammatory process was taking hold. Chronic pain brings its own form of exhaustion and the inflammatory process its own inexplicable malaise.

Ankylosing spondylitis is now treated with a range of drugs and strengthening exercises but when my mother was diagnosed in the 1940s the recommended treatment was intensive radiation of the lower spine to stop the progress of the disease. For a woman of childbearing years this had the effect of also irradiating her reproductive organs and bringing on premature menopause. Other less radical treatments included basking in front of an infra-red lamp wearing sunglasses, applications of heat by hot water bottles followed by various anti-inflammatory unguents, and the indignity of colonic irrigation.

My mother consulted doctors and specialists: diagnosticians, physicians, rheumatologists and orthopaedic surgeons – in Sydney, New York and London. When they could offer no effective treatment, she tried homeopaths, naturopaths, cleansing diets and health farms. None of these options, traditional or alternative, had much effect because, in truth, by the time her disease was diagnosed her spinal vertebrae were on their way to becoming completely calcified, thus depriving her of skeletal support. Her body gradually diminished in height as it caved in on itself, reducing her by the end of her life to not much more than half her full adult height.

Writing of my mother's illness has caused me to anguish whether I gave her sufficient support. Certainly I was of little assistance as a sulky introspective teenager, when the first changes occurred.

I remember my mother taking me shopping in town; I was bouncing along beside her, no doubt excited about something she had bought me.

'I love going to town,' I enthused. 'Don't you, Mum?'

My mother replied in a strained voice: 'No, I don't. All I can see most of the time is the footpath.'

In my twenties I was more sensitive but also consumed with my own new life of marriage and motherhood. My mother and I talked frequently by phone, which she called 'the bed-to-bed hotline' (it was the sixties!), and David and I would visit my parents at weekends or they would come and stay with us, much to the delight of our four small children. So it was not that we didn't have opportunity to speak frankly, rather that she rarely referred to her increasing difficulties.

My mother made few concessions to the changes in her body. When she needed a stick to walk with, she had one made, disguised as a stylish umbrella. She had always dressed with careful elegance and loved natural fabrics – ravishing silks, polished cottons and finely woven wool – and so when ready-made clothes no longer fitted her shape, she found a creative dressmaker who could design and make her clothes, sensitive to the contours of her body. She had her fine blonde hair coiffed by a hairdresser who could adapt washing methods appropriately, as she could not lean back in a chair. Challenges were not an issue so much as an opportunity for creative thinking.

As time went on and her disability became more severe, my father took an increasing share of domestic responsibilities. Observing the progress of the disease, he decided to retire from his ABC career of thirty years at the age of sixty. Publicly he gave the reason as wanting to address himself full-time to writing, but he privately admitted that he wanted to have more time with his Coral to enjoy the interests they had always shared: the literary life, the arts, travel and family – now with their clutch of seven grandchildren. My mother immortalised them as 'The Seven Little Shoe-Buttons' in her book, *What Happened After*, published just months after her death.

The last six years of Coral and Les's life together were rich with their day-to-day companionship and the excitement of moving into the first home they ever owned, a modest apartment situated right on Sydney's Balmoral Beach, looking out over the shining waters of Middle Harbour towards the bulk of North Head. They were also productive years for their writing collaboration. In 1970 *People of the Big Sky Country*, a collection of their best separate pieces of travel writing about remote parts of Australia and the characters they met, came out in a glossy large-format edition, lavishly illustrated by some of my father's best photography. It was a great success, selling 50,000 copies. They were also still writing radio documentaries together for broadcast on the ABC.

My father was at this time president of the Sydney Centre of International PEN, a worldwide writers' organisation with a strong interest in the humanitarian concerns of people caught in oppressive regimes, restrained from speaking or writing freely. So there were plenty of occasions to get together with their literary friends, for worthwhile work as well as social enjoyment. They wrote, travelled, visited and entertained, and even bought their first ever new car, a Holden station wagon of such untold luxury my mother dubbed it 'the Silver Mink'. Just months before her death, they drove across Australia to Perth for reunions with my eighty-three-year-old grandmother Sylvia, their siblings and a bevy of lifelong friends, my indomitable mother taking the wheel across the Nullarbor, balancing on a pile of cushions so she was high enough to see through the windscreen.

On 17 February 1972 *The Sydney Morning Herald*, a paper they had both written for, proclaimed:

AUSTRALIAN WRITER DIES

Coralie Rees, the Australian writer, died at her home at Balmoral Beach on Monday, aged 63. Mrs Rees and her husband, Leslie Rees, a former drama editor for the ABC, formed one of the best known Australian literary partnerships.

She was born in Perth and met her husband while they were attending the University of Western Australia. Later they went on travelling scholarships to London where they were married. In addition to travel books, Mrs Rees wrote poetry including *Silent His Wings*, children's plays, short stories and radio and journalistic features. She is survived by her husband and two daughters.

Tributes flowed, obituaries were published and an avalanche of letters to my father arrived at Balmoral. People who had known Coralie Clarke Rees throughout her life and those who had known her briefly all expressed admiration for qualities that I had more or less taken for granted. I had been a small child when she first became afflicted with AS and was barely thirty when her life came to an end.

Nancy Robson, who later became Australia's First Lady as Lady Anne Kerr, was one of my mother's closest female friends. At the time of my mother's death she wrote:

What all those who loved her are remembering is the flowering of her spirit, the rich and positive personality – to friends and family an unfailing source of warmth and radiance, of strength, of help that was infinitely practical yet given with boundless love.

When, as a beautiful and still young woman, Coralie was attacked by an illness the full implications of which she faced from the very beginning and without self-pity, she displayed moral and physical heroism in surmounting – in what can only be called disregarding – her physical condition, so that her personality remained unflawed and her activity as generous, diverse and fruitful as before.

The West Australian, a newspaper to which my mother had contributed for some years as London correspondent, ran an obituary by EW Irwin entitled 'A Woman of Quality':

She typified the best of her generation, the one that grew up in Australia between the wars, an era which, whatever its tragedies, saw Australian writing come of age, and a notable advance in the emancipation of women – matters that were among her primary concerns. [...]
   In her early travels off the beaten track she proved her physical courage, but when still a beautiful young woman she was attacked by an illness that demanded courage of a different kind. The illness severely crippled her body but not her spirit for she met the challenge with outward serenity and her life remained zestful and her personality unflawed to the end.

Tom Inglis Moore, writer himself and one of Australia's eminent literary scholars, published his tribute in *The Australian Author*:

Coralie was an exceptionally fine personality, as rich in courage, sympathy and understanding as in intelligence, humour and zest for life. Staunch and generous in friendship, she inspired affection and admiration in a large circle of friends. In her later years she triumphed over physical disability and suffering through sheer gallantry of spirit.

Some people, in personal letters of sorrow to my father, remarked upon his constant care for his Coralie – one 'for the way he helped to make her disability quite inconspicuous', another for 'looking after her with such love and understanding'. Leslie did not see it this way, not at all. To him, they were partners in life, in work, in family, in interests, neither one being to a more or lesser degree dependent on the other.

Dymphna Cusack remembered:

> I shall always see Coralie as she was the first night we met over 35 years ago. Lovely – she was a true beauty – gay, gracious.

Dymphna was married to a writer herself so had a more realistic view of the equity of the Rees partnership. She wrote to my father:

> It wasn't easy – for either of you. I remember one day – I think it was our last lunch together – that Coralie told me how marvellous you were. Indeed we had a competition, comparing *our* marvellous husbands and *our* marvellous luck!

Many of the letters remarked upon the way Coral and Les had managed to combine their writing and broadcasting output, travel and family life in a sustained and harmonious way:

> You grew up together and have done everything that mattered to you both together which is a rare and wonderful thing in a marriage.

One of Coralie's friends, a staunch feminist and pillar of the League of Women Voters, wrote to my father:

> Your partnership is one of those all too rare True Life stories. What wonderful times you have shared. Leslie, may you find some comfort in taking your memories out of storage.

As I look over the collection of letters and expressions of sorrow I've so long kept, I see how many of my mother's qualities, 'her generous outgoing warmth', 'her stimulating intellect', 'her graciousness and sensitivity' were admired and respected, 'an inspiration to all her friends'. But the word that appears again and again is 'courageous' – everyone seemed to admire her 'admirable fortitude under so obvious difficulties'. Gwen Meredith, creator of the ABC's long-running serial *Blue Hills* and one of Coralie's circle of close women friends, wrote:

> I am deeply distressed and cannot really believe it. Although I have known for years that Coralie was ill and suffering, she was always so magnificently courageous that somehow I had come to regard her as capable of going on indefinitely.

Doris Fitton, grande dame of the Independent Theatre, North Sydney, recalled:

> The last time I saw her was at Kenneth's Hair Salon where she was so happily attending to her glamour. She was such a charming person, so clever and brave.

But it was the letter to me from a family friend that shone a light on the source of Coralie's enduring strength, her inner fortitude:

> Over the years my admiration and affection for your mother has deepened. I shall never forget her. I shall remember our laughter and good times shared, and I shall remember too the evening we spoke of serious things, and she told me of her faith which enabled her to live without fear of the future. We only talked once this way but it helped to explain part of her incredible bravery.

Coralie grew up with an Anglican view of God in a family that, while not rigorously devout, followed Christian principles and practice. Leslie, however, described himself as agnostic, interested in religion purely from an intellectual point of view and in churches for their architecture. When my sister and I were growing up, our parents encouraged us to explore various faiths by going to all the different denominational scripture classes offered at school. 'Try them all and make up your own minds,' was my father's liberal advice. When I was in primary school, I was so enthused by winning a Scripture prize that I asked my parents if I could go to Sunday School. 'Certainly, if you would like to,' was their reply. So every Sunday I would dress in my very best clothes and take myself on the tram up to the Presbyterian enclave just a block away from my school at Neutral Bay Junction, sometimes even staying on for the church service, a lone child among the adult congregation. My sister had a later phase of churchgoing and in her teens was confirmed in the Anglican Church, my parents supporting her choice and attending the service.

When I was preparing for my marriage ceremony with its Christian rites and values, my mother revealed regretting that for her nuptials she had not also chosen the age-encrusted words of the *Book of Common Prayer* rather than that terse bureaucratic exchange in a London registry office for the price of 'seven and sevenpence, please'.

On her journey through the challenges imposed by ankylosing spondylitis my mother became interested in forms of meditation and spiritual healing: she was seeking some inner sustenance and trying to find the right form for her particular needs. Then she was introduced by a thoughtful friend to Subud, a practice and belief system that allowed her to become strong and peaceful in her inner life.

Subud is not so much a faith as a practice called 'Latihan'. As a path to God it has more in common with true yogic meditation than with any form of ritualised worship. Latihan, like other forms of structured meditation, aims to bring about an inner quiet, a sense of peace and contentment, whatever trials or chaos the outside world presents. Subud is non-denominational and non-discriminatory. It has no particular dogma or teaching. It originated in Indonesia and is now spread throughout the world.

Subud Latihan became an important part of my mother's life and was critical to the last seven years of her journey. She attended Subud meetings as often as she could and my father supported her in her practice. For Subud purposes, the name 'Stella' was bestowed on her – just as it was on me by Miles Franklin.

In 1969 my parents travelled to Toronto, Canada, to see Megan and her family and decided to go via Indonesia in order to meet with Bapak, the world leader of the Subud movement, at his headquarters in Tjilandak.

While at Tjilandak, my mother apparently wrote a letter to Bapak after her first formal meeting with him. It was full of questions she hoped he could answer, questions that were burning in her, questions that reveal much about her responses to the challenges she faced. Only recently I discovered a draft of this letter, written on odd bits of paper stowed inside the cover of a Subud book, *Songs of Submission*. I do not know if Bapak responded to her questions.

Tjilandak
April 25, 1969

To Bapak

First I would like to thank you for receiving my husband and me in your home last Saturday night and for welcoming us to Tjilandak. It is a great joy and a privilege to be here, and our visit will be all too short – just a taste or a prelude, I hope, to a longer visit in the future. While we are here I would like to ask you, if I may, a few questions:

Is my name Coralie right for me or is it slowing up my spiritual progress? I like it very much and have always been happy with it, but could you tell me whether it has anything to do with the deformed shape of my spine? This deformity did not start to become evident till I was about 40 years old (I am now 60).

Doctors are uncertain whether it started with a small injury to a vertebra when I was a child or is wholly due to an arthritic condition inherited from my mother. My mother (now 80) has a similar curvature but mine is very much worse than hers. Is there a meaning in Subud for the physical ills we have to endure? Have they anything to do with our ancestors? Or are they the expression of our own wrong living? In other words, is there possibly a deeper reason than the medical ones why I have been afflicted with this unusual condition of the spine?

I know that ill-health which has resulted from my spinal condition has brought me into closer touch with spiritual values of life through Subud. So in that I was regarding my deformity as a blessing and I give thanks to God that it has led me to Subud – or made me ready for Subud to find. At the same time, if I do Latihan patiently and sincerely is there hope that my spinal condition will improve? I have been in Subud nearly five years and during that time the shape and strength of my spine has become worse with increasing age but my patience to bear it has improved.

I would also like to ask you what is the Subud belief in the afterlife? I think about this a great deal. When my husband asks me to explain Subud to him, on this I cannot.

I would be most grateful if you could grant me a short interview to answer these questions. Our all-too-short visit to Tjilandak ends next Tuesday afternoon (April 29th) when we have to take our plane to Greece, England, Canada (to see our daughter) and so back to Sydney across the Pacific. If you cannot spare the time for an interview perhaps you could have your answers to these questions posted to me.

I wish to thank you deeply and sincerely for the unforgettable experience of visiting Tjilandak. I feel sure the strength of Latihan here will be a great help to me during the strenuous journey that lies ahead. My husband, who is not yet ready for Subud, has been deeply impressed by all his experiences here – by the quality of the people he has met, especially the Indonesian people, and by the effect Subud has upon them in creating an all-embracing world brotherhood. He is a writer and intends to write a book for Australian children about children in Indonesia.

Please give my affectionate respects to Ibn. I hope she is feeling better.

Yours very sincerely

Coralie Rees

25

The Dream Museum

With Coralie's death came the end of that productive literary partnership of forty plus years. In reality, the writing would go on for many years – but differently. There was a seismic shift from the plural Rees to the singular, bringing an end not only to their published and broadcast collaborative works but to the detailed planning, vociferous discussions, honest debate, ruthless critique and mutual encouragement on which they both had relied and which was the substance of their writing teamwork.

Of course Les's life was immeasurably changed, losing in one blow his wife, writing partner and best friend. At sixty-six, he was still distinguished-looking, vigorous and energetic, in excellent health and brimming with ideas. His buoyant and gregarious enthusiasm was temporarily dimmed but not extinguished.

Domestically, he put his energies into the new generation. At the time of our mother's death, Megan and I had seven children under ten years of age between us so the ministrations of a devoted grandfather were greatly appreciated. Besides, we had lost our adored mother, our role model, confidante and supporter, and were struggling to cope while keeping on bravely with the endless demands small children bring. Les found it very lonely living in their small home so resonant of his Coral and the daily patterns of their shared life. He would spend part of each week at my family's boisterous ménage on the rural outskirts where he bashed away at his typewriter in the dedicated small space we called 'the Mouse House'. Our children called him 'Mouse' after an early attempt by our daughter Christiana, his first grandchild, to articulate his chosen title of 'Gramps'. Mouse was known to protest that he wished she'd chosen a marsupial rather than a rodent, as the name stuck.

These were productive years for Les as he turned to a subject that was truly his passion: drama. He drew on his accumulated experience as a critic, playwright, editor, adapter and producer, as well as his twenty-five-year term as chair of the Playwrights Advisory Board. He had made his entrance as a drama historian in 1953 with *Towards an Australian Drama*, the title indicating the goal of a truly indigenous drama was yet to be achieved. After 1966 he addressed himself to a wider and more complex analysis: the birth and development of Australian drama from the earliest European beginnings, the convict era, right up to the 1970s. It was an enormous effort of research and writing, culminating in *The Making of Australian Drama*, published in 1973.

Such a wide-ranging study had never been made before and the book's publication coincided with a rising interest in Australian literature, particularly in academia. It became a seminal reference, regarded as the Bible of Australian drama, and the first edition sold out quickly. The publisher planned a second edition and asked for a companion volume to bring the history up to date with developments in the period from 1970 to 1985. So the monumental two-volume *History of Australian Drama* of over seven hundred pages covering the period from the 1830s to 1985 became 'the most comprehensive work in its field and the most consulted'.

What separated Leslie Rees's critical history from academic analyses that followed was that he had been an active participant in much of the development of drama in this country, particularly in the forty years from the late 1930s.

There were achievements in the children's books arena, too. Right in time for a second wave of eager family readers, Leslie's *Digit Dick* series and the series of Australian animal biographies were republished by Hamlyn with new illustrations and in colourful large-format editions, bringing the characteristic Rees model of children's literature to a new generation of readers. As environmental and conservation concerns started to become more mainstream in the 1970s and 1980s and the list of Australia's native creatures facing extinction became longer and longer, these children's books with their educative message became more widely relevant.

Always a West Australian at heart, Leslie was now an acknowledged member of the State Library of Western Australia's Hall of Fame. He is there with Randolph Stow, Elizabeth Jolley and Tim Winton, among others.

Les made frequent returns to Perth, including as writer-in-residence at the Fremantle Children's Literature Centre, where he would stay in accommodation at the old jail and give talks to children and their teachers about his books. The Leslie Rees Fremantle Lecture continues to be held there every year in his honour.

Despite losing his travelling companion, Leslie's thirst for adventure remained unquenchable. He was forever planning travels to parts of the globe not yet explored. He made two trips to Russia where some of his children's books were published in translation with peculiar illustrations of Australian animals by an artist relying heavily on imagination rather than observation. Here he was escorted around by members of the Russian literati and was able to make a splash with the roubles, as he wasn't able to take his royalties out of the country. He visited Yugoslavia in his capacity as 'a writer-spokesman on the move', assisting the Australian ambassador to achieve a reciprocal cultural agreement. In Bucharest he spoke with the head of Romanian radio and attended the office of the Romanian Writers' Union, impressed with their reading and translation of some Australian works. In Bulgaria he was surprised and delighted by the Bulgarians' unremitting enthusiasm for book publishing. He returned again and again to holiday in California where he was welcomed by a community of like-minded people and where he had valued friends for many years.

One of the happy outcomes of my father's adventures in Russia was his meeting with Irina Golovnya, who made a specialty of translating Australian works, including Steele Rudd's bush-battler classic *On Our Selection* and Marcus Clarke's *For the Term of His Natural Life*. Irina had also translated some of Dymphna Cusack's novels and the two women had become friends. My father arranged for Irina to come to Australia in December 1990 and to stay with him at Balmoral. In January she was invited to discuss Russian translations of Australian fiction with Robert Dessaix at an event for Sydney Writers' Festival.

But first there was Christmas.

My father was expected to join us for a family celebration at our property on the north coast of New South Wales. Several of our children would be there, two with partners, so it would be quite a houseful. I invited Irina to come too. Imagine her face when the small plane landed on the strip of Grafton airport, where a man was engaged in keeping the kangaroos off the tarmac! On the twenty-five-kilometre drive back to the property, I called in to a roadside shop and came out with four litres of milk. Irina couldn't believe it. Such luxury! She told me milk was rationed in Moscow and they had to stand in long queues to get it.

Our charming guest delighted in her bush Christmas amid two hundred wild acres and kept looking out over the Orara River and beyond to the forest of eucalypts, murmuring in amazement, 'Zee bush! Zee bush!' Around the table, she entranced us all by her stories of how glasnost had been achieved – and by preferring to drink the local milk rather than the more festive libations the rest of us were downing. Three days after Christmas we packed up the four-wheel drive and David drove us through the national park and down a spectacular and rocky incline to where the Nymboida River flows over glistening river stones, sparkling in the sun. In that remote and beautiful spot, we celebrated my father's eighty-fifth birthday: an Australian picnic I was sure Irina would not forget.

Between his adventures, Les set about documenting his fifty years in theatre, radio, television and books. *Hold Fast to Dreams* was the result. Intended to be about his working life and participation in literary fields of creative activity, it focuses mainly on the professional rather than the personal.

When it was published, my then seventy-seven-year-old father gave a talk called 'The Agonising Art of Autobiography' to an audience of fellow writers, revealing that the writing of it had been particularly difficult for him as in everyday life he was shy about self-disclosure.

There was still one aspect of his craft he longed to master: the sophisticated adult novel. Les had completed his first weighty fiction manuscript in his twenties but even in his eighties he was slaving on an ambitious magnum opus, one that eventually defeated him. He privately expressed his sense of failure in a wistful cry from the heart:

> To have written and been thanked for that dream-novel, a novel in which I would have put my knowledge and experience and understanding of life and its people, as well as transmitting a worthy yarn – that would have been the great fulfilment. To have captured a world in imaginative and holding terms, imposing my own sense

of shape, movement and character in keeping with the truth of Life's fundamental design, eventually finding some 'central stillness' (Vivian Smith's words). To have had the joy of writing it well so that it found its mark and won its own kind of celebration …

Alas, alas!

Perhaps it was not only his Edwardian reticence about exposing human inner lives that held him back. His childhood had been mired in poverty, his innocence throttled by family violence. Smothering his feelings was his survival strategy. How is a small child able to process these assaults without curling up inside himself? Little wonder he was so inhibited about exploring fictional journeys in the country of the mind and heart.

However, in *Hold Fast to Dreams*, he at last cast his reticence aside to reveal the struggles of his early life and to give a riveting depiction of the horrors of his childhood, the fear and humiliation he endured from his alcoholic father.

But he could also now perceive his father's addiction with some compassion:

> Looking back, it is hard that one should have to think in such terms of the man who fathered us, but the truth is that, after a few years of marriage and despite potentially good qualities, he had never been anything but a wretched nuisance to himself, to his wife and to us, his multiple progeny.

From the terrified small boy who grew up in the dark shadows of domestic violence and who dreamed of being a writer, Leslie could reflect that his tally of published books was now nearly fifty. He'd carried off all the gongs, including the Order of Australia in 1981 for services to literature, the first ever Children's Book of the Year Award – in 1946 – for *Karrawingi the Emu*, and in 1999 the NSW

Premier's Special Award for Services to Literature. His 'practical and general encouragement to generations of Australian writers' was acknowledged in his Premier's Special Award and appreciated by many of those he mentored who became well known. Ruth Park and D'Arcy Niland had once written: 'A thousand sincere thanks to Leslie Rees from two people who learned a great deal from his wise direction and who valued his encouragement at a time when encouragement was all there was.' In 1999 he also won the Townsville Foundation for Australian Literary Studies Award for his drama histories. The award he most valued was the honorary title of Australia's best-loved children's author.

Ever passionate in dreaming up new titles and book ideas, he never stopped writing, right through his eighties and into his early nineties when he published his last new book, *The Seagull Who Liked Cricket*. (He liked cricket, too.) The typewriter sat permanently on the dining room table, the same table on which we had done our homework and which our parents had used for literary production and many a dinner party. Now it was covered by piles of paper: scruffy manila folders containing notes and concepts scribbled on bits of paper, correspondence awaiting answers and drafts of whatever work was in progress. If one was invited to dine with him at Balmoral, the literary detritus would be shifted to one end and an appropriate space cleared.

In mining the rich but chaotic literary archive bequeathed to me, I came across a fragment in such tiny scrawl I could hardly discern some of the words. It was dated 'late 1992' – his eighty-seventh year. From it I detected him essaying another autobiography, perhaps this time a more contemplative one, far less emotionally controlled and private. It seemed he had reached the confidence of allowing the reader into his intimate reflections. He'd given this intended work the provisional title *Boy of O Five* in reference to 1905, the year of his birth. He wrote:

'The power of the story lies in its being experienced through the imagination of both the teller and the receiver, its elements being an amalgam of common truths already apprehended plus of things newly conceived and transmitted in a creative continuity.'

Mr X lies in bed thinking over the past, meanwhile gazing over his shelffuls of books.

He thinks back to when he was a small boy, living in a slummy bungalow cottage with open verandahs giving space to rickety beds with thin worn blankets and homemade patchwork covers. It was here his first consciousness of boyhood began, of himself as a boy removed by seven years from the next older members of his family. Later he would realise how the very drabness and disorder and isolation of that islanded boy spurred the beginning of a life of break-away, of wanting to explore the perimeters of the wider world without restriction but while still needing to remain imbedded in the family matrix.

He had never been able to part with a book, so they'd accumulated densely. When he had bought his apartment many years ago, he had put up his own shelves, up to the ceiling and stretching the length of a wall. And he had hundreds of books on all subjects. Novels were in the top row (once read they could rest in a less reachable space). Next down were books of poetry – Australian and general – (grimy from schooldays), travel books, collections of plays, essays and books of history. Eight long shelves of books, probably a thousand. They were arranged with minimum orderliness and chronology. He liked them that way, liked having his eye on the whole collection when he was searching for one particular reference. Many he'd had for nearly seventy years, not textbooks but special titles bought for a shilling or so in a second-hand shop with pocket money earned as a butcher's delivery boy or doctor's car cleaner.

From his bed he smiled guiltily that in all that time he hadn't yet got round to reading some of those early-bought treasures: always intended to, kept putting it off. All those books represented his life and trying to make some sense out of the facts, dilemmas and reality, the truth about the world and its people. Yes, of thinking and of word-enjoyment.

But these were rather ponderous reflections. No need for them to throttle the simple fact that learning things (but not too deeply) had for him been sheer fun. A pity that too many items absorbed through one metaphorical ear went on to flirt with the corrugations of his brain and decided to journey to the other ear and out of it and be lost to him.

He had always been given to this massive perambulation of the memory, re-tapping one phase of his experience after another, letting it flow through his head and senses: relationships with male friends, narrow escapes, adventures, wild phases with women after Coral had left (still readily desirable in image after so many years), the substance or magic of books, of a good film or painting or string quartet, Beethoven, Boccherini, Haydn, Hummel and of course Mozart, Mozart, Mozart. And *The Brothers Karamazov*, Chaucer, Milton (yes, he'd read the whole of *Paradise Lost* at age 16), de Maupassant, Pirandello, Goldsmith ('wrote like an angel even if he talked liked Poor Poll'), the incredible quantitative record of the immortal Bard. The plays he'd seen in so many places, Moscow, New York, London's Shaftesbury Avenue, Sydney: plays by Chekhov, O'Neill, George Bernard Shaw, Marlowe and Williamson.

So his little room that was a cave was also a dream museum. Yes, the drums would so often beat and the sounds roll. And how he thanked his stars forever that he'd acquired this greatest gift … the power to open the door – to revel in the output of most centuries and most cultures and countries … even the popular idiom of the present day too, though much of it escaped his understanding.

He rose, legged it into his shorts and set off for his morning walk around the bay.

The dawn was just breaking. And what a dawn. Because he was looking towards the east or northeast, the many tethered yachts were all seen in black – bobbing black against the creeping pink light flooding the sky and the great width of water. Beyond those waters, the curve of the coastal hills was also black and above them stern grey clouds were, at their higher edges, burnished with red-gold, strips and masses of living fire. And above them the pale blue sky arching over towards him.

26

Small Volumes

It was the last year of the twentieth century and my father was battling pneumonia.

After he had been some weeks in hospital, it became clear to me that he was too frail to go home. Although recovered, the illness had cost him his sparkle and physical vigour: his signature lust for life. I now had to do the second hardest thing I have ever had to do as a daughter: I had to tell him there was no option but the respite care I had arranged at a retirement hostel. He would need to go there to be cared for and get proper meals.

'But oh I want to go back home,' he pleaded. 'How long will I have to stay there?'

I doubted he would ever be able to live in his Balmoral unit again.

He was desolate. The respite room was a rhomboid-shaped chamber with interior-looking windows. There was little space for anything besides a bed and chair. The walls and furnishings were a bleak indeterminate shade. He could have his meals there or go down to the dining room and sit with others at a small table.

He hated it. He hated it with a passion. He hated the fact that well-meaning staff told him when to take his pills. He hated sitting for meals with a group of people he had never met and with whom he had few common interests. He hated that there was no 'good conversation' (one of the joys of life he prized above all others). He hated being boxed in, his freedom lost, and that he could not see the stars.

I grieved for him and carried the burden of being the agent of his distress. He was a man of the outdoors; he craved fresh air and light; he was a walker, a swimmer, a delighter in nature in all its tiny detail and vast expanses. Now to be confined to this small room in an alien place, none of the objects of his richly lived life around him, nothing to identify him, to give him meaning or purpose or the strength to go on … It was a terrible incarceration.

My father had an ebullient nature. He passed on to all who would listen his belief in what he called 'the bump of wonder'. His theory was that the bump of wonder gave life its savour – it was the salt that brought out the flavour of all things wise and wonderful. The bump of wonder was a mixture of curiosity and delight in all creation.

His challenge now was to turn his confinement in respite care into a channel for small joys, thus making life endurable again. He came up with a plan. He found there was an hourly bus that passed the hostel and went down the hill to the beach. As soon as he was strong enough, he set up a pattern of catching the two o'clock bus down Raglan Street so he could spend a couple of hours sitting in his own home with his beloved collection of books, pictures, *objets d'art* and memorabilia around him, gazing out on the blue waters of Middle Harbour and musing over his life and loves and many adventures. At five o'clock he would catch the bus up the hill and be back at the hostel in time for tea. This way he established a bearable compromise. He had not been irrevocably torn from his former life – he could still touch it and feel it and take pleasure in its familiar detail.

Some afternoons I would pick him up from the hostel and we'd go down to his place in my car. On one occasion, I felt oppressed by the way everything was gathering dust. The air seemed thick with it. Even when he had lived there, my father had always vigorously refused to have anyone in to help him clean or do anything else. He preferred to do it himself, he said. He couldn't bear the interruption to his time and concentration. However, his attention to the cleaning became more and more cursory and now that there was no-one living in the apartment full-time, it was apparent that something should be done.

With reformist zeal, I got out the ancient Electrolux and began to thrash around the floors with it, complaining about the state things were in. Suddenly my father became very agitated. His blue eyes were blazing, his voice rising.

'Stop. Stop. Don't waste time on that! Put it away.'

'But, Dad, the place needs cleaning.'

'Now is not the time. I've got something I want to show you.'

My father was usually very slow to anger. He had the mildest of tempers, so I was shocked. With some resentment, I bent down and turned off the machine.

My father's urgency, his irritation were palpable. When I look back now, I realise that from his perspective, the wisdom of his years, he knew that there would always be mess and detritus in human lives, but that the small moments when two people could share things of tender memory, precious detail and enduring love are rare and to be fought for.

Over the inert frame of the vacuum cleaner he passed me a small leather-bound book, the size of a pocket diary.

'Darling, I want to tell you about Coral. I want to tell you about our love for each other.'

He was speaking as if it were yesterday. He went to his oak bookcase with its leadlight glass doors, the first piece of furniture he had ever owned. In it he kept all the first editions and author copies of the many books he had written, along with precious signed volumes by other writers.

He pulled out another small book and passed it to me.

'I've got something to show you. You know when I left Western Australia to go to London, we exchanged these little books. We had each written in them verses of poetry to read to help us endure our separation.'

I opened one of the books, holding it carefully in the palm of my hand.

My father then took out a larger shiny black book held together with ribbon. 'I've got something else for you. When I went on that long journey by ship from Australia to England, every night after dinner I went to my cabin and wrote a letter to Coral. Of course I couldn't post them. But I wanted to tell her every little detail of what I was experiencing. Here they all are, all the letters I wrote to her on that voyage. When she eventually received them, she pasted them into this book. Now I'm giving it to you.'

I took the book and opened it, seeing its pages stuck with small parchment papers crammed with lines of handwriting in faded black ink. I had not seen the letter-book before. I had no idea of its existence.

My father's face was now alight with the memory of the girl he had first loved more than seventy years ago and whom he had never stopped loving. He had never spoken to me of these matters before and he never would again.

27

A Place in the Sun

'Let's go for a walk,' I said. These were our favourite pastimes: walking and talking.

It was a Sydney winter's day, the sun's watery rays gilding the sparsely placed splashes of colour, the sky a pale dome of cerulean blue. A faint wind stirred the brush box and, here and there, a bloom (or was it a rosella?) lit the grey green leaves with a stab of vermilion.

I found the wheelchair surprisingly heavy to push: even the slightest incline made me strain. This surprised me because the load seemed so fragile, so reduced: his form under a heavy jumper swayed with the movement of the chair, one hand inert on his lap, fingers curled, the other clutching his knee rug, which concealed a urinal bottle, just in case.

I chose what looked like a shortish street opposite – squat houses facing onto cottage gardens but quiet, with no through traffic. The footpath looked relatively even and had grass on the verges. I chatted away as I pushed.

Halfway along the block I parked the chair on the strip of grass and sat myself opposite on a low concrete wall. The owner of the wall looked up from sweeping her porch but seeing the chair and its tenuous contents, resumed her task. Thus we sat facing each other in the winter light. Nearby a eucalypt drooped its arms of tapering silvered leaves.

He said, 'My mind's gone funny today. I'm having delusions.' But he added with a laugh: 'They're not all unpleasant, you know. For instance, I can see your face – only it seems about ten feet wide.'

I stood and picked a small spray of leaves from the tree. First I laid them on his lap. Then, fearing they might blow off, I placed them in his inert hand, curling the fingers over. But how much love can a few leaves convey?

He looked long at them then looked at me, his eyes very blue. 'It's so lovely to be out in this wonderful sun after being cooped up inside.' After the strain of speaking he slid into a little half-sleep, his head drooped forward.

'Come on,' I said. 'Let's explore a bit further.' The bumping of the chair along the uneven pavement seemed to rouse him and occasionally I had to stop and rest.

The sun was now lower in the sky and a quiet, sharp wind began to move the leaves about.

'I suppose we'd better head back before the wind gets too cold.'

To get back, I had to navigate the chair across a busy road. I discovered there were little concrete ramps when you came to the corner, access ramps for small vehicles such as prams and strollers, perhaps even wheelchairs.

The down ramp onto the road presented no problem: gravity took care of that. But, having crossed, I found I needed several goes at the up ramp. Nevertheless, I could not make headway. Dragging is easier than pushing so I turned the chair around. As I started to drag it up that very small incline I noticed my passenger had slumped forward, his head over his knees. His weight thus shifted, I found it impossible to move the wheelchair.

'Hey,' I said, a trifle testily. 'Dad. Just sit back and relax. Otherwise I can't budge this thing.' Cars were whizzing by.

From the chair there was no response. With one foot on the rear cross-bars of the wheelchair to hold it on the slope and with one hand hanging onto the handle, I leaned forward and placed my arm diagonally across him, trying to move his weight even a fraction back onto the seat to balance the chair.

The weight thudded gently back against the chair. But as I tried again to pull the chair up the small ramp, his weight shifted forward again, head on chest. Nothing for it but to lean over and place one arm tightly around his inert form to try to hold him in the chair then heave and haul with all my strength, one hand on the chair to guide its direction, up along that little incline and then along the straight until we reached the garden. Bent forward over him and holding him as tightly as I could, I propelled us both along the street in that ungainly embrace.

I parked him in the late sun on a little terrace amid some wordless onlookers. His body seemed shrunken, sagging and askew in the chair. One hand still clutched the emergency bottle under the knee rug, the fingers of the other curled around the leaves on his lap.

I raced inside and found the nurse, a young bloke with beefy arms.

'I need some help,' I said, my voice rising in desperation. 'He's nearly falling out of the wheelchair. I can't seem to keep him in it. Come quickly.'

'Probably had another little stroke,' the nurse said matter-of-factly. 'I'll take a look in a tick.'

Later, after my father had been transferred and was trussed up, his inert arm in a sling, the gate sides in place to keep him from falling out of his cot, he opened his blue eyes. He looked and looked into my face as if trying to drag recognition from some deep mire within.

'It's me, Dad.'

He stared at me wonderingly. I picked up his good hand and held it tenderly against my cheek. I probed gently: 'What's my name, Dad? Come on, you know me.'

Then I insisted: 'Dad, you *do* know who I am.'

He kept gazing at me intently, his mouth puckering like a purse, trying to shape a sound, a name, an image. His concentration was immense. His whole face was straining and his eyes burning into my own.

At last, with a triumphant breath, he brought forth an explosive sound. 'D…D…darling!' he shot out. A lopsided smile of triumph followed. His head fell back on the pillows and his eyes half-closed. Depleted utterly.

Whether he realised it was me or whether he was seeing his beloved Coral waiting for him I'll never know. For that was the last recognisable sound he ever made.

Epilogue

After my mother died, I wanted to write her story. I wanted to record her literary and personal legacy but, more deeply, to keep her alive to assuage the ache of my grief.

When I told my father I intended to write her biography, he asked, a trifle peevishly, 'What about me? Aren't you going to write my story, too?'

I responded with all the indignant hauteur a thirty-year-old can muster. 'But Dad, you can write your own!'

Which indeed he did.

Through my adult years, my father would occasionally bring to my attention that he was counting on me to keep the literary fires burning. I must admit to being somewhat stung when I found, towards the end of an oral history recorded in Western Australia, that he had spoken about me in what I could only interpret as a tone of grave disappointment. 'We always hoped she'd be a writer,' he revealed, adding, 'She teaches English,' as if that was perhaps a shameful alternative. However, that was in 1981, before my career had really taken off. And he did go on to describe me as 'a considerable reader' and said, 'She's one of the people I can really discuss literature with. We have great old talks on poetry and so forth.'

After my father died on 10 August 2000, my life took yet another direction. I was besieged by that mountain of paper. Right next to my worktable stands an imposing glass-doored bookcase, a heavy piece of oak furniture I bought after my father's death to house my parents' published works, their many titles and editions. But it is the messy boxes under the table and stacked up the walls that closet much of their unpublished work, as well as the letters which were never intended for publication, letters which were to reveal to me so much about them, their eager aspirations, their idealism and the realities that failed to puncture it, their passion for each other and for becoming writers.

So overwhelming did I find the range and complexity of my bequest that I was tempted to call in an archivist to help sort it all out. But I could not envisage letting a stranger poke about in such a private sphere.

I was sunk in a deep pool of sadness at my father's passing. He had been my only parent for half my lifetime. What I missed most was that I could no longer discuss literary matters with him. I had grown used to being part of an intensely literary family. The written word was my parents' joyous and abiding focus, throughout their lives a continuing frame of reference. Most of their friends and associates were writers too. Such was the rich fabric of their life, a life I had absorbed and breathed as naturally as air.

Now I was surrounded by their ghosts. In a room of my own (a luxury my mother never achieved), I explored options, ways to creatively refashion the chaos of my paper inheritance. And there was that other longing, housed in me so long, to breathe new life into the generous-spirited, staunch-hearted Coralie, the beautiful and talented woman who had shown so much resilience.

Most precious to me among her papers were her handwritten letters from the time before I was born. Into these she had freely poured so much of her inner life, her desires, her plans, her fears, allowing me to see her in a different light: like a familiar, separate and unassailable.

Nearly three decades had passed since I had told my father I wanted to write her story. But while my father lived, my writing about her had not been possible. In his eyes, she was more his than mine. He was the custodian of her secrets, written and unwritten, and he did not offer me the key. Because of his restraint about matters that touched the heart, my father would only talk about her briefly and objectively, or in some throwaway remark, like, 'A very clever girl, your mum' – as if I didn't know. It was almost as though, after she left us, the pain was too much for him. He kept her and all her precious detail locked deep inside himself.

But it was my turn now.

~

My parents' passion for the literary life flavoured the daily pattern of my first two decades, imposed its constraints and poured upon me rays of illumination. The fertile interchanges of a creative and intellectual hothouse stood in counterpoint to the drab discipline of the everyday plod: the endless daily work of bringing ideas and experiences into a concrete form. But I was ambivalent about being a writer. I knew I *could* make that choice. I've always delighted in the writing process: the way one can shuffle words around in a sentence to alter the finer shades of meaning, the struggle to find *le mot juste*, the exact word that encapsulates a particular thought or concept. There's an exhilaration in exploiting the deep riches of the English language, stretching it to suit purpose and genre. But did I want my life to be a pale imitation of my parents'? Did I want to be endlessly compared? Besides, I harboured no illusions about the literary life. Miles Franklin, right at the end of her days, wrote in a letter to Pixie O'Harris, 'why do we go on? Writing is an affliction worse than TB [tuberculosis] for TB can be cured.'

My father, near the end of his life, put together a personal notebook about his writing life, subtitling it: *Unveiling Further Secrets, Minor Scandals, Conspiracies, Disillusionments, Hazards, Rewards, and Untoward Anecdotes of the Writing and Publishing Mystique.*

In my own life, I didn't turn my back on the language but I employed it in other ways. My career as an educationist in the disciplines of English and humanities involved some fulfilling work, embedded – as it was – in a philosophy of access and equity. There's something precious about introducing a class of adults to a beautiful work of literature they never knew existed or helping recent immigrants practise the language skills they will need to get through each day. A particularly rewarding experience was running an outreach class on creative writing for a group of tired middle-aged women. (I was one myself at the time.) I took this class as an extra after a long day at college, driving thirty kilometres to a straggling outer suburb where it was held one night a week over nine weeks in a room at the otherwise dark Baby Health Centre. None of my students had picked up a pencil in years – probably since they escaped from their dreaded schools. But one by one, magic happened as each person discovered confidence and then the joy of expressing thoughts and distilling experiences, sharing parts of themselves that had lain deeply buried for years. One woman even went on to win a poetry competition.

In the 1980s I was given a brief to design a new core subject for New South Wales TAFE's tertiary entrance course to replace the traditional subject of English. I came up with *Language & Learning Skills*, a practical approach to language using the skillset required to get through a post-secondary course of study: writing, oral, research, critical and evaluative skills. The course and the textbook

I wrote for it went on being used in colleges across the state for a couple of decades.

Perhaps my most valuable legacy was in the area of Aboriginal studies. In the 1990s, I was appointed general editor of a complex package in book and CD-ROM format: *Indigenous Australians: An Aboriginal community focus*. It was designed as an educative tool for any students or adults who in the course of their work needed increased cultural understanding and sensitivity. The teaching and learning handbook I wrote was complemented by a rich resource bank of hundreds of photos, recorded interviews, documents and videos. I sought as much input and advice from Aboriginal educators and community people as possible.

I learnt during this process that many of my colleagues were of the Stolen Generations and so had been deprived of their own history and culture – even their names, birth dates and parentage in some cases. Some told me of childhoods as servants for wealthy pastoralist families, others grew up on missions without any freedoms at all. They now wanted to fill those deep gullies in their own cultural birthrights. So, with support and ongoing advice from Aboriginal educators, I developed the first Diploma of Aboriginal Studies, aimed specifically at Indigenous students who had been denied their own heritage through the process of dispossession and forced removal.

After twenty years I retired from TAFE and put my energies into an area that is rarely discussed and widely misunderstood: schizophrenia.

The youngest of our four children had suffered from this challenging disease since teenage years, resulting in a gruelling learning curve as we grappled with psychiatric hospitals, clinicians and the vastly inadequate resources of mental health services. Intractable psychotic illness brings with it a challenging journey for the whole family and endless anguish for the sufferer, the most painful being social isolation and, for sometimes quite long periods, mandatory detention in a locked ward. I spoke at all sorts of forums, including an international conference on schizophrenia, explaining to this audience of clinicians and brain researchers just exactly what the personal repercussions of this illness are for sufferers and for those who love them. For five years I volunteered my services to an NGO that advocates for families in situations like ours. This led me to retrain as a counsellor and family therapist. I chose to work with women and children escaping family violence and trauma. It was rewarding work for which I had to draw upon everything I had ever learnt.

Then my sister, Megan Clarke Wintle, died suddenly in February 2016. I was asked by her son Derek to prepare a eulogy on her early life, our twenty years of growing up together at Shellcove. This set me thinking about our experiences as children of writers and how that had affected the course of our adult lives.

At her funeral service, I acknowledged our true good fortune.

One of life's greatest blessings was ours – a 'golden childhood' which gave us a strong foundation and shaped the rest of our lives: our directions, our choices, our values. Our parents were a creative team, liberal-minded intellectuals who had the rare capacity of combining their literary ambitions with a balanced and inclusive family life.

I also talked about the delights of the Rees family language, arising from the fact that all four of us had studied French and Latin for at least five years and completed majors in English language and literature at university.

What emerged from these learnings and passions was a patois, a complex creole studded with quotations from literature, phrases in French and Latin, names of characters in our father's books, witty sayings, colourful coinages and our mother's penchant for a play on words. Throughout our lives, whenever we talked or wrote to each other, Megan and I would revert to this form of exchange. It was something that drew us together and reminded us that though we were very different people, we had a deep well of shared knowledge and experience that we both treasured.

Then I came to the shadow sides of our upbringing. One was being left with other families for such long periods when our parents went off adventuring. While they were away, we sisters became much closer, clinging together like orphans. Our parents travelled in risky and remote regions by haphazard means of transport. We rarely heard from our travellers. Nor could we contact them should an emergency arise.

I also spoke of another disadvantage to having such multi-talented parents with glittering reputations. Although Megan and I never articulated this, throughout our lives I think we both had a nagging sense of inadequacy. Whatever we achieved, it always seemed mediocre by comparison.

To me this was especially so in literary matters. Even with several titles published, quite a few articles and one literary prize for my poetry, another for the heritage edition of my father's most popular title, I've never considered calling myself 'a writer'. Just as one swallow does not make a summer, one book, even two or three, does not make a writer. Or not the concept of 'being a writer' that my parents shared with their literary contemporaries. To them and their cohort, the term 'writer' was not about how many titles you had on the shelf. The term embraced a unique and passionate lifestyle, a pilgrimage, a vocation that was pursued with total commitment, despite the economic and social inconveniences it brought.

When Megan died, I had been the manager of my parents' literary archive for nearly sixteen years but I was now the last of our Rees family. So I was the only person who could record the intimate story of Coral and Les by drawing on firsthand experience. Clearly, there was no option. It was time for me to embrace the literary life and to pick up my pen.

When I perceive my parents through my daughterly lens, I must admit to admiring how they lived their lives, their professional integrity and the tenacity with which they pursued their literary ambitions. Any niggling ambivalence over the choices they made is outweighed by what was known in our family as 'fp' – filial piety, a delicious term used by the Romans, which I scooped up when translating Ovid and Virgil. The word *love* in English is so tired and overused and covers everything from the object of one's desire to tomato sauce. Like the four Greek words for different types of love – *philia, storge, eros* and *agape* – I like the capacity of *filial piety* to encapsulate that particular love a child has for a parent, one that has implicit boundaries, that demands respect, that acknowledges the unique place of the parent in the child's psyche. It is a term that honours the difference between generations and the passing of knowledge, skills and values as part of the essential parental gift.

I had my father for nearly sixty years, my mother for half that time, but both are equal in that deep place where those we have cherished flit in and out but are never far away.

Dymphna with the 1970 portrait of her parents, Coralie Clarke Rees
and Leslie Rees, by Sydney artist Dora Toovey.

Acknowledgements

I'm delighted to be associated with UQP, a publisher with such a long and proud history and I thank Publishing Director Madonna Duffy for embracing *A Paper Inheritance* the way she has, so letting a light shine on Coralie and Leslie Rees's place in Australian literary history.

Other people have contributed their expertise during this book's long gestation. Caroline Baum read an earlier draft and Patti Miller critiqued some chapters during her 'True Stories' course. Both made invaluable suggestions. Kathryn Heyman restored my self-belief as a writer. Jacqueline Kent, herself an accomplished biographer, undertook the delicate task of a structural edit. What could have been a tussle ended in friendship. At the start, UQP Senior Editor Margot Lloyd and I agreed to work happily together. And we have done so.

I thank my fellow writers of the Lit. Lunch: Francesca, Sharron, Catherine and Amanda who encouraged me out of such a bottomless Slough of Despond that I was ready to give the game away and concentrate on growing vegies. With other valued friends, members of the BT Book Club, I've shared many a long lunch on the regular occasions we talk the afternoon away and, at some point, get round to considering other people's books. I thank my friend Bea for setting up our group many years ago and for our GTs, now on FaceTime.

In middle age, I contracted an eye disease linked to my mother's AS. Over the years of working on this book, I've been treated by a skilful ophthalmologist for another eye disease: a form of macular degeneration, the most common cause of blindness in Australia. I thank Dr Jerry Vongphanit for saving my sight and for taking such an interest in my work each time he injects my eyeball with sight-saving medicine. I also thank Dr Stella Rumsey, a GP with literary interests, who checked the details on ankylosing spondylitis.

I thank two stunning women, my daughters, Christiana and Lisa, for their belief in me and for sharing books and laughter; I thank two beaut blokes, my sons, Simon and Damien, for who they are and what I have learnt from them. As little ones my grandchildren, Charlie, Dylan, Saffron, Piper and Natasha, brought the sunshine back into my life. I'm proud of them all, now young adults and navigating their own courses.

Then there's David. We've travelled the long road, together – though not in each other's shadow. We've shared its twists and turns, disasters and delights. Ever loyal, ever true, he might have complained of reading about the exploits of his parents-in-law, Coral and Les, over and over again. But I don't remember him doing so. What I never forget is how graciously he always welcomed my mother and father into our home and how he lent his practical skills to help them whenever needed.

For all the fine people who have sustained my journey, I'm ever grateful.

Biographical Timeline

1905	Leslie Rees (LR) born 28 December, Maylands, Bayswater, WA
1908	Coralie Clarke (CC) born 23 October, Perth, WA
1914–18	LR attends Subiaco State School
1919–23	LR attends Perth Modern School
1921–25	CC attends Perth Modern School
1924	LR works as a student teacher
1924–28	LR attains a Bachelor of Arts, UWA
1925–29	LR works as a journalist on *The West Australian*
1926–28	CC attains a Bachelor of Arts, UWA
1927	CC and LR meet when LR is editor of *The Black Swan* (UWA literary magazine) and CC is appointed sub-editor; May, CC plays lead in University Dramatic Society's *The Whole Town's Talking* and LR reviews her favourably in *The West Australian*
1928	LR and CC meet on holiday on Rottnest Island and their 'future was sealed'; CC's play *Shielded Eyes* published in *The Black Swan*;
1929	LR works as the drama and art critic on *The West Australian*; CC becomes editor of *The Dawn*; 2 December, LR departs for London on RMS *Orford*
1930	LR studies at the Slade School of Fine Art, University College London; 1 June, CC departs for London on SS *Orsova*

1931	CC studies dramatic theory at London University; LR appointed drama critic of *The Era*; CC becomes sub-editor of *The Children's Sketch*; 19 September, CC and LR marry at St Pancras Town Hall
1931–35	LR writes a weekly column, *This Week at the Playhouse*, for *The Era*
1932–35	Coralie Clarke Rees (CCR) writes *London Woman's Diary*, syndicated in Australian major dailies, and other freelance journalism published in England and Australia
1936	February, Coralie and Leslie (C&L) leave London with Eileen Joyce; April to June, EJ and CCR travel across five Australian states on ABC concert tour; June, C&L settle in Sydney; LR works for *The Sydney Morning Herald* as drama, art and film critic; CCR freelances and broadcasts on the ABC; December, LR joins the ABC as federal drama editor
1937	March, C&L move to Shellcove, their home for almost thirty years; LR co-founds the Playwrights Advisory Board, Sydney
1938–63	LR is chairman of the Playwrights Advisory Board
1938	30 August, Megan Clarke Rees born at Saba Hospital, Neutral Bay
1940	5 November, Stella Dymphna Clarke Rees born at Saba Hospital, Neutral Bay
1942	LR appointed air-raid warden; CCR, M and D evacuated to Glenbrook, then Young, NSW
1944	1 January, CCR's brother Max Clarke killed in Canada
1946	C&L's first trip to Alice Springs and Northern Territory; LR's *Karrawingi the Emu* awarded the Children's Book Council of Australia's first Children's Book of the Year
1947	LR's *Sarli the Barrier Reef Turtle* Australian Book Society's Choice
1949	1 January, CCR's father, Guildford Clarke, dies; 24 April, LR's mother, Mary Elizabeth Rees, dies; May, M&D stay with Jess in Bridgetown, WA, while C&L hitchhike around remote north Australia, researching for *Spinifex Walkabout*
1950	October, CCR diagnosed with ankylosing spondylitis; deep ray treatment on spine
1951	C&L's New Guinea trip; research for *Danger Patrol*

1953   October, C&L's *Spinifex Walkabout* on bestseller lists

1954–55   May to February, C&L's *Westward from Cocos* trip (Mauritius, Cocos Islands, Africa, Europe, America, New Zealand); M&D board in Sydney

1956   LR's play *Sub-Editor's Room* on ABC TV produced by LR (first Australian play produced on Australian television)

1957–66   LR is deputy director of drama, ABC

1957   C&L's *Coasts of Cape York* adventure

1960   C&L visit APY Lands, Simpson Desert, Uluru, researching for *People of the Big Sky Country*

1966   22 July, LR retires from the ABC; 1 August, C&L move from Shellcove to Balmoral Beach

1967–75   LR is president of the Sydney Centre of International PEN

1968   C&L's radio series *London Life in the 1930s* broadcast on ABC (based on *Seven and Sevenpence, Please*)

1970   Dora Toovey paints C&L's portrait, which is a finalist in the Portia Geach Memorial Award and then purchased by Dymphna

1972   14 February, Coralie Clarke Rees dies in her Balmoral home

1979   LR's two-volume *History of Australian Drama* awarded a Foundation for Australian Literary Studies award

1981   LR awarded the Order of Australia (AM) for services to Australian literature

1999   LR awarded NSW Premier's Special Prize for his contribution to Australian literature

2000   10 August, Leslie Rees dies in Sydney in his 95th year; Dymphna Stella Rees becomes manager of her parents' literary archive

2012   LR's classic *Shy the Platypus* published by the National Library of Australia in a heritage edition and with an introductory essay by Dymphna (wins the Australian Museum's Whitley Award)

2016   February, Megan Clarke Wintle (née Rees) dies

2021   *A Paper Inheritance* by Dymphna Stella Rees is published

Select Bibliography

Brennan, Christopher (1960) *The Verse of Christopher Brennan*, Angus & Robertson, Sydney.

Brunton, Paul (editor) (2004) *The Diaries of Miles Franklin*, Allen & Unwin in Association with State Library of NSW, Sydney.

Davidson, Dianne (1997) *Women on the Warpath: Feminists of the first wave*, University of Western Australia Press, Crawley.

Davis, Richard (2001) *Eileen Joyce: A portrait*, Fremantle Arts Centre Press, Fremantle.

Davison, Frank Dalby (1936) *Children of the Dark People: An Australian folk tale*, illustrations by Pixie O'Harris, Angus & Robertson, Sydney.

Davison, Frank Dalby (1944) *Man-Shy* (10th edition), Angus & Robertson, Sydney.

Fox, Mem (1990) *Mem's the Word: The inspiring story that created Possum Magic*, Penguin Books Australia, Ringwood.

Franklin, Miles & Cusack, Dymphna (1939) *Pioneers on Parade*, Angus & Robertson, Sydney.

Inglis, KS (2006) *This Is the ABC: The Australian Broadcasting Commission 1932–1983*, Black Inc., Melbourne.

Kinnane, Garry (1986) *George Johnston: A biography*, Nelson, Melbourne.

Lane, Richard (1994) *The Golden Age of Australian Radio Drama (1923–1960)*, Melbourne University Press, Carlton South.

Palotta, Grace (1907) 'A Woman's Way' in *The Lone Hand,* Vol. 1. No. 4, Angus & Robertson, Sydney.

Park, Ruth (1993) *A Fence around the Cuckoo*, Penguin Books Australia, Camberwell.

Park, Ruth (1993) *Fishing in the Styx*, Viking Australia, Ringwood.

Peterson, Dymphna Rees (1978) *Coralie Clarke Edits The Dawn: A chapter in the life of Coralie Clarke Rees*, held in State Library of Western Australia, Perth.

Rees, Coralie Clarke (1968) *An Interview with Hazel de Berg*, Oral History Collection, National Library of Australia, Canberra. (Verbatim transcript.)

Rees, Leslie (1967) *An Interview with Hazel de Berg*, Oral History Collection, National Library of Australia, Canberra. (Verbatim transcript.)

Rees, Leslie (1980 and 1981) *An Interview with Chris Jeffery, Oral History Officer*, J.S. Battye Library of West Australian History, Perth. (Verbatim transcript.)

Rees, Leslie (1982) *Hold Fast to Dreams: Fifty years in theatre, radio, television and books*, APCOL, Sydney.

Rees, Leslie (1988) *Interview with Don Grant and Marg McIntyre*, Oral History, State Library of Western Australia, Perth.

Roe, Jill (1993) *My Congenials: Miles Franklin and friends in letters*. Vol. two: 1939–54, Angus & Robertson, Sydney.

Roe, Jill (2008) *Stella Miles Franklin: A biography*, Fourth Estate, Sydney.

Von Bissing, Ronimund (1962) *Songs of Submission: On the practice of Subud*, Latimer, Trend & Co, Great Britain.

Wheatley, Nadia (2001) *The Life and Myth of Charmian Clift*, HarperCollins, Sydney.

OTHER NON-FICTION BY UQP

BEYOND WORDS
A year with Kenneth Cook

Jacqueline Kent

In 1985 Jacqueline Kent was content with her life. She had a satisfying career as a freelance book editor, and was emerging as a writer. Living and working alone, she relished her independence. But then she met Kenneth Cook, author of the Australian classic *Wake in Fright*, and they fell in love.

With bewildering speed Jacqueline found herself in alien territory: with a man almost twenty years older, whose life experience could not have been more different from her own. She had to come to terms with complicated finances and expectations, and to negotiate relationships with Ken's children, four people almost her own age. But with this man of contradictions – funny and sad, headstrong and tender – she found real and sustaining companionship.

Their life together was often joyful, sometimes enraging, always exciting – until one devastating evening. But, as Jacqueline discovered, even when a story is over that doesn't mean it has come to an end.

Shortlisted, 2020 National Biography Award

'There is nothing "buttoned" about Jacqueline Kent's memoir of her brief relationship with Kenneth Cook, author of *Wake in Fright* (1961). Indeed, she brings a striking degree of verisimilitude – an almost eerie recall – to the project.'
The Sydney Morning Herald

ISBN 978 0 7022 6039 1

THEA ASTLEY
Inventing her own weather

Karen Lamb

Thea Astley: Inventing her own weather is the long-overdue biography of Australian author Thea Astley (1925–2004). Over a fifty-year writing career, Astley published more than a dozen novels and short story collections, including *The Acolyte*, *The Slow Natives* and, finally, *Drylands* in 1999. She was the first person to win multiple Miles Franklin awards – four in total. With many of her works published internationally, Astley was a trailblazer for women writers.

In her personal life, she was renowned for her dry wit, eccentricity and compassion. Although a loving mother and wife, she rose above the domestic limitations imposed on women at the time to carve out a professional life true to her creative drive.

Karen Lamb has drawn on an unparalleled range of interviews and correspondence to create a detailed picture of Thea the woman, as well as Astley the writer. She has sought to understand Astley's private world and how that shaped the distinctive body of work that is Thea Astley's literary legacy.

Winner, 2016 Prime Minister's Literary Awards – Non-fiction

'An engaging, affectionate account of Astley that relishes the writer's contradictions and opens up new ways to understand her novels.' *Inside Story*

ISBN 978 0 7022 5356 0